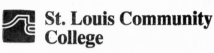

SCREENING THE SACRED

SCREENING THE SACRED

Religion, Myth, and Ideology in Popular American Film

EDITED BY

JOEL W. MARTIN
Franklin and Marshall College

CONRAD E. OSTWALT JR.
Appalachian State University

WESTVIEW PRESS
Boulder • San Francisco • Oxford

Copyright © 1995 by Westview Press, Inc.

Published in 1995 in the United States of America by Westview Press, Inc., 5500 Central Avenue, Boulder, Colorado 80301-2877, and in the United Kingdom by Westview Press, 12 Hid's Copse Road, Cumnor Hill, Oxford OX2 9JJ

Library of Congress Cataloging-in-Publication Data
Screening the sacred : religion, myth, and ideology in popular
   American film / edited by Joel W. Martin, Conrad E. Ostwalt, Jr.
      p.   cm.
   Includes bibliographical references and index.
   ISBN 0-8133-8829-5 — ISBN 0-8133-8830-9 (pbk.)
   1. Motion pictures—Religious aspects.   I. Martin, Joel W., 1956– .
II. Ostwalt, Conrad Eugene, 1959– .
PN1995.5.S36   1995
791.43′682—dc20   94-40252
                                                                                          CIP

Printed and bound in the United States of America

The paper used in this publication meets the requirements
of the American National Standard for Permanence of Paper
for Printed Library Materials Z39.48-1984.

10   9   8   7   6   5   4   3   2   1

Contents

11   Women Spoken For: Images of Displaced Desire

12   Conclusion: Religion, Film, and Cultural Analysis

Preface

Film is an extraordinarily popular medium today, but films do much more than simply entertain. Films, as with other cultural forms, have the potential to reinforce, to challenge, to overturn, or to crystallize religious perspectives, ideological assumptions, and fundamental values. Films bolster and challenge our society's norms, guiding narratives, and accepted truths. In short, films can and do perform religious and iconoclastic functions in American society.

Peter Williams, in *Popular Religion in America,* argues that in our society popular cultural forms perform some of the religious roles usually associated with ecclesiastical institutions. For example, Williams notes that in the United States sacred time has been transformed by a cycle of holy days independent of any traditional religious institution. Holidays such as the Fourth of July, Memorial Day, Thanksgiving, and New Year's have redefined "the idea of sacred time," expanding it far beyond traditional religious holidays such as Yom Kippur and Easter. Religion, in other words, is not confined strictly to what happens in a synagogue or church but is manifested in diverse cultural formations in our society, including popular films.[1]

In this study of Hollywood films, we avoid the elitism that finds intellectual and aesthetic value exclusively in canonical works of art. Rather, we think an investigation of popular expressions of art is integral to understanding the culture that produced it. If we want to understand American culture, we need to study Hollywood films. This is the reason we have brought these chapters together: to examine critically the way popular films relate to religion. The authors of the chapters collected in this book define religion in different ways, some much more broadly than others, but all assume that religion is an important part of our world and that popular films are powerful vehicles for communicating religious meanings, mythic stories, and bedrock ideological values to millions of people. Their chapters teach us to recognize the explicit and implicit presence of religion in one of the most important media of our contemporary culture. These chapters demonstrate that "religious" longings and values pervade the public sphere. This should change the way we think about religion as well as about film. Movies can no longer be viewed as "just entertainment," and religion can no longer be viewed as an antiquated or a peripheral institution in a predominantly secular society. Rather, films, perhaps because they are presumed to be "just entertainment," provide a key means for millions of Americans to grapple with religious issues, mythic archetypes, and fundamental ideological concerns. By looking critically at films, we can learn a good deal about religion in the United States.

Joel W. Martin
Conrad E. Ostwalt Jr.

Acknowledgments

The creation of this book took many years of collaborative effort between coeditors Joel Martin and Conrad Ostwalt. We attended professional meetings in both film studies and religious studies, wrote dozens of letters soliciting manuscripts, posted notices in scholarly newsletters, and edited the chapters in this collection. We worked well together. Often, when one of us grew tired, the other would come up with a good idea or a new approach. We thank Marykay Scott, Jane Raese, and the entire staff at Westview Press for their enthusiasm for our work. In addition, Cheryl Carnahan provided invaluable editing suggestions. And to our contributors—thank you for your patience and excellent work. Throughout the project, we were sustained by the enthusiasm and insights of our students, many of whom were as excited by the project as we were. In recognition of their role, we dedicate the book to them.

The resulting collection is exceptional, and we think it will be groundbreaking. Each chapter makes an original contribution to the subject of religion and film. Several of the chapters (Martin, Rushing, McLemore, Makarushka) directly engage the problematics of race, class, and gender. Readers will be challenged to think critically about the ways popular films encourage racism, encode class, and construct gender even as they are asked to ponder the various ways films screen the sacred.

It goes without saying that I owe a debt to former teachers and mentors who, in one way or another, have shaped my study, teaching, and writing. Wesley Kort has guided me thoughout my preparation and study and has provided a theoretical framework for viewing the relationship of religion and culture. Peter Kaufman and Grant Wacker have been mentors and friends since my undergraduate days. The work of Giles Gunn and Kenny Williams challenged and guided me during my graduate studies. And Carolyn Jones and Mark Ledbetter continue to provide critical assessment and feedback on my work. My colleagues and friends at Appalachian State University provide support and encouragement—thanks especially to David Ball, Graduate Studies and Research, Jessie Taylor, and Alan Hauser. Finally, my family always supports my endeavors: to parents, Conrad and Doris Ostwalt; my family, Donna Goodin, Mark Ostwalt, Angela Hines, Bobby Goodin, Tracey Ostwalt, David Hines, Carrie Goodin, Amy Goodin, Jordan Ostwalt, Jacob Hines, Kadi Ostwalt, John Davidson, Martha Davidson, Marcia Williams, Mike Williams, and Emily Williams; and especially my wife, Mary—thank you.

C.E.O.

I owe thanks to many extraordinary teachers for their inspiring scholarship, friends for stimulating conversation, and family for steadfast love—Robert Wuthnow, James Welsh, Joel Williamson, Marilyn Massey, Peter Wood, Charles Long, Catherine Albanese, William Hutchinson, Conrad Cherry, Gary Ebersole, Charles Hudson, Fredric Jameson, Dan Frick, Tamara Goeglein, Steve Cooper, Kabi Hartman, Annette Aronowicz, Bob Mickey, Andy Manis, Matt Glass, Caroline Carvill, Rodger Payne, Keith Naylor, Wendy Young, David Hackett, John Stackhouse, Madeline Duntley, Gerald McDermott, Val Ziegler, Steve Prothero, Rosemary Gooden, Laurie Maffly-Kipp, Tom Tweed, Betty DeBerg, Tony Fels, Jane Rossetti, Bill Martin, Patty Martin, Stan Martin, Sophia Martin, Allen Martin, Melanie Martin, and Caroline Martin. To all of them, I give my heartfelt gratitude.

J.W.M.

1

Introduction:
Seeing the Sacred on the Screen

JOEL W. MARTIN

MANY YEARS AGO a college classmate went to see the first *Rocky* film. Afterward, he declared, "It makes me want to get into the best shape possible." We were shocked. Jack was not known for discipline or drive. Up to that point, he had spent most of his college days and nights playing poker, drinking beer, and listening to rock and roll. Stallone's film changed his life. He started jogging and pumping iron; he lost weight and became a respectable athlete. When he began attending classes, I was impressed. However, despite this convincing evidence of the movie's power, it was not until years later that I finally saw it.

The very first image shocked me, for it is not of Sylvester Stallone or even of the city of Philadelphia. The film begins with a full-screen image of the face of Christ. The camera tracks down from this image, represented in a mosaic on the wall, to Rocky, the palooka boxer who has squandered his natural gifts. Rocky, it turns out, is fighting in a gymnasium that used to be a church. Suspended above the ring is a banner reading "Resurrection A.C." (presumably the initials stand for Athletic Club). Several other Christ-figure motifs follow. Just as Christ consorted with a prostitute named Mary Magdelene, Rocky advises a girl named Marie to stop being promiscuous; like a Good Samaritan, he rescues a bum from the street; finally, like a scapegoat savior or human sacrifice, he suffers physical violence in order to redeem the hopes of the common people. Full of Christian themes, the movie is also full of civil religion, the ideology that sanctifies the United States as God's chosen nation-state. *Rocky* features sacred symbols such as the flag, repeats cherished narratives about patriotic heroes such as George Washington, and affirms the basic creed that the United States is the land of opportunity. As I watched this film, I wondered: Could the use of powerful symbols from Christianity and U.S. civil religion account for the film's mass appeal and its life-changing power?

Scholars Out to Lunch: Take One

In pursuing this question, I turned to two areas of scholarship: film criticism and the academic study of religion. I expected to find models of how to analyze the relationship of religion and film. What I found was disappointing. Scholars engaged in prevailing modes of film criticism have had almost nothing to say about religion. And scholars who study religion have had almost nothing to say about Hollywood film. Instead of encountering an ongoing and stimulating dialogue about religion and film, I encountered silence.[1]

Whether influenced by Marxist, psychoanalytic, feminist, post-structuralist, or auteur theory, film critics ignore religion and the academic study of religion. Apparently, critics assume that secular values, forces, and perspectives matter more than religious ones. If this is the case, film critics are like those historians, sociologists, economists, or psychologists who, in Bryan R. Wilson's words, "take secularization for granted. Their overwhelming tendency … is to regard religion as a peripheral phenomenon in contemporary social organization, and one which, in their studies of the broad contours of social change, productivity, economic growth, or human psychology, they rarely find need to consider."[2] Similarly, rarely does a film critic publish an article that deals with religion.

It is almost as if the discourse of cutting-edge film criticism is designed to exclude attention to religion. The index of a recent introduction to the vocabulary of contemporary film criticism is revealing. Terms such as *alienation, ideology, plenitude,* and *resistance* appear. Six types of realism and four types of discourse are indexed. Freudian terms abound—hysteria, ego, drive, oedipal complex—as do key words from the theoretical lexicons of Lacan, Derrida, Kristeva, and Saussure. But religion is not listed; nor is myth or ritual, let alone eschatology, soteriology, or theology.[3]

If religion is not in the vocabulary of film scholars, it is also true that they give almost no attention to the academic field of religious studies. In an introduction to a series of books on film, Edward Buscombe and Phil Rosen declare that the field of cinema studies has been hugely enriched "in interaction with a wide variety of other disciplines." They list "literary studies, anthropology, linguistics, history, economics and psychology."[4] They do not mention religious studies, even though this well-established, widespread discipline involves the labors of tens of thousands of professional scholars. Perhaps this is a simple oversight. Perhaps it reveals an assumption that film studies has little to learn from religious studies. Whatever the cause, it is hoped that the present collection will make such omissions less likely in the future.

It behooves students of American film to take religion more seriously, especially as historians and sociologists argue that religion, particularly varieties of fundamentalism, is increasing in importance throughout the world and will likely do so at an accelerated rate as the dawn of the new millennium approaches and passes.[5] Ironically, the power of religion was recognized by many of the thinkers whose theories have influenced contemporary film criticism. Several wrote extensively on religion (Marx, Freud, Kristeva, Derrida).[6] Others advanced theories that can be reconciled with the continued powerful presence of religion in our society. Consider the theory of ideology developed by structuralist-Marxist Louis Althusser. Many film critics have appropriated Althusser's definition of ideology as a "system (possessing its own logic and rigor) of representation (images, myths, ideas or concepts as the case may be) existing and having a historical role within a given society."[7] Ideology works, according to Althusser (quoted in Stam), through "interpellation, i.e., through the social practices and structures which 'hail' individuals, so as to endow them with social identity, constituting them as subjects who unthinkingly accept their role within the system of production relations."[8] Using this theory, film critics have maintained that films shape spectators as social subjects.[9] There is no reason critics could not use such an approach and give direct attention to religion. They could say, for instance, that the religious images and myths represented in *Rocky* "hailed" Jack and made him desire to become fit. The Christian and civil religious impulses in the film shaped his social identity.

Scholars Out to Lunch: Take Two

If film criticism has ignored religion and religious studies, religious studies has given little attention to popular film and film studies. It was not until the 1980s that the largest professional association of scholars of religion, the American Academy of Religion, included in its annual convention a forum on religion and film. A few books have appeared on the subject, including some pathbreaking ones by James Wall, John R. May, and Thomas M. Martin, but as late as 1993 Joseph Cunneen could still conclude that "serious study of religion in narrative film has been extremely limited." Cunneen thinks the paucity of scholarship reflects not a problem among scholars but an inherent limit of the medium of film itself, its "inevitable bias toward realism." Given this bias, it is difficult to represent the sacred in a convincing way, so an actual shortage of truly religious films results. The Hollywood production system does not help matters, Cunneen argues. Oriented toward profit and a mass audience, this system does not allow directors "to make personal movies that suggest the depth of religious mystery," films such as those by great "artists" like Robert Bresson (*Diary of a Country Priest*), Carl Dreyer (*The Passion of Joan of Arc*), Eric Rohmer (*My Night at Maud's*), and Ingmar Bergman (*The Seventh Seal*).[10]

Cunneen's list of directors reveals an assumption common in religious studies scholarship; namely, that only a highbrow film can be truly religious. As recent books such as *Religion in Film* and *Image and Likeness* show, religion scholars gravitate toward European films or established U.S. classics. Almost no one in religious studies deigns to study a Stallone or Schwarzenegger film. A person interested in religion in popular Hollywood film will find very few interpretative models and almost no exemplary published articles. This book is designed to correct for these blind spots in religious studies and film criticism.

Religion and Film Intersect but Also Diverge

Although the editors and authors of this volume find a good deal of religion in contemporary films, we are aware that the medium fails to express many significant aspects of human religiosity. In some key ways, religion exceeds film. For instance, the film *Black Robe* calls attention to the brutal way colonial Native Americans tortured some of their enemies but provides viewers with no hint of the complex spiritual motivations and narratives that shaped Indian actions and values. According to ethnohistorians, when colonial Indians tortured captives (usually adult males), it was to avenge the wrongful death of one of their kin, but more than that, it was also to free his or her soul, which was perceived to be bound in a sterile limbo until proportionate justice was exacted.[11] Since the film gives viewers no real appreciation of the spiritual traditions and practices of the people it depicts, viewers will conclude incorrectly that Indians were simply sadists who enjoyed inflicting pain. Similarly, in the 1993 version of the *Last of the Mohicans,* there are far too many scenes of bloody combats. Set in a beautiful landscape, these acts are not situated within the context of the cultural and religious life of the Iroquois people. The film shows us battles, not visions; military campaigns, not sacred rituals; attractive Indians with the wind blowing through their long hair, not spirits circulating through all life-forms. In this film as in *Black Robe,* Native American religion has been inadequately represented.

If we realize that many aspects of human religiousness have not been and probably never will be represented in film, we also realize that little is to be gained by examining every film in relation to religion. In some key ways, film exceeds religion. The *Police Academy* movies, for instance, do not appear very promising case studies for our purposes. An interpreter might find a quasi-Christian morality encoded in these movies (the first shall be last, the last shall be first), but the yield hardly seems worth the effort, and a person advancing such an interpretation will appear humorless and driven. We have no desire to squeeze blood from turnips. Fortunately, most films fall somewhere in between those that are explicitly "religious" in theme (like Scorsese's iconoclastic *Last Temptation of Christ* or Redford's meditative *A River Runs Through It*) and those that have almost nothing to do with religion. It is in this large middle ground that we focus our efforts. We concentrate on films that make our job as interpreters of religion challenging but not impossible. Most of the films discussed in this book are Hollywood blockbusters, and two won the Academy Award for best picture (*Rocky* in 1976, *Platoon* in 1986). By examining religion in commercially successful films, we hope this anthology will, on the one hand, convince students of film that they should take religion seriously and, on the other, convince students of religion that they need to take popular films seriously. We all need to rethink the relations of religion and film, of religious studies and film criticism, and of religion and contemporary culture.

Ours is an interdisciplinary project. It brings religious studies and film criticism into contact with each other but, additionally, taps other fields important to cultural studies today. Our contributors teach in departments of religious studies, philosophy, English, American studies, and communication studies. Their diverse backgrounds and perspectives enrich this collection considerably. The common focus on religion and film unifies the entire collection.

To create an even stronger sense of unity, the editors (Conrad E. Ostwalt Jr. and Joel W. Martin) have constructed an organizing framework for the book. This framework assumes that there are three distinct ways to theorize the relation of religion and film. Accordingly, we group the contributors' chapters in three separate categories. We feel confident about the decisions we have made, but we also realize that by putting chapters together in this way, we have shaped to an extent the way any given chapter will be read. By defining the context, we influence the text's reception. Individual authors may not agree with our argument, organization, or conclusions.

Since the editors are trained in religious studies, we have relied chiefly upon this field to guide our work and structure this book. Religious studies, it must be emphasized, is an academic discipline and is not beholden to any religious institution. Its first home is the university or college, not the church or synagogue. As with other fields in the humanities and the social sciences, it is committed to the pursuit of knowledge, not the saving of souls. What distinguishes it from other fields in the academy is the fact that religion itself represents a distinct subject matter. Religion, like literature or history or art, warrants its own academic discipline and specialized modes of study. Some scholars of religion express this claim by saying that religion is sui generis—that is, religion constitutes a domain of human activity "of its own sort." Religion orients communities toward something or someone or some place sacred or inviolate.

Not all scholars of religion accept the idea that religion is sui generis. They fear this idea makes religion seem too remote from the rest of life. The editors of this volume interpret the phrase less absolutely. We do not think it means that religion is completely autonomous and cannot be interpreted in relation to politics, economics, psychology, or social context. Rather, we think religion is a semiautonomous domain of culture deserving serious academic study, and we contend that scholars should "press for religious explanations when presented with religious data."[12] If they want to understand a Buddhist monk, scholars of religious studies will argue that it is important to understand something about monastic traditions in general or Buddhism in particular. Similarly, if they want to understand religion in a contemporary Hollywood film, they will assume that it is important to understand the religious traditions informing the cultural context in which the film was made and viewed. Looking for religion, they will examine the film to see if traditional religious teachings or values are present, if any of the common forms of expression normally associated with religion are present, if religious symbols are being invoked, and so on.[13]

Three Approaches to Religion

During the period in which the field of religious studies has been recognized as an academic discipline, it has had time to develop considerable internal diversity. We cannot pretend to introduce the many ways in which scholars approach the study of religion; we refer curious readers to more detailed surveys.[14] For the purposes of this text, however, we can describe three basic approaches to religion current in the field: the theological, the mythological, and the ideological. Their conception of what constitutes religion varies greatly. Nevertheless, because all three of these approaches take religion seriously and have found a home in the academy, we feel justified in grouping them together under the rubric of religious studies. We have structured the book around these three approaches.

In their purest, "ideal" versions, these approaches diverge significantly. Theological thinkers analyze how religious texts and thinkers in various traditions, particularly Judaism and Christianity, have talked about God. Theologians try to relate these representations or teachings concerning God to modern and postmodern contexts, translating teachings about such things as the covenant, sacrifice, Incarnation, fallibility, and justice into modern philosophical categories or critiquing society in their light. Theological scholars tend to equate religion with Judaism and Christianity. Since these traditions have had a tremendous impact upon Western culture and all of its art forms, theological scholars are positioned to make many valuable insights about the modern Western art of Hollywood film.

Other scholars, often associated with the study of comparative religion, do not equate religion with monotheistic religions or with any single tradition, deity, belief, or institution. Rather, they see religion as a universal and ubiquitous human activity; they assert that religion manifests itself through cross-cultural forms, including myth, ritual, systems of purity, and gods. Myth consists of stories that provide human communities with grounding prototypes, models for life, reports of foundational realities, and dramatic presentations of fundamental values: Myth reveals a culture's bedrock assumptions and aspirations. Ritual concentrates human attention and orchestrates action in order to sanctify time. Systems of purity enable people to deal with negativity, with things that threaten the order of their world. Finally, gods include all superior beings that humans engage religiously. Different cultures fill these forms with different contents.

As we shall see in this book, Hollywood has filled these basic forms with a tremendous variety of contents, projecting onto screens a rich diversity of myths, rituals, systems of purity, and gods for us to contemplate. Some of the projections are Christian, many are not. The luminous character of Rocky may resemble Christ in many ways, but in even more important ways we will see that he represents a distinctively American, indeed, a peculiarly white American, savior. Studying the ways Hollywood reinterprets, appropriates, invents, or rejects inherited archetypes, mythic stories, ritual acts, symbolic figures, and spiritual values will teach us a great deal about religion in the contemporary United States.

In contrast to theologians and myth critics, still other scholars interpret religion in relation to what is not religion; for example, the social structure, the unconscious, gender, and power relations. Although not reducing religion to something nonreligious, they think it is important to situate religion in its historical, social, and political contexts. They focus especially upon how religion legitimates or challenges dominant visions of the social order. In other words, they study the relation of religion and ideology. For this reason, we label them ideological critics.

These are suggestive, not exhaustive, characterizations, but they point to basic paradigms that prevail in our nation's divinity schools and universities. By making explicit the existence of these paradigms, and by showing how each engenders a distinct type of criticism of film (theological criticism, mythological criticism, ideological criticism), we hope to contribute to the current debates concerning the definition of religion and the interpretation of religious texts and actions. More than that, by putting these paradigms into motion, by fleshing them out through the study of film, we hope to bring to the debates an unprecedented degree of concreteness and color. Films are fascinating and popular visual texts. By focusing on films, we think we have found a graphic way to explicate the major intellectual divisions in the study of religion. Finally, we argue that each of the three major types of criticism has commendable strengths but also inevitable weaknesses. All are valuable; none is perfect. This suggests that a new, fourth type of criticism is needed. Perhaps it will be a blend of theological, mythological, and ideological criticism. This book raises the question of what this type will look like; only future study and discussion will provide the answer.

The authors grouped under the heading Theological Criticism tend to equate religion with specific religious traditions (e.g., Christianity and its scriptures). The authors grouped under the heading Mythological Criticism tend to define religion more broadly in terms of universal mythic archetypes (e.g., the figure of the sky god). The authors grouped under Ideological Criticism focus on the political and social effects of religion (e.g., its ability to convince dominated people to accept or resist their lot).

Our tripartite classification system has evolved as we worked on this collection. It has also been shaped by our experiences in the classroom. Whereas our classification system is our own and we have arrived at it independently, and although it is not intended to be the definitive or ultimate typology, we note that other scholars, operating in different subfields of religious studies, have come up with similar typologies to describe how religion is studied today. For instance, William Paden identifies three ways scholars have approached the study of world religion: Christian comparativism, universalism, and rationalism. The first is confessional: It focuses upon Christianity as the true religion; in comparison, other religions seem inferior or false. In contrast, universalism finds truth in all religions; it looks for deep commonalities beneath surface differences. Rationalism represents a third distinctive approach: It is reductionistic and says all religions are equally invalid, all are inferior ways of knowing the world, and all will eventually be replaced by

rationalistic thought. Paden thinks each of these perspectives has limits and problems. Christian comparativism is ethnocentric, universalism levels important differences, and rationalism does not take religion seriously on its own terms.[15]

In a strikingly similar way, Catherine Albanese in *America: Religions and Religion,* identifies three major ways scholars of U.S. religion have defined religion.
"*Substantive* definitions of religion focus on the inner core, essence, or nature of
religion." Such definitions "tend to emphasize a relationship with a higher being
or beings." This way of defining religion is favored by theologians. "*Formal* definitions of religion look for typically religious forms gleaned from the comparative
study of religions and find the presence of religion where such forms can be identified," even if there is no reference to a higher being. Religious forms highlighted
by Albanese include myths, rituals, moral codes, and communities. Formal definitions tend to be favored by historians of religion and scholars of myth engaged
in cross-cultural study. In contrast, "*functional* definitions of religion emphasize
the effects of religion in actual life." They stress the ways religion helps people
"deal with the ills, insecurities, and catastrophes of living." Functional definitions
tend to be favored by social scientists.[16]

Substantive, formal, functional; Christian comparativism, universalism, rationalism; theological, mythological, ideological. Although our typology does not
exactly parallel those of Paden and Albanese, these similarities across the subfields
of religious studies convince us that our classification system is not arbitrary or
artificial. Although we employ our tripartite system only to explore the relation of
religion and film, it could be useful in the broader study of religion and culture.
Indeed, we are tempted to think that this classification system makes a theoretical
contribution to the field of religious studies. It may provide a useful means of interpreting our culture's running dialogue with religious values, themes, archetypes, and narratives. It could enable us to examine this dialogue from three critical perspectives. It definitely helps us to analyze some of the key ways religion and
film are related.

Three Types of Criticism

Theological criticism draws upon an incredibly rich tradition of ethical reflection
and exegetical commentary. When Larry Grimes considers the meaning of resurrection in relation to *Psycho;* when Ted Estess explores how *Ironweed*'s humble
characters experience a redemptive mystery; when Avent Beck shows how the
Christian narrative informs the plot of *Platoon;* when Conrad Ostwalt examines
how the apocalypse is imagined in current films, they are not writing in a void but
are engaging questions that have been asked by many generations of Christian
scholars. It is little wonder that in this section of the book we encounter elegant,
soul-searching writing. Among other things, these authors' criticism reveals that
many contemporary films engage traditional religious themes. Their criticism
helps us to realize that our popular culture, even though it may present itself as

thoroughly secular, continues to wrestle with Christian claims, symbols, and expectations.

For this and other insights, we need theological criticism. As Larry Grimes argues, some things in films simply make much more sense if interpreted through traditional Christian theology. However, if the theological approach makes an irreplaceable contribution, it is also true that we need additional approaches to religion and film. Theological critics are most at home in talking about religion in its Christian or Jewish forms. Their first impulse is to link modern cultural expressions to scriptural antecedents. When they examine films, theological critics inevitably focus on films that feature Christ figures and that deal with classic theological themes such as the existence of evil and the nature of God. Such specificity characterizes the chapters in a book such as *Religion in Film* and *Image and Likeness.* Concerning the latter a reviewer wrote, "The reader is left uneasy with the way in which the stories of the films—including *Citizen Kane, 2001: A Space Odyssey, The Wizard of Oz, Casablanca,* and *One Flew Over the Cuckoo's Nest*—are meshed with the stories of the Jewish and Christian scriptures."[17] Theological criticism is important, even essential in cultures strongly shaped by Christianity and Judaism, but it is not sufficient. It defines religion too narrowly and tends toward ethnocentrism. If we want to understand the relation of religion and film, we will need to employ nontheological approaches as well.

A more inclusive, cross-cultural understanding of religion is exemplified in the works of scholars of comparative mythology. As Mircea Eliade, Joseph Campbell, and others have argued, religion can be defined in a nontheological manner as the quest of humanity for contact with the sacred. Such a definition leads myth critics to search for religion in all cultures, in art and architecture, in dreams, in all symbolic activities, and especially in mythic narratives—stories that reveal the foundational values of a culture. Employing an expansive definition of religion, myth critics find much to analyze in popular film. Eliade recognized the fertile relationship between myth and film: "A whole volume could well be written on the myths of modern man, on the mythologies camouflaged in the plays he enjoys, in the books that he reads. The cinema, that 'dream factory,' takes over and employs countless mythical motifs—the fight between hero and monster, initiatory combats and ordeals, paradigmatic figures and images (the maiden, the hero, the paradisal landscape, hell, and so on)."[18]

Eliade's contemporary Joseph Campbell not only observed the connection between myth and film; his work on myth informed the making of Hollywood films. Campbell summarized what he felt was the basic plot of all hero stories: "The standard path of the mythological adventure of the hero is a magnification of the formula represented in the rites of passage: separation-initiation-return. ... A hero ventures forth from the world of common day into a region of supernatural wonder: fabulous forces are there encountered and a decisive victory is won: the hero comes back from this mysterious adventure with the power to bestow boons on his fellow man."[19] This plot was appropriated by director George Lucas, who credited Campbell as the inspiration for Lucas's *Star Wars* trilogy.

Part 2 focuses on films that reinterpret myths to make them vital for contemporary viewers. Andrew Gordon employs Joseph Campbell's description of the monomyth to show that Luke Skywalker in *Star Wars* follows the classic pattern of the mythic hero. Caron Ellis, influenced by Eliade's willingness to see the sacred beyond Christianity, finds beneficent power in the sky. Specifically, Ellis argues that the friendly aliens that come to earth in science-fiction films serve to alleviate our anxieties regarding nuclear proliferation and global pollution. Meanwhile, in the films *Alien* and *Aliens* Janice Rushing identifies the reemergence of the earth goddess as a vital cultural power. Drawing on Jung's theory of the collective unconscious, Rushing identifies the earth goddess as a transcultural archetype, a primordial image of profound importance to humanity. It does not matter if such a figure has a biblical prototype. The earth goddess is older and more primordial than the Bible, than Christianity, than all organized religions. She symbolizes a kind of spiritual power with which we must come to terms if we are to live fully human lives. If she is appearing now in our cultural myths and on the screens of our movie theaters as a monstrous fury, it means we need to change the way we relate to both feminine power and nature.

Myth criticism employs a much broader definition of religion than does theological criticism. This enables myth critics to perceive religion when a theological critic might miss it or deny its presence altogether. For all of its breadth and vitality, however, myth criticism has some limits. If it is adept at identifying the presence of non-Christian, mythic powers in film, myth criticism does a much less satisfactory job of showing how these powers relate to the kinds of mundane power social scientists and historians analyze. In short, sky gods and earth goddesses tend to be treated as ahistorical archetypes the human unconscious throws up in response to existential challenges. Myth critics focus on our psychological quest for meaning but tend to ignore the way meaning is always politicized and historicized. Not surprisingly, Campbell, Eliade, and Jung have been attacked on political grounds.[20]

To appreciate how myths affect society, we need another type of criticism. Ideological criticism, in contrast to myth criticism, focuses primarily upon the political effects of cultural expressions; the quest for meaning is secondary, and the relationship to a traditional religious figure or theme is even less relevant. Ideological critics tend to be historicists. This means they think culture and art do not transcend politics but shape and are shaped by politics, and they consider claims that symbols and archetypes are transcultural or timeless to be naive and incorrect. Ideological critics want to know how a specific cultural expression reinforces or undermines the structure of power relations in a given society at a particular time, not how such an expression fulfills a universal human need for meaning. Ideological critics study the relationship of religion and society. Thus, when Joel W. Martin examines the film *Rocky,* he is not primarily concerned about

seeing if the film's hero acts like a Christ figure (which Rocky does) or understanding how the film provides mythic meaning for its audience (which it does).
Rather than treating the film primarily as a theological or mythic text, he interprets it as a political and social text that employs religion for ideological ends. The
film, in this reading, blames African Americans for real social problems experienced by working-class people who are not African American. It turns religious
symbols and mythic meanings toward concrete political and social ends. In a different vein, Elizabeth McLemore, in her treatment of *Blue Velvet*, shows how this
postmodern film subverts interpretative schemes that presuppose fixed, archetypal meanings. Whereas some critics would like to see *Blue Velvet* as an allegorical battle of good and evil, McLemore thinks the film does not allow such a simple
interpretation. Finally, when Irena Makarushka views *Nine and a Half Weeks*, she
is not concerned first with showing how the film mediates theological or mythic
meaning to viewers but, rather, with tracing how the film reveals the political and
social effects of religious images on young women. She argues that gender relations have been defined in relation to female archetypes (Eve, Mary) created by
male desire. She is concerned with the effects these archetypes have on women
and asks if women's experience can be reclaimed and named by women. She finds
some intriguing answers in the film.

Race, class, gender, and the postmodern are a few of the central interpretative
categories for ideological critics. Without question, they can be used to shed considerable light on most Hollywood films and on the form of film itself. However, if
critics rely too exclusively on these categories, they may overemphasize only one
dimension of religion and ignore or distort others. Some ideological critics focus
so tightly on politics that they end up treating religion simplistically. Because they
have forgotten the complexity of religion and its relative autonomy as a domain of
culture, these critics cannot properly be said to be practicing religious studies.
Such is the case with ideological critics such as Michael Ryan and Douglas Kellner.

In their recent book, *Camera Politica: The Politics and Ideology of Contemporary
Hollywood Film*, Ryan and Kellner do not even define religion, although they refer
to it many times. Influenced by Marxist criticism but lacking Marx's rich vision
regarding the contradictory impact of religion on society, they assume that religion can only be the opiate of the people, a mystifying set of symbols and ideas
that always promotes individualism and conservatism. In their view, religion is always regressive.[21]

Even with such a limited perspective, Ryan and Kellner produce some valuable
insights regarding religion and popular films. For instance, *Saturday Night Fever*
(1977), in their view, provided the white working class with visions of transcendence from their historical and economic situation. In the movie, temporary escape from working-class drudgery is as easy as immersing oneself in the world of
disco. Permanent escape can be obtained by crossing the bridge into Manhattan.
Such a vision captivated viewers and seduced them into believing again in the
American Dream. Ryan and Kellner would much prefer that Americans perceive

the ways in which gross social inequities and differential income levels are integral parts of a capitalist, sexist, racist system. They want viewers to be skeptical of visions of transcendence.[22]

All this is well and good, except it sounds the only note Ryan and Kellner know how to play regarding religion. Although they are willing to grant that films can be politically self-contradictory, they do not explore the complexity of religion, its ability to reinforce the worst injustices, and its prophetic ability to move people into the street to resist injustices (e.g., the U.S. civil rights movement, the anti-shah marches in Iran, the People Power movement in the Phillipines). In their view, religion is a fixed, known, stable force not requiring interpretation or deconstruction. In fact, it is a much more complex phenomenon. Not only can it serve contradictory ideological purposes, it can also affect human beings on multiple levels and in manifold ways. To do justice to this multidimensional phenomenon, we need to rely not just on ideological criticism—which focuses exclusively on the political dimension—but also on theological and mythological perspectives. Although not as sensitive to the political effects of religion, these approaches are at least "bold enough to take the things of the spirit spiritually."[23]

As we study the relation of religion and film, we need to learn how to tap the strengths of theological criticism, mythological criticism, and ideological criticism while recognizing their respective weaknesses. Each type of criticism is necessary; none alone is sufficient. This book makes these points clearly in the way it is structured. Each type is given its due in a tripartite structure. Whereas such a structure is the best one possible at the present moment—a kind of federal system involving three branches that check and balance each other—we can imagine a future synthesis of these types of criticism. Such a synthesis will be a criticism deeply grounded in generations of thought about the sacred, broadly open to the diverse ways in which the sacred manifests itself, and acutely sensitive to the political and social effects of religious and mythological texts.

Such criticism, as yet unnamed, may emerge. Indeed, we can catch glimpses of it in this book when our critics show an awareness of the limits of the various approaches they employ. So although it is true that our theological critics focus on classic Christian themes, it is also true that they know religion encompasses mythological traditions beyond Christianity and that religious stories can serve ideological ends. Our mythological critics may emphasize the archetypal qualities of the gods and goddesses they examine, but they also suggest that these sacred beings tell us something about our political situation, the fear of nuclear weapons, and our desire for a new relationship with nature. Finally, whereas our ideological critics are very concerned with the way race, class, and gender are represented, they are also sensitive to the ways in which sacred traditions—Christian and otherwise—shape these representations. This book, then, can serve as a model both of types of criticism as they are practiced today and for criticism as it may be practiced tomorrow.

PART ONE

THEOLOGICAL CRITICISM

And the cathedral, where congregations gather to see the great illuminated stories in glass, to watch the ritual performances on the stage of the altar, to follow, through the calendar, the great epic of Christianity with its heroes, its villains, its disputes and digressions, its strange character parts, its compelling story-line, can be seen as the cinema of the pre-celluloid era.[1]

This is Melvyn Bragg's description of "cinema" before the advent of film in his book *The Seventh Seal*. What is refreshing about his statement is the way it reverses the normal trajectory of criticism, which typically moves from spiritually oriented past to secularized present and tries to find traces of the former in the latter. Bragg sees art and religion as always linked, each relying on the other to find expression and purpose. For him a cathedral is the site of something akin to cinematic experience, and the reverse is true as well. A film participates in the construction of an overarching religious sensibility and perspective on ultimate matters, a theology. Ingmar Bergman affirmed this: "Thus if I am asked what I would like the general purpose of my films to be, I would reply that I want to be one of the artists in the cathedral on the great plain. I want to make a dragon's head, an angel, a devil—or perhaps a saint—out of stone. It does not matter which; it is the sense of satisfaction which counts. Regardless of whether I believe or not, whether I am a Christian or not, I would play my part in the collective building of the cathedral."[2]

Theological criticism studies the "cathedrals" being built in the cinema, the ways in which films express classic religious concerns, sensibilities, and themes. Theological criticism helps us identify the dragon's heads, angels, devils, and saints of a celluloid era. The basic assumption behind theological criticism is that certain films can be properly understood, or can be best understood, as an elaboration on or the questioning of a particular religious tradition, text, or theme. Thus, underlying certain films there must be some basic moral, ethical, or theological position upon which the meaning of the film depends. Theological criticism hinges upon the notion that the critic, director, screenplay writer, or some other creative force behind the film develops a certain theological agenda or concept, and the distinctive goal of the theological critic is to uncover that concept.

Theological criticism draws upon traditional theological concepts such as good and evil, redemption, grace, hope, and salvific potentiality. The theological critic will choose these concepts as the window to understanding the film's intent, even if it means discounting other dimensions of the film. Even in films that are strongly charged ideologically, for a theological critic religious concepts and symbols will hold the key for understanding the real meaning. For example, *Places in the Heart,* set in the segregated South, explores racial tension, gender subordination, and prejudice in society. However, the film takes on a whole different light with the surprising ending, which portrays black and white, the living and the dead, sharing a meal. The vision of the kingdom of heaven catches the viewer completely off guard and forces a reexamination of the film's events from a theological angle. *The Fisher King,* set in contemporary New York, dramatizes the impossible gulf between the rich dwelling in high-rise heavens and the homeless poor hidden away in subterranean hells. Nevertheless, class conflict is not the primary story for a theological critic but is merely the background for an exploration of the experiences of forgiveness and grace that liberate the two lead characters (Jeff Bridges, Robin Williams) and free them from the demons that haunt them. In both cases, it is the religious dimension of the films that will attract the theological critic's attention, not the social and political meanings conveyed. In other words, when identifying traditional religious meaning is the major goal of the film critic, theological criticism is taking place.

Another way to recognize theological criticism is through its reliance on allegorical interpretations that find in film traces of a familiar religious story and worldview. Allegorical interpretation has long been a favorite of Christian commentators. Originating as a "strategy for assimilating the Old Testament to the New, for rewriting the Jewish textual and cultural heritage in a form usable for Gentiles," allegorical interpretation is "grounded in the conception of history itself as God's book, which we study and gloss for signs of the prophetic message the Author [God] is supposed to have inscribed within it." Thinking that God had caused history to happen in a way that always pointed to Christ, Christians reinterpreted the Hebrew Bible in light of the New Testament. Thus, when they read about Israel's bondage in Egypt, some Christian commentators understood it as a true historical occurrence and also as a representation of the descent of Christ into hell after his death on the cross. As Fredric Jameson concludes, "Allegory is here the opening up of the text to multiple meanings, to successive rewritings and overwritings which are generated as so many levels and as so many supplementary interpretations."[3]

Given its historic importance among Christian interpreters, it is not surprising that some contemporary critics employ the allegorical standard to view film. Unfortunately, this is sometimes taken to ridiculous extremes when critics, focusing on the didactic function of film, look for "Christ figures" around every corner in order to impart Christian teaching. "Rewriting" virtually every film in terms of the Christ story or as a battle between good and evil, they dilute and undermine the power of this interpretative standard. Nevertheless, if we resist the idea that every Hollywood hero is Christlike and that every villain is the beast of the apocalypse, many films incorporate Christian symbolism and call for allegorical interpretation. It is hard to ignore the references to Christ in films such as *Cool Hand Luke, One Flew over the Cuckoo's Nest, Rocky,* and *E.T.* In Part 1 of the book, Avent Childress Beck's chapter, "The Christian Allegorical Structure of *Platoon*," provides a good example of how the allegorical interpretative standard can be used to provide additional insight to a film. Dripping with references to Elijah, Christ, and the beast from the Book of Revelation, *Platoon* begs for allegorical interpretation.

Regardless of whether allegory is the basic standard for criticism, if one approaches a film from a theological perspective it is not enough to show that the film recapitulates or borrows figures or symbols that resemble those of an established religious tradition. To do that alone would merely locate religion elsewhere, outside the film; it might imply that the religious meaning of the film is available only to those who know the religious texts and traditions. A truly theological approach, in contrast, will show how the film communicates religious meanings, even to those viewers unfamiliar with specific religious texts and traditions. Theological critics should show us how films function theologically; that is, encourage viewers to ask ultimate questions. This is precisely what the authors represented in this section of the book do. They argue that films such as *Psycho, Apocalypse Now, Ironweed,* and *Platoon* stimulate viewers—even those who know little about Christianity—to think about profound religious themes such as the finality of death, the possibility of resurrection, the end of time, the experience of grace, and the meaning of sacrifice.

Whereas each author employs a distinct method and style to tease out the religious meaning, it is worth noting that with little distortion, various approaches could be fused into a fairly unified or systematic method for interpreting religion and film. The method strongly resembles that developed by some literary critics who study religion and literature. After all, films are stories, and they share characteristics with fiction. Could we be witnessing the birth of a new subfield of religious studies? This subfield focuses on a distinct aspect of culture but uses methods developed by literary scholars. This possibility warrants fuller development, if for no other reason than because film and literary critics share the ability to choose how to interpret texts or films.

Literary critics such as Frank Kermode, Robert Scholes, Robert Kellogg, and Wesley Kort have stressed the religious power of literature by examining the elements of narrative or storytelling: atmosphere, character, plot, and tone.[4] Of particular importance to this study is the theory of Kort regarding religion and narrative. In *Narrative Elements and Religious Meaning,* Kort discusses how the four basic elements of storytelling (atmosphere, character, plot, and tone) can lend any particular narrative a religious quality by mediating an encounter with "otherness"—that which is beyond the known world of experience. In most religions, the encounter with otherness transforms a person's life by giving new and expanded meaning, altering one's perception of reality, and instilling a more profound belief. The encounter with otherness is the goal of the religious quest, the transformed life its desired effect. Kort argues that an encounter with otherness is mediated in literature by the four basic elements of narrative. Atmosphere describes the limits of life within an imagined world. Because atmosphere constitutes "the range of possibilities [and] the borders of human influence" for the fictional world, it points to that which is beyond human control, that which is other.[5] Likewise, "character in narrative ... [provides] an image of human possibilities or a paradigm of human potential."[6] Plot orders time and processes and makes them meaningful, giving meaning to the passage of time, which appears beyond human control.[7] Finally, tone, or the presence of the author in the work, allows the inclusion of personal and subjective belief.[8] Often, the presence of the artist infuses the work with a transcendent, omniscient voice (otherness) and lends the work a religious quality or a theological point of view.

Kort's method suggests that the very nature of narrative is religious; narrative contains within itself a structure that confronts the reader with that which is transcendent and beyond mundane experience and grants meaning to human experience by exposing it to the sacred realm, the realm of realities beyond human control. Even if the content of the specific story seems secular, the very form of the story, as narrative, can mediate an awareness of otherness, of the transcendent and, hence, can serve a religious function by providing access to the sacred.

Films incorporate the same four elements of storytelling and, thus, have the ability to confront the audience with otherness, thereby expanding and altering worldviews. For example, one of the premises behind the theological method of criticism is that there is some creative force behind the film that infuses the film with meaning. Critics generally point to the director as the theological or philosophical force behind the film. Critics are accustomed, for instance, to tracing the religious power of such films as *Mean Streets* and *Taxi Driver* to the moral vision and background of these films' director, Martin Scorsese. As the director he had a privileged role in shaping these films. When he says that he made *Mean Streets* to tell the "story of a modern saint," we take the statement very seriously and allow it to influence the way we interpret the film.[9]

In this section of the book, Larry E. Grimes demonstrates how the director of *Psycho,* Alfred Hitchcock, infuses the film with a "traditional Christian vision" and a "discourse of hope" that "sets it apart from ... films such as *Blood Simple,*" films that view humans as destined to live in a world without hope of transcendence. Likewise, Avent Beck makes the case that Oliver Stone employs allegorical methods as a central driving force of *Platoon*. Ted L. Estess focuses on William Kennedy, the author of the novel *Ironweed*, as the philosophical force strong enough to overshadow the director of the movie, Hector Babenco. Kennedy's regard for the experience of mystery informs both the novel and the film.

In each of these examples, the theological approach to film suggests that there is a driving theological purpose behind the films. This purpose shapes the tone of the film and, thus, provides the interpretative standard for the critic. The critics become theologians as they uncover the theological implications in the film under question. For example, Grimes looks at death through "Advent eyes" in order to see the hope of resurrection in Hitchcock's work, and although he talks about the director's "theologies," it is clear that the critic's theology is at stake as well. In addition, Estess deals with theological concepts such as redemption, expiation, grace, and guilt in light of his purgatorial setting.

Similarly, close examination of the remaining narrative qualities of film can provide the critic with gateways to theological ideas and concepts. Focusing on character development, the critic can trace how films build heroes and present Christ figures, individuals who transcend their surroundings and, through sacrifice, redeem their communities. Focusing on setting, the critic can probe how films manipulate the existential stage to produce, for example, a heavenly utopia or a hellish dystopia. Finally, focusing on plot, the critic can reveal how films interpret the meaning-granting possibilities of time. This last point is well illustrated in Conrad Ostwalt's chapter, in which Ostwalt explores the way film has experimented with the modern view of the end of time and time itself becomes the vehicle for a kind of secularized theology.

So, if the film student defines religion in terms of theological precepts, film can be religious because it can be a vehicle for theological speculation, can offer theological insight through allegory, and can give the viewer cause for reflection. In any event, theological criticism searches for underlying philosophical claims to truth about human existence within a particular religion or theological tradition and deals with theological concepts such as grace, forgiveness, good and evil, and redemption. Therefore, whether focusing on the didactic function of film, the creative force behind film, the narrativity of film, or some other characteristic of film not considered here, film has the capacity of "screening the sacred" through the urgent and endless search for meaning.

2

Shall These Bones Live? The Problem of Bodies in Alfred Hitchcock's *Psycho* and Joel Coen's *Blood Simple*

LARRY E. GRIMES

WHAT TO DO WITH a dead body is a difficult problem for both the practitioner of crime fiction and the preacher of the Gospel. A common response from both quarters is to skip over the presence of the body as accidental to truly significant mysteries that demand our attention. No genteel mystery writer holds our gaze for long on legs protruding from the flower bed; nor does the sensitive modern clergy preach a eulogy over an open casket.

Nevertheless, in 1960 Alfred Hitchcock, long-time practitioner of the art of cinematic murder, focused his gaze and ours unblinkingly on a dead body. For eleven minutes nothing else is of concern to actor, director, or audience. Marion Crane is dead. In 1985 Joel Coen repeated the venture. In *Blood Simple,* he allowed exactly eleven minutes to lapse between the time Julian Marty is murdered and the disposal of his body. Then, to go Hitchcock one better, he extended the burial scene for another nine minutes, finally, like Hitchcock, ending the scene with the suspense-laden "departure" of a car.

Although Hitchcock and Coen both attend directly to bodies dead and corruptible, they do not gaze on them with the same stare, nor do they tell the tale of death and dying using the same narrative strategy. This is so because they see life from different theological angles, and, as one would expect, their differing theologies give peculiar and distinct narrative shapes to the tales they tell.

My intent here is to underscore the traditional Christian vision in *Psycho*, which sets it apart from post-Christian, postmodern films such as *Blood Simple*. Vision and narration are inherently connected; since narration is by far the more concrete, I begin my theological quest with the observation that Hitchcock and Coen encounter and resolve very different narrative problems in their films. For

Hitchcock the central narrative problem is closure, the matter of an ending. Central to Hitchcock's struggle with the ending of *Psycho* is his conviction that film narrative is at once communal and manipulative, a conspiracy of audience and director, of director against audience. In an interview with François Truffaut, Hitchcock singles out *Psycho* as an example of this conspiratorial art, saying, "*Psycho* has a very interesting construction and that game with the audience was fascinating. I was directing the viewers. You might say I was playing them, like an organ."[1] His highly manipulative, deeply communal understanding of film art supports my contention that Hitchcock was an idealist in search of universal truths about the emotional, if not the cognitive, life of human beings. He told Truffaut, "If you've designed a picture correctly, in terms of its emotional impact, the Japanese audience should scream at the same time as the Indian audience." Across cultures and languages, "the image remains intact, even when the projection is faulty. It's your work that's being shown—nothing can alter that—and you're expressing yourself in the same terms everywhere."[2]

Although Coen is clearly impressed with Hitchcock's film art, he does not share Hitchcock's quest for truth through film. The central narrative problem in *Blood Simple* is not the matter of closure. It is, rather, the disparity between event and discourse, a disparity that diffuses force and dissipates truth every time there is an attempt to correlate discourse with historical event or to align one person's understanding of events with another's. Discourse and event never harmonize. No body of meaning exists in the film; thus, there can be no communal meaning, no community of meaning. In *Blood Simple* words such as myth, truth, and saga are as dead as Julian Marty and the fish on his desk.

Psycho: Establishing the Body, Remembering the Parts

Recent studies of *Psycho* have called attention to its complex composition and have isolated two very distinct movements in the film.[3] Certainly, the film is divided into parts. But I think the division is best understood as an extension of narrative practices common in literature[4] rather than through the analogy of musical tropes. Literary, not musical, models best explain the rehearsals and repetitions that divide *Psycho* into its various parts. What Hitchcock has built, I think, is a single film with multiple endings—five to be exact.

Psycho stands as a completed film, a unified narrative unit, the moment Marion Crane's car is swallowed by the swamp. Hitchcock knows this and marks the event with the only complete screen wipe in the film. This, I suggest, is the body of the film. Untouched by alternate endings, the body of the film speaks of corruption and death. Its biblical message is clear: The wages of sin is death. The first ending to *Psycho* provides no way for Marion to extricate herself from the sin-death trap into which she has stepped.

Hitchcock then adds four other possible endings. Ending two, the longest of the alternative endings, requires a reiteration of the body of the film. Marion is "resurrected" in the flesh of her sister, Lila, and joins Sam Loomis (Marion's lover) and Detective Arbogast in the search for Marion. This repetition of the story literally mirrors and frames characters in setups borrowed from earlier mise-en-scène (all the visual components of a single shot or frame). The body of the film as resurrected in ending two is a classical Hollywood film. Its narrative structure is simple. The terrible story of Marion Crane is subsumed into a murder-mystery plot. And the horror of it all is exorcised through ritual repetition of scenes until the murderer, Norman/mother, is unmasked. Significant variations are inserted in this reiteration of the original story. Two variations are the most important: Murder is now an attack on person rather than body (cleanup is no longer a time-consuming matter), and the audience role shifts from action to reaction. The second ending allows primal horror to become a predictable horror story. Conventions of the classical Hollywood film stand between viewer and action in such a way as to make corruption and death a mere celluloid fantasy. As the swinging light bulb flashes a "laugh" across mother's mummified skull, we are encouraged to think of it all as a nasty little joke.

A third ending is offered by Hitchcock. This ending is applicable only to the reiterated story and is a supplement to it. In the third ending a psychoanalyst explains the origin of Norman's insanity. This ending provides a rational explanation for the horror we have seen, an (en)lightened conclusion to a very dark film.

The fourth ending comments on the third ending and so is still a part of the reiterated story or second ending. In the fourth ending we see Norman/mother sitting in a cell and hear the mother voice assert her gentle innocence. This is the mad-house ending from which enlightened reason is completely banished. Mother denies the horror of it all—and that is her great madness. Her denial is a distorted version of the "denial" offered by the psychiatrist; hence, this mad ending is a complement to the enlightened one that preceded it.

The final ending provided by Hitchcock is connected by a series of process shots to endings two and four and by its own imagery to ending one. Hence, it takes on particular significance since it does, in fact, (re)member the entire film. The camera moves from ending four to ending five through an extreme close-up of Norman/mother's face, which is then superimposed on mother's mummified skull through which we dissolve to a shot of Marion's car being craned up from its grave in the swamp. This fifth and final ending lasts only seconds, but it (re)members the entire film as no other ending does.

To come to terms with the (re)membered film, one must first examine the body of the film, that part that traces a complete and conscious action embodied in Marion's attempt to unite her life with that of Sam Loomis. The film begins as a disembodied camera eye surveys the cityscape of Phoenix, Arizona. The camera eye moves at the will of the director, and its apparently objective view is, in fact, the subjective gaze of Hitchcock. The aerial establishing shot merges audience, director, and camera into a single eye from which to view the filmic action embodied in Marion Crane. The moment of merger is very important because it gives flesh to the camera eye. And the flesh is ours. We become the (em)bodiment of camera/frame/discourse just as Marion becomes the (em)bodiment of story. The story, then, is Marion's. Discourse, however, is a function of angle and frame, of the camera eye; therefore, it is controlled by the director and by us since audience and auteur are merged in the establishing shot.

The story of Marion Crane is easily summarized. First, she and Sam engage in sex outside marriage because economic factors mitigate against marriage. Nevertheless, Marion wants either marriage or the dissolution of their union.

At work Marion is provided with a way out of her dilemma. She can steal $40 thousand and shatter the economic wall that separates her from Sam. Quite consciously, Marion takes the money and plans to abscond with it.

Marion's intention is clear (she will steal the money, journey to Fairvale, pay Sam's debts, marry Sam, and they will live happily ever after). However, after her long conversation with Norman Bates, she modifies her intention and makes plans to disrupt her journey. But she never gets to act on those plans; instead, she is brutally murdered. Her story (along with her intentions) is slashed to pieces in the shower. Hitchcock's powerful montage sequence disembodies Marion (flesh, intention, and story) before our eyes.

The murder of Marion and the consequent termination of her story are particularly difficult for viewers of *Psycho* because the abrupt ending is unconventional. Movie-going convention dictates that films last approximately ninety minutes. Genre convention says that characters who embark on journeys arrive at suitable destinations. Hollywood convention says that stars are not brutally murdered. Therefore, as the camera watches Marion's blood swirl down the drain, as it gazes in extreme close-up on her lifeless eye, the viewer attributes life to the corpse as, for a moment, water drops seem to be tears. But Hitchcock will not tolerate such hope. He superimposes Marion's lifeless eye over a shot of the bathtub drain and, in the tight dissolve that follows, forces us to watch as all hopes for life disappear down the drain. Perhaps because Hitchcock uses a visual cliché here, some viewers still hope against fact that Marion is alive, but it is not so. As the viewer waits for convention to overcome madness, for life to defy death, Norman spends eleven long minutes cleaning up the mess that was Marion's life.

It is important to understand another way Hitchcock maintained viewer interest during the long cleanup scene. Early in the film Hitchcock not only made the audience codirector of the film, he also suckered us into the story. Our story is subtly scripted and very carefully framed. The point of contact between our story and Marion's occurs when she returns to her office from her rendezvous with Sam. Outside the office the camera records the presence of a man in a Stetson. That man is Hitchcock making his conventional signature appearance. This time he uses his appearance to link two important stories of temptation and fall. His appearance in a Stetson hat outside Marion's office anticipates the appearance of Mr. Cassidy, the unscrupulous dirty old man from whom Marion steals $40 thousand. Like Hitchcock, Cassidy wears a Stetson, and he (or at least his money) is Marion's tempter.

Our tempter, Hitchcock, is much more subtle. We are already fallen creatures when we first see our tempter. He hooked us when we willingly became the embodiment of the camera eye. At that time we joined him in willing the discourse of *Psycho*. Few viewers avert their eyes when the camera turns voyeur and enters the lovers' nest. Nor do they wish for Marion to abort her plan to steal Cassidy's money. Movie convention tells them Marion's behavior is bad. She has changed her undergarments from white to black. We know what that means. We also know Marion has the money with her when she is awakened by the state trooper, but we take her side when fixed in his powerful stare. We okay Marion's journey toward Fairvale again and again. And to make sure we know what we are saying, Hitchcock finds an ingenious way of presenting us with a script of our moral sentiment.

As she changes cars, Marion buys a newspaper. In freeze frame the full headline of the paper can be read: "Voters Okay New Water District." Hitchcock has smuggled a prompt card into the film for us, reminiscent of the clever way he made his signature appearance in *Lifeboat*. From this point on, Hitchcock begins to shape our story against Marion's story through strategic use of close-ups of the folded newspaper. Again and again he uses point-of-view shots, our point of view, to ask us if Marion's actions are "okay." In this manner we embody the will of the director and confirm his discourse. Our story is the story of a people who ogle the semiclad bodies of fornicators Marion and Sam, who adapt quickly to a Marion clad in black, who view lawful authority as menacing and oppressive. In particular, we okay Marion's decision to sign in at the Bates Motel as Marie Samuels. We okay her decision to wrap the money in the newspaper. Our last line in the film comes as Norman makes a final inspection of the motel room. The blood has been mopped up, and Marion's body is in the trunk of Norman's car. In a fitting severance of story and discourse, the camera dumps us for Norman. His camera/eye scans the room, coming to rest on the folded newspaper. We read or, rather, we say "Voters Okay," affirming all Marion has done and all that has been done to her. The actions were hers, but the discourse is ours; therefore, all that is done to Marion, including that which thwarted her intentions and drained her life of meaning, is codirected and determined by us and cannot be palmed off on Hitchcock alone. Whatever deep, dark pervasions may have motivated Hitchcock in his attack on Marion's body, he has managed to generalize and universalize them in such a way as to make many, if not all, viewers conspirators in the crime.[5] And like any good blackmailer, Hitchcock has carefully recorded our part in the conspiracy, should we ever seek to deny our guilt.

Psycho as Advent Film

Two matters remain in the body of the film that need attention before we turn to a final assessment of the film (re)membered. First, there is the matter of the opening title, which identifies the time and place of the film's action. It was shot in Phoenix in December. But the inclusion of this title does more than anchor this "psychotic" film in human time; it also gives the film a symbolic frame. Phoenix and Advent are juxtaposed. According to legend, the beautiful Phoenix reproduced itself by first consuming itself in flames then rising from its own ashes. This version of death/rebirth is both ahistorical and asexual. On the other hand, Advent hails the coming of God in the flesh. Advent is the season the church celebrates in the weeks before Christmas. It prepares Christians for the birth of Christ. A time of joyous anticipation, it affirms the significance of physical, sexual, historical existence.

Hitchcock, I argue, has made an Advent film. And it is the Advent context that helps us to address the problem of bodies in the film and to arrive at an answer to the question, Shall these bones live? Hitchcock's commentary on the Advent theme in his film is carried by a much repeated money motif. As Leland Poague has pointed out, money matters are important parts of every scene in what I have called the body of the film. However, I think the money motif makes much more sense if interpreted through traditional Christian theology. The problem is that of debts and debtors rather than of capitalism and Ford automobiles, as Poague would have it.[6] Athanasius, the fourth-century theologian who concentrated on the doctrine of the incarnation, justified the incarnation—the central concern of Advent—by noting that death and corruption had gained a legal hold over humankind through sin and that "the handiwork of God was in process of dissolution."[7] Only radical action on the part of God could both satisfy the just sentence of death imposed on human beings and maintain the glory of God's chief handiwork. That radical act of satisfaction, according to Athanasius, was the act of the word become flesh.

Anselm, French theologian of the eleventh century, extended the observations of Athanasius and concluded, "When you pay what you owe to God, even if you have not sinned, you must not count this as part of the debt you owe for sin. But you owe God all those things you have mentioned. For in this mortal life there ought to be such great love, and longing to reach that for which you were made. ... What then will you pay to God for your sin?"[8] Anselm answered this question by evolving from incarnation theology an economic theory of atonement, which he summarizes as follows: "It would not have been right for the restoration of human nature to be left undone, and how it could not have been done unless [humans] paid what was owing to God for sin. But the debt was so great that, while [humans] alone owed it, only God could pay it, so that the same person must be both God and [human]."[9]

The concern for debts that cannot be repaid runs through the film. Sam is trying to repay his father's debts. He must also pay his wife alimony. When Marion steals the $40 thousand to pay off Sam's debt, she incurs a debt of her own. This is made most clear after she confesses the error of her ways and decides to return to

Phoenix and make restitution. However, the calculations in her checkbook show that she cannot even repay the full amount of her financial debt, let alone her legal and moral debts. Cassidy may be right when, in his role of tempter, he says he buys off unhappiness. But neither his money nor anything else human beings possess can buy off death, which is a central point in Athanasius, Anselm, and Hitchcock. The wages of sin is death, and sin will have its due.

This said, we are ready to (re)member *Psycho*. First, to do so we must sort out discourse from story. We must find *Hitchcock's Psycho* as it is embedded in this Hollywood film, for the credits make it clear that the proper title is "Hitchcock's Psycho." As far back as *The Lodger,* Hitchcock told Truffaut, he was aware that there was a difference between the film he wanted to make and the film the studio system would allow him to make.[10] In *Psycho*, I suggest, he has it both ways. Through his clever use of multiple endings he makes a one-hour film to his own satisfaction while delivering a feature-length movie to the studio. "*Hitchcock's Psycho,*" I think, denies the asexual, ahistorical Phoenix-like thesis of endings two, three, and four, which reiterate the original story and bend away from the radically incarnational Advent motif. His *Psycho* is the film that is completed when Marion's body sinks into the swamp, and it is (re)membered through the powerful, although ambiguous, shot of her car being resurrected from the depths. But *Psycho* is an Advent and not an Easter film. Like the season, it is marked by waiting. The waiting is long and empty. First, there is the unprecedented eleven-minute scene in which Norman disposes of the dead body. Then there are the multiple endings, alternate and bogus, that seek to divert our gaze from the problem of bodies, sin, debt, and death, which we have made our own by sharing deeply in Marion's guilt, Hitchcock's guilt, the guilt of the "framing eye."

The violent phallic murder of Marion is an attack on womb and earth, against the goddess, against life. Yet for all its terrible violence, it is an empty action. Marion is not freed from her trap by it, nor is Norman freed from his. Violence against the mother/body does nothing to lessen the problem of bodies; in fact, it heightens the terror of life in the flesh. But, I think, Hitchcock's conclusion is neither gnostic nor nihilistic. Rather, he demands of the audience that it watch and wait, that it not be distracted by fanciful solutions to the problem or rational solutions or madness. The audience must live in its flesh, know its guilt, its debt, and its death, and watch and wait. To wait is to not foreclose. To wait is to beat the trap, to deny (en)closure. To wait is to have hope, to adopt a discourse that keeps the life story open. And the discourse of *Hitchcock's Psycho* is a discourse of waiting, a discourse of hope. Given the discourse of hope that informs the story of *Hitchcock's Psycho*, it is possible to read the last scene, the fifth ending, through Advent eyes. One can hope, as the car is pulled from the swamp, that the dead shall be raised incorruptible. Although such hope may deny the events of the film, the events of life, I do not think such hope is contrary to the Advent-based, incarnational discourse, which (re)members the body of the film for all who watch and wait without averting their eyes.

Blood Simple: Down Here You're on Your Own

Like *Psycho, Blood Simple* is a film with two titles. Although cataloged as "Blood Simple," the title recorded in the film's opening credits is a simple sentence: "Blood simple." And the title appears, I think, as the closing sentence to the prologue of the film. The prologue is delivered by an unnamed private investigator. As the private investigator makes his remarks, the camera provides us with panoramic shots of Texas oil country framed between close-up shots of an asphalt highway. The private investigator drawls, "The world is full of complainers. The fact is, nothing comes with a guarantee. And I don't care if you're the pope of Rome, the president of the United States, or man of the year, something can go wrong. Go ahead, ya know, complain to your neighbor. Ask for help and watch him fly. Now in Russia they got it mapped out so everyone pulls for everyone else. But what I know about is Texas, and down here you're on your own." Then the title appears in sentence form: "Blood simple."

And so it is, at least down in Texas. Elemental desires and fears motivate all of the action in the film. Event overrides discourse. Art becomes style. Much happens in the film, but it means little. This film does not express or support a theological vision. The film story (events) begins as Ray drives Abby toward Houston. Abby is married to Julian Marty, a bar owner (Ray's boss), and has decided to leave him. Rain strikes the windshield *Psycho* style. The two, at Abby's instigation, decide to pull off the main road (*Psycho* deja vu again), find a motel, and satisfy their sexual appetites. The private investigator from the prologue, who is in Marty's hire, follows them to the motel, takes pictures, and informs Marty of his wife's infidelity. Ray loses his job but keeps Abby. An angry cuckold, Marty hires the private investigator to kill Abby and Ray. The private investigator agrees. He sends Marty out of town on a fishing trip and takes photographs of Abby and Ray, which he doctors to make it appear that he has murdered the couple. When he gives Marty the pictures, he collects his fee and then shoots Marty with Abby's gun. According to the investigator's plan, the police will find the body and the murder weapon and arrest Abby. However, it is Ray who finds the body and the weapon. Thinking that Abby has killed Marty, Ray goes through a *Psycho*-like cleanup at the murder scene, then bundles Marty's body into his car. Unfortunately, Ray is wrong on two counts: Abby did not kill Marty, and Marty is not dead.

Problems with Marty's body dramatize the disparity between event and discourse, between the brutality of life and the attempt to create higher meaning. As the burial scene unfolds, the humor of the film becomes dark, bold, and ironic. Coen does not use this graveyard scene, as Shakespeare might have, to take us through gallows humor from corruption toward a deeper meaning or the hope of redemption. He only plays at the idea of raising bodies from the dead, and he plays it well. Viewers cannot contain the horrible laughter they emit when Marty, lying near death at the bottom of his grave, raises himself and attempts to shoot Ray, only to fail and be hastily buried alive. Coen's foray into "bodies raised" ends in slapstick laughter, gallows humor, and gross indifference to human life. It offers no sign of redemption or hope.

The remainder of the film centers on the investigator's efforts to kill Abby and Ray, thus leaving no witnesses who can connect him to Marty's murder. In the end, Abby kills the investigator, thinking he is Ray. The story ends there, but no dominant discourse emerges from the film. The characters are all trapped in private discourses, which the audience finds inadequate as responses to the story. Because no communal discourse has developed during the film, the terribly cynical emptiness of the prologue (oral and visual) haunts us at its end. These bodies will not rise. Indeed, the living seem almost dead. One wants to complain but remembers the voice of the investigator: "Go ahead, ya know, complain to your neighbor. Ask for help and watch him fly. … Down here you're on your own." "Blood simple."

Coen's film draws out most clearly the connection between naturalism and absurdism that is so critical to postmodernist thinking. Human behavior is blood simple—we do as our bodies direct—and physical desire is the discourse of human life. All meaning is biological, private, and blood simple. In this context old-fashioned idealist theology makes no sense, for between idea and sense there is always the problem of the body. And bodies do not rise. They do not rise from the dead, nor do they rise beyond themselves to form some ideal corpus called humanity. "Down here you're on your own."

To ensure that the philosophical and theological implications of his film are integral to the narrative, Coen does two things. First, he borrows Hitchcock's signature role from *Psycho* and adapts it to the demands of his own work. The gross Mr. Cassidy and the manipulative Hitchcock from *Psycho* are merged in *Blood Simple* to create Coen's vulgar, cunning, Stetson-wearing tempter—the private eye. Although nameless, the detective has a definite identity. As his cigarette lighter proclaims, he is/was "the man of the year." Unlikely as the designation seems, given the laid-back sleaziness of the character, the label makes sense as Coen subtly reveals the name of this tempter. He is Beelzebub, Lord of the Flies. High on a cliff overlooking the Rio Grande, the private eye wheels and deals to corrupt human souls as a lone fly crawls along his brow. The fly is present again as he shoots and double-crosses Julian Marty. Evil incarnate is present in this film. But evil as (em)bodied in the investigator is as limited as any other force at work in human life. Although it has some agency of its own, its discourse by no means determines or encompasses events. Event exceeds discourse, even the discourse of evil, tumbling on beyond the control of any evident agency until even the Lord of the Flies bows to the pressure of story and lies dead with eyes fixed on the plumbing of a bathroom sink.

The second mark of emptiness in the film is created through the careful mixing of sight and sound. Early in the film we become aware of the endless round of overhead fans as the camera tilts back to watch them turn or shoots down through them as they chop-wipe scenes of human life and death. Connected with the chop-wipe of the fan blade is the swush-swush of its blades, which record on the sound track like the slow pump of the human heart. Together they create an oral/visual equivalent of the theme that life is blood simple. Integrated into this image of the blood-simple life are two objects that have symbolic importance in the film. The first is a stringer of dead fish. The second is the detective's cigarette lighter. The fish and the lighter are crucial props in the scene in which the investigator murders Marty. What is important about the fish is that they are dead. Close-up after close-up reinforces this fact. Traditionally a symbol of the Lordship of Christ, the dead fish balance the Lord of the Flies symbol, indicating that neither redemption nor evil is an effective agent in a world that is blood simple. As for the lighter with its inscription to "the man of the year," it is lost under the scales of the dead fish. No one ever retrieves it. Like the fish, its traditional symbolic worth is negated here. No light shines in the darkness. Salvation and damnation are both empty words in this blood-simple world. What dominates is the chop-wipe of the ever-turning blade, the swush-swush of the pumping heart. Community and ideality are necessary to give life to abstract concepts such as evil and good. But there is no community here. Again we feel the force of the prologue: "Down here you're on your own."

What I conclude from the study of these two films is that the problem of bodies is serious and significant for modern people. Hitchcock is deeply troubled by the problem and slashes out at it visually. But his frenzy of cinematic violence only produces death ineluctable. Gazing fixedly at death, he then turns to the power of human community and religious discourse to (re)member us all. The best he can do is to unite us in bodies hopelessly corruptible as he joins with us in a seemingly unending wait for resurrection. Without Advent eyes, one must read the film as William Rothman and so many others have, insisting that

> Every film image is a death mask of the world. The world of film is past. The camera fixes its living subjects, possesses their life. They are reborn on the screen, creatures of the film's author and ourselves. But life is not fully breathed back into them. They are immortal, but they are always dead. The beings projected on the screen are condemned to a condition of death-in-life from which they can never escape. What lures us into the world of a film may be a dream of triumphing over death, holding death forever at bay. But *Psycho* demonstrates what Hitchcock's work has always declared: The world of film is not a private island where we may escape the conditions of our existence. At the heart of every film is a truth we already know: We are born into the world and we are fated to die.[11]

Yes, *Psycho* supports part of this reading but not all of it. We are fated to die. Death is embedded in life. But through Advent eyes, eyes provided in this film, life can be (re)membered. In Hitchcock's *Psycho,* I think Christian discourse finally shapes story into the affirmative with regard to the question, Shall these bones live? *Blood Simple,* on the other hand, confirms the worldview through which so many contemporary critics read *Psycho.* There people are fated to die; to die empty, private deaths that end lives that have mattered not at all. What is most striking about Hitchcock's film, I think, is that it can be viewed back-to-back with the coldly naturalistic *Blood Simple* and not seem sentimental or trite. Hitchcock gives traditional Christian discourse credibility in *Psycho.* In fact, the conclusions he reaches with regard to the problem of bodies seem more complex and more fresh than the stylish but clichéd postmodernism of Coen.

3

Angels in the Primum Mobile: Dimensions of the Sacred in William Kennedy's *Ironweed*, Novel and Film

TED L. ESTESS

The empyrean, which is not spatial at all, does not move, and has no poles. It girds with light and love, the primum mobile, the utmost and the swiftest of the material heavens. Angels are manifested in the primum mobile.

—William Kennedy

The major thing is not to get on in the world but to get home.

—Italo Calvino

The squabble over the relative merits of a novelistic as opposed to a cinematic rendering of a story is like the argument about the relative importance of pitching and hitting in the World Series: often predictable, eventually tiresome, but unavoidable. We sometimes wish for the clarity of an Ingmar Bergman, who, although subtle and nuanced on most subjects, is blunt about this one: "We should avoid making films out of books" (quoted in Kennedy 1988, 21). In contrast, Hector Babenco, the Argentine-Brazilian director who received a 1985 Academy Award as best director for his rendering of Manuel Puig's novel *Kiss of the Spider Woman,* is almost nonchalant on the matter: "Translating a novel into a film is just re-creating the emotions the novel inspired when you first read it" ("Dialogue" 1986, 14). William Kennedy, a former movie critic and the screenwriter for Francis Ford Coppola's *Cotton Club* and for Babenco's translation of *Ironweed,* complicates the matter from a novelist's perspective.

> When a writer undertakes the writing of a script from a novel of his own, it is tantamount to self-amputative surgery. You eventually pose in front of the mirror without a left ear, a right thumb, with a thigh partly sliced away, the left leg dangling at the an-

gle, and then you decide that you're ready for the premiere. Just comb the hair a little to the left, wear gloves, bulky trousers, and a high shoe, and who'll notice? You may even set a new style. (1988, 22)

Turning a Novel into a Film

In Babenco's translation of Kennedy's novel *Ironweed,* we are aware that an ear is missing and that other extremities have been carved, but we still encounter a work sufficiently powerful to make us think Bergman is too austere in his magisterial pronouncement. Films can be made from books and be well made at that. Babenco's film, in fact, re-creates much of the emotional energy of Kennedy's book, even at the cost of massive "self-amputative surgery" suffered by its author-screenwriter. Gone, necessarily, is much of the soaring lyricism of the novel. As the camera moves from the train up to sky and on to the stars in the opening sequence of the film, we perhaps see Babenco's desire to evoke that lyricism, as he does later, in the use of soft, amber tones to intensify key scenes. But the film, although conveying the novel's elegiac sadness, is bleaker, in large part, I think, because the film ultimately cannot represent the lyricism of Kennedy's poetic prose. Gone as well is the book's linguistic expansiveness, which draws the reader into contemplative engagement with both the subject and the style of the written text. In its place we have memorable linguistic nuggets and sufficient dialogue to carry the plot, but the language of the film hardly matches that of the novel, nor should we expect it to.

The film does transpose, with mixed success, two crucial strategies that are prominent in the novel. First, the film retains, although in far less explicit terms, literary allusions to deepen and enlarge the canvas of the story. Much of the power of the novel arises from Kennedy's melding of literary allusions, drawn especially from the epic tradition, into the narrative pattern. He credibly associates literary antecedents with a bum's life in the United States, such that the story of Francis Phelan unmistakably evokes the American ethos—first because the story occurs in depression-burdened Albany, New York, but, more important, because it employs that which above all else, including the cowboys, renders a hero quint-essentially American: baseball. Kennedy's protagonist achieves mythic proportions distinctly American because he has played on fields, almost elysian, with the great Ty Cobb and the immortal Walter Johnson. Along with situating his characters in relationship to ancestors in the worlds of both literature and baseball, Kennedy's novel energetically deploys a second narrative strategy, that of *magical realism* (Gibbs). We know magical realism best through the genius of Gabriel Garcia Márquez. Although Kennedy's novel lacks the zany, almost absurdist dislocations of sensibility Márquez practices, it bears a family resemblance to the Columbian's work in its opposition to the minimalist commitments of many other recent fiction writers. Kennedy's novel—and likewise the film—share Márquez's sense that magical possibilities reside in commonplace reality. Reality, for both novel and film, is more than it seems to be. Reality is not exhausted by linear, rationalist expectations but is subject to eruptions of the unexpected, to rapid, miraculous transformation by the irrational. Similarly, time does not move ahead in a single direction through unique, discrete moments but persistently cycles by again and again, such that the past becomes undeniably, *really* present again. For the magical realist, time is reversible. In *Ironweed,* novel and film, even the dead are alive.

The film, I should add, does achieve effects unavailable to the written text. First, it seems more concretely, because it is more visibly, rooted in historical circumstance than the novel, especially since Kennedy's linguistic soaring tends to detach the reader from the specifics of the socioeconomic situation of the characters. The film, moreover, makes audible—hence more palpable—the music, which, as we presently see, has important thematic implications for both the written and cinematic forms of the story. In addition, the film gives us faces in a way a book can never do. "The close-up," Italo Calvino has written, "has no equivalent in a narrative fashioned of words" (1986, 75). He expands: "Literature is totally lacking in any working method to enable it to isolate a single vastly enlarged detail in which one face comes forward to underline a state of mind or stress the importance of a single detail in comparison with the rest" (1986, 75). In *Ironweed*-as-film this technical advantage creates an immense expressive advantage, especially given such faces as those of Jack Nicholson, Meryl Streep, Hy Anzell, and Tom Waits. No writer is equal to the mystery and expressive capability of a human face or, for that matter, a human voice; whereas the visual image the camera provides of, say, Jack Nicholson limits the viewer to one face, what the visual image loses because it is more specific is more than compensated for by what it gains by presenting, with greater immediacy, the mystery of a single human being. Finally, *Ironweed*-as-film gains in coherence over the novel, as William Kennedy would have it do. Film, Kennedy writes,

> yearns for coherence. The novel does also, but the novel can tolerate sideshows and excrescences that wouldn't be allowed by most modern filmmakers. Because the novel requires an exercise of the intellect, an intimacy with the reader's mind and reasoning powers, it can meander and ruminate, it can luxuriate in language alone, and gain in depth from these excursions. But because film is an exercise in immediacy, of raw life perceived in the instant that it happens, those meanderings are judged to be irrelevancies that dilute or divert the principal focus of the story. Stay in the center ring and never mind the sideshows, is the revered wisdom. (1988, 25)

Although such comparisons of the novel and its cinematic rendering are almost inevitable, we might try another approach. Instead of placing novel and film in competition and judging the one by the standards of the other, it is finally more fruitful first to see each as a work in and of itself, subject to its own conventions and rules of creation; expressive of the vision and concerns of novelist and director, respectively; and capable, in more or less satisfying ways, of exploiting the narrative and visual materials and strategies at Kennedy's and Babenco's disposal. But such an ideal rendering of the relationship of a novel and a film is just that:

ideal. As with many ideals, it is neither practicable or attainable. More desirable, because it is more true to the interpretative situation in which the reader-viewer of a novel-film is placed, is to allow the novel and film to resonate with each other but in a complementary rather than a competitive way. It is unavoidable that a person who walks into a theater having read the book on which a movie is based will view the film differently from other, "unread" viewers. But it is feckless for that "informed" viewer simply to respond by saying, "This is different from, or less than, or better than the novel." Better, I think, to juxtapose the two works so as to allow for insights that might not emerge were one dealing with the film or novel alone; one thereby might see more clearly what lies at the source of both works—the vision of William Kennedy.

Kennedy's Purgatorial Vision

In aiming the hermeneutical task at the vision of William Kennedy, I do not wish to distract from the creative activity of the director, for Kennedy is correct in saying "film is a director's medium." He goes on: "Who would doubt it? Well, producers sometimes, writers sometimes, actors sometimes, also critics, charwomen, and rachitic, one-eyed shut-ins, who all know how to do it better. But if Babenco isn't in charge then it's the committee system at work, the bureaucratic underworld: Casey, North, Poindexter, doing a soft-shoe imitation of Ronald Reagan shuffling off to Managua" (Kennedy 1988, 22). Babenco certainly knows how to make films, but in making this particular film, he places his artistic and technical powers and skills in service to the work that initially energized his imagination for the project. Indeed, he sees himself, as I have noted, as re-creating the emotions *Ironweed* inspired when he first read it. He is a co-respondent to that to which William Kennedy responds; his response, then, is in an important sense subject to the novel and to the novelist, even more so since he engaged Kennedy to write the screenplay for the film.

My concern in discussing Kennedy's religious vision is with the way in which the stories of Francis Phelan and, to a lesser extent, of Helen Archer achieve mythic proportion and theological weight. The stories of these two characters, so firmly rooted in the time and place of Albany during the Depression era, resonate with deep, archetypic significance. In the stories of their humble lives, ultimate concerns are addressed, the profane and the sacred are fused. This blending reflects the Catholic sacramental perspective, the deep sense that God becomes present in human flesh in a fallen world. The stories evoke the abiding, deep-down mystery of the human situation in time and eternity; and mystery, William Kennedy says, is "the basic element in all works of art" (Kennedy 1987, 4), certainly, we might add, in all works that achieve mythic proportion and theological profundity. Such works place the self in relation to time in all its modalities, past, present, and future; they measure the self against eternity, often in relationship to the dead; they display the self in struggle with the material conditions of the time and locale without implying that the self is exhausted by those conditions; they situate individuals in relation to their fellows and explore the limits and promises of human communities, often reconstituting community after a season of social chaos; they allow for hierophantic moments and constitute special places, which we might appropriately call sacred times and sacred spaces; they follow a recognizable and enduring structure, such as a journey; they give narrative pattern to the exploration of unavoidable human concerns, such as love, death, suffering, guilt, betrayal, fidelity; they plumb the interior life and give a human face to the energies, benevolent and malevolent, that shape the psyche; they show human beings doing business with gods and goddesses.

The critical response to the book and the film has made much of the connections between Kennedy's character and Dante, and, to be sure, the connections are manifest and many. The epigraph to the book, which consists of the opening lines of part 2 of Dante's great cartograph of the soul, establishes a purgatorial soulscape:

> *To course o'er better waters now hoists sail*
> *the little bark of my wit, leaving behind her a*
> *sea so cruel.*

A subtle change from the novel establishes a similar situation for the film. Early in the morning of October 31, Francis Phelan and his companion in distress, Rudy (played by Tom Waits), are working in a cemetery; for the first time since 1916, when he inadvertently dropped his thirteen-day-old son, breaking his neck and killing him, Francis Phelan comes to the grave of his child. In the book the epitaph reads "Gerald Michael Phelan, born April 13, 1916. Born on the 13th, lived 13 days. An unlucky child who was much loved" (Kennedy 1984, 18). But in the film—as we clearly see in a photograph that appears in Claudio Edinger's *The Making of Ironweed*—the gravestone reads "LUCKY CHILD: He lived 13 Days and leaped over Purgatory" (1988, 16). Why lucky? No doubt because Gerald had gone directly to the heavenly paradise; but in view of his father's story, Gerald is lucky because he has "leaped over" the long purgatorial anguish that is, in the world of *Ironweed,* human life.

To place Kennedy's character in a purgatorial situation is not to suggest that Francis Phelan has been in an inferno stage while on the bum and that now, on Halloween 1938, he emerges for the first time on the purgatorial slopes. Rather, it is to suggest that William Kennedy views all human life, from start to finish, as purgatorial in character. Whether one realizes it or not, redemption is needed, expiation is required. Francis Phelan is a "failing" human being, and, as such, he is Kennedy's representative of all human creatures who in varying ways transgress in word, thought, and deed. If one forgets—and Francis Phelan has forgotten—that purgation is needed or even possible, then life will be experienced as infernal; but even while in the state of forgetfulness, a person such as Francis engages all the time in one purgatorial activity after the other, blind to where redemption might reside but nonetheless incipiently aware that something is needed to relieve the guilt and sorrow and regret that cling to one in this journey through time. In Kennedy's world, the question, then, is not whether one will engage in purgatorial activity but whether one's activity will bring one near the much-needed redemption. For twenty-two years Francis Phelan has kept himself away from redemption and forgiveness, and he has done so by flight. But now, in the late hours of his fifty-eighth year, he returns to his hometown to remember that he has forgotten that forgiveness is possible. In the three days of this story, he engages in acts of expiation. These lead finally to his regeneration as he moves back into Annie's home, indeed, back into *his* own home with *his* own family.

In one of those excrescences in which Kennedy says a novelist can indulge but that a screenwriter must necessarily amputate, the narrator of the novel accentuates the Dantesque situation of Francis Phelan by reporting from the perspective of the long-dead infant: "Should [Gerald] absolve the man of all guilt, not for the dropping, for that was accidental, but for the abandonment of the family, for craven flight when the steadfast virtues were called for?" (Kennedy 1984, 17) Of special note here is that in the world as construed by novel and film, the dead have a reality independent of Francis Phelan's consciousness. Reality includes both the living and dead; reality is accretive, which is to say, the dead do not go away even when they are dead. Writer and director do not want us to conclude that Francis is, as some early critics have remarked, simply suffering the effects of alcohol-induced DT's, "the shakes," or is experiencing some other kind of intrapsychic hallucination. For Babenco, it is technically more difficult to make clear that these "spooks" exist apart from Francis, especially since Francis alone perceives them; but in the novel Kennedy's intent is clear, as in this passage, which shows Gerald thinking, even acting, independently: "Gerald, through an act of silent will, imposed on his father the pressing obligation to perform his final acts of expiation for abandoning the family. You will not know, the child silently said, what these acts are until you have performed them all. And after you have performed them you will not understand that they were expiatory any more than you have understood all the other expiation that has kept you in such prolonged humiliation. Then, when these final acts are complete, you will stop trying to die because of me" (Kennedy 1984, 19).

Without being aware of what is going on, then, Francis Phelan performs acts of expiation that, when complete, will lead to his recovering his own life. The goal toward which he unknowingly traverses is that self-sovereignty Vergil ultimately bestows on Dante in *Purgatorio* 27: "I crown and miter you over you yourself" (Dante 1983, 142). But the traverse to that point is arduous, especially on Halloween, "the unruly night when grace is always in short supply, and the old and the new dead walk abroad in this land" (Kennedy 1984, 29).

We can, at this point, better appreciate William Kenndey's purgatorial sensibility by relating it to other currents in the literary world. First, by envisioning the human predicament in purgatorial terms, Kennedy emerges as a Catholic writer.

He is so not because his current beliefs accord with the teachings of the church but because his imagination has been thoroughly shaped by Catholic education and Catholic culture and by the way in which that education and culture have appropriated the ancient sources of the Western tradition. These sources include the Greeks and the Romans, especially the epics of Homer and Vergil (who lead, of course, to Dante and Joyce, both of whose marks are explicit in the novel, implicit in the film). But second, to characterize Kennedy's as a purgatorial sensibility is to differentiate him from another powerful current in the literary temperament of the past one hundred years or so. We might term that current *infernal;* in so doing I have in mind such figures as the Malcolm Lowry of *Under the Volcano,* the Franz Kafka of *The Trial,* the Jean-Paul Sartre of *No Exit,* and the Samuel Beckett of *Endgame.* In designating the work of these great masters of distress as infernal, I do not wish to imply that no possibility for regeneration resides in their imaginative territory; nor do I deny that the negative, which they so unrelentingly and severely intensify, can make present the possibility of regeneration, if only by force of its absence. Still, there is a vast distance between the territory of the infernal and the purgatorial soulscape of William Kennedy, where the arc of spiritual movement, after a long period of descent, seems characteristically to curve upward, moving his protagonists toward brighter, consolatory moments.

If we are, then, to conjure the mythic dimension of *Ironweed,* we must trace the purgatorial journeys Francis Phelan and Helen Archer follow on Halloween and All Saints' Day, 1938. Francis is brought consciously into the process by a bit of news delivered by his son, Billy. Again, the scene in the cemetery is crucial for establishing Francis's situation as unremittingly purgatorial. Francis drops to his knees before the gravestone; with bleary, tearing eyes and scruffy, dissolute countenance, he speaks to the infant in the grave: "You know, I saw Billy a week or so ago and the kid looks good. ... We talked about you. He says your mother never blamed me for dropping you. Never told a soul in twenty-two years it was me let you fall. Is that some woman or isn't it?" (Kennedy 1984, 19).

Having spent twenty-two years in guilty flight, Francis finds it incredible that his wife, Annie, has not castigated him for Gerald's death. Four times in the film—first to Gerald in the cemetery, then to Helen during their late-night walk on the street, then to Annie, and finally to a collection of bums in a shantytown called the "Jungle"—Francis recalls Billy's report. The repetition establishes this news as pivotal in Francis's consciousness, as we clearly see when he talks with Annie, who simply tells Francis it "wasn't your fault" (Kennedy 1984, 159). The voluble Francis, never without ample reply, is moved to silence—and gratitude: "No way I can thank you for that, Annie. Thanks just don't touch something like that. That's something I don't even know" (Kennedy 1984, 159). He has sloshed for years through sour days and bitter nights, living in ramshackle tenements and fleeing railroad cops; all the while, homebound Annie has remained steady and faithful, angry at times but ultimately forgiving and accepting. Realizing this,

Francis can only remark, "You're some original kind of woman, Annie. Some original kind of woman" (Kennedy 1984, 159).

Before following the journey of Francis to its appointed end, I turn briefly to Helen, who, unlike Francis, is more sinned against than sinning. Years before, while a promising musician at Vassar, Helen first experienced life's harshness when her father committed suicide. Helen's mother deviously arranged for all of the inheritance to go to her son, thus betraying and blocking Helen's future. With the inheritance, the brother finished law school and prospered; with nothing, Helen left Vassar in 1906 to work in a music store, only later to skid toward homeless destitution. Her life has been unremittingly sad, so that when we meet her in Kennedy's story she passes her sorry days regretting what might have been.

Although she is a bundle of unfulfilled possibilities, Helen still comports herself with dignity, struggling all the time to maintain self-respect. To Francis Phelan, Helen Marie Archer is "a great soul"; and she is so, not only because she has loved Francis but because her soul has been shaped and enlarged by that art which, above all others, is purgatorial: music. Indeed, for Dante, purgatory is the realm of music. Why might this be? Perhaps because music acts directly on the soul, without the mediation of thought and reason; music expands and opens the soul, making one susceptible to the ministrations of grace; music quiets discords within and attunes one to the harmonies of the spheres; music transports one from the finite to the infinite, from time to eternity: "Oh the lovely power of music to rejuvenate Helen" (Kennedy 1984, 118).

In Babenco's translation of the story, three of the most memorable scenes center on Helen's music. First, as she sings "He's My Pal" at the Gilded Cage—where Meryl Streep gives an extraordinary performance—Helen mistakenly fantasizes that she is making a big hit with her audience. Then, in a music store—after telling a little girl "music is one of the greatest things in our lives; we ought to be willing to die for our music"—Helen prepares for death by playing a haunting piano composition. Finally, in Palombo's Hotel, she dies with the plangent chords of the third movement of Beethoven's *Ninth Symphony* sounding from a phonograph. Significantly, in the novel Helen's death music is the "Choral Ode" from the fourth movement. In addition to choosing a more somber tone generally for the film, Babenco perhaps changed movements because of the great difference between reading on the page that Helen hears Beethoven's setting of *Freude, schöner Götterfunken/Tochter aus Elysium* and actually hearing these triumphant sounds from the screen. The fourth movement would simply have overwhelmed the scene, but with the third movement Babenco maintains emotional control while still allowing the music to console and enlarge this "great soul" as she moves from this world.

Helen's journey, like Francis's, is purgatorial. In addition to being cleansed by music, she enacts explicit rites of purgation on All Saint's Day, 1938. At dawn, after "paying" for the night's shelter in Finny's car by masturbating him, she crawls out,

wiping her hands, even picking up dust to use as a cleansing agent. At Saint
Anthony's Church, Babenco has her gingerly wash her hands in the holy water before she kneels to confess "forgive me for I have sinned. But, for me, they are not
really sins, but *decisions*." Helen displays "a will to grace, if you would like to call it
that, however elusive that grace has proven to be" (Kennedy 1984, 134). As if to emphasize that even when grace is elusive the unexpected can happen, Babenco has
Helen find a $10 bill as she gets up from the prayer, and with this gift she goes to
Palombo's Hotel to redeem her things and enact her final purgative rites. There, in
a scene powerfully rendered by Streep, Helen composes herself for death. She constitutes the lonely hotel room as a haven; for her, it is home. Before her bath, and
with Beethoven sounding from the phonograph, she places on a table her few enduring objects—a brush and a mirror and, most important, a picture of herself as
a child with her father. The picture of her father makes present the only family she
has; the picture of herself as a child mitigates the scars of time.

Together, I suggest, the picture and the music and her bath challenge, even reverse, the effects of time. The reversal is a mythic, mysterious reversal like the resurrection, which cannot undo, in an empirical, publicly verifiable way, the scars of
time; but, I venture, in the felt experience of Helen the reversal is nonetheless real,
such that the "great soul" that is Helen Marie Archer dies in harmony with the
spheres. In this scene we have both historical and religious experience: In history,
Helen's life is lonely and relentlessly sad, but concurrently, in the mythic sacramental realm, she is absolved, purged, transported. In evoking this double truth
of Helen's last moments, Kennedy has earned the reader's permission to intensify
even further the poetic fervor of his prose. As she dies, Helen thinks of Beethoven,
"Ode to Joy,"

> *And hears the joyous multitudes advancing,*
> *Dah dah-dah,*
> *Dah dah-de-dah-dah,*
> *And feels her legs turning to feathers and sees that*
> *her head is*
> *floating down to meet them as her body bends under the weight of*
> *so much joy,*
> *Sees it floating ever so slowly*
> *As the white bird glides over the water until it comes to*
> *rest on the Japanese kimono*
> *That has fallen so quietly*
> *So softly,*
> *Onto the grass where the moonlight grows.*
> *(Kennedy 1984, 139)*

Homecoming

As Helen self-consciously constitutes her place and composes herself for death in
Palombo's Hotel, Francis arrives at Annie's house across town on Pearl Street,

there to enact similar rites of confession and purgation and to reconnect with enduring things from his past. The return of Francis after such a long absence reminds one of the most famous traveler of all, Odysseus. In a bath scene reminiscent of Odysseus's in Book 19 of the *Odyssey,* Francis scrubs the sediment of street and junkyard from his scarred limbs, to emerge resplendently attired in the suit and shoes he had left behind twenty-two years before. The associations with Homer's traveler are as manifest as those with Dante's. Away for twenty years, Odysseus returns to a wife who is exemplary in her fidelity and resourcefulness; after twenty-two years, Francis returns to Annie, who says she "only had one man" (Kennedy 1984, 161). Odysseus stays for seven years with the nymph Kalypso, and Francis spends nine years with Helen. Odysseus makes a name for himself at Troy, fighting with and against legendary heroes on the field of battle, whereas Francis gains fame playing baseball on the field of sport, first at nearby Troy and later in the majors with the Washington Senators.

More important than these similarities are correspondences between the character of Odysseus and that of Francis Phelan. First, both are great talkers and storytellers. Accordingly, we might recall Odysseus's singing his adventures to the Phaiakians in Books 9–12 and to Penelope in Book 23 of the *Odyssey* as we watch Francis enthrall his family with stories and as we read of Rowdy Dick Dowlan's response to Francis's crafty wordsmithing. "Why should any man," Rowdy Dick thinks of Francis, "be so gifted not only with so much pleasurable history but also with a gift of gab that could mesmerize a quintet of bums around a fire under a bridge?" (Kennedy 1984, 73–74). A clue to why Odysseus and Francis have so much history to relate, and a clue to the character of each, lies in their names. We have already associated Phelan with failing, but we can also pause with Odysseus. In Homer, the name connotes trouble, pain, strife, difficulty. Contentious Odysseus could well be named Trouble, for he characteristically is both a troublemaker and the recipient of trouble (Dimmock). And so with Francis: Everywhere he has gone, he has dished out trouble and received trouble in return. That right hand of his, which was the source of glory on the baseball field, is also the bane of his existence. Just at the time he was shining at third base, he killed his first man by throwing a stone during an Albany trolley strike. Toward the end of the novel, in one last spasm of violence, he kills a man with a baseball bat. So it has gone throughout his life: He has exacted payment and respect from others by force of his hands, but all the time the load of guilt has mounted on this failing and violent, yet gifted and grand, creature.

The scene in which Francis Phelan returns to his house on Pearl Street is superbly rendered in both novel and film. Beginning with Annie's startled reception of Francis at the steps and culminating in the family meal of thanksgiving (featuring the turkey Francis incongruously presents), the scene portrays Annie, Billy, Peg, and grandson Danny's receiving Francis as belonging in the family with them for all time. Even when he abandoned them, he was one of them; home was always there, awaiting his return. As in Helen's death scene, the effects of time, at least for a few moments, are undone; we enter a mythic realm in which life in the family is

reconstituted as it was in the beginning, before the failing and betrayal and abandonment, in *illo tempore*. We especially sense this reversal of time as Francis goes
into the attic, there to open the trunk to find artifacts from his earlier life. His
glove, the ball with the Ty Cobb autograph, the photograph of his early Albany
team, his suit and shoes—these objects are there, solid, enduring; they signal that
human affiliations can endure as well. Annie's fidelity and acceptance, the affection of Billy and Peg, although tried and tempered by their father's failings, endure no less solidly than the objects in the attic. In Kennedy's world, it is possible
to come home again. So, even more mysterious than the appearance of the spooks
singing the "Dies Irae" from Mozart's *Requiem* outside the house is the mystery of
what occurs inside as Annie absolves Francis with the simple words "wasn't your
fault" (Kennedy 1984, 159) and the family receives into its midst a guilty yet chas-
tened husband and father.

We may not be amiss in seeing correspondences between what happens in the
Phelan family and that inexhaustible source of mythic lore, the game of baseball.
For one thing, baseball provides the means by which the long-lost grandfather can
connect across the generations with his grandson, Danny. The boy has heard stories about his grandfather, and as Francis takes him into the backyard to teach
him how to throw an "inshoot," we sense that this passing of baseball lore enacts
and seals a primordial tie between generations. This tie endures despite the passing of time. By passing the gifts—of his glove to his son, Billy, of the Ty Cobb–au-
tographed ball and how to throw an inshoot to Danny, of the stories to the entire
family—Francis blesses those persons whom he has wronged.

But in addition to providing material to bind the family together, the national
pastime may do more in *Ironweed*. Indeed, the structure of Francis's progress
seems oddly to correspond with structural elements of the game. In baseball, one
starts at home and moves counterclockwise around the bases, always heading
back toward home. This structure roughly corresponds to what Francis is doing:
turning the clock of his life counter to its unremittingly linear impulse, yearning
to get home before he gets put out. (Again, we remember Dante, who creates a
soul such as Belacqua whose purgatorial rite is to remember his life backward.)
Also, we might see a correspondence between undoing the effects of time in the
story and the nature of "baseball time." In baseball, one experiences the elasticity
of time, a factor that makes the game all but intolerable for some persons who prefer the boundaries of fifteen-minute quarters and thirty-minute halves. The
game-time can stretch, in principle, into infinity. Also, in baseball the effects of
time can be reversed: In a single at bat, a team can undo all that has taken place before and can arrive back where it was at the beginning of the game. Similarly, in
the film and the novel, clock-time is elongated as events from Francis's past return
and the effects of his many misdeeds are cancelled or transcended. Francis, in
short, faces the possibility of coming home, and homecoming emerges as the
guiding mythologem of the entire story.

But coming home is not easy, either in baseball or in Francis Phelan's life. Looking out at the backyard from Annie's kitchen, Francis is captivated with all the "niceness" but must admit to himself that "everything [is] easier than coming home, even reducing yourself to the level of social maggot, streetside slug" (Kennedy 1984, 160). Coming home is difficult for Francis precisely because it would require him to receive the graciousness the family extends. But more than that, coming home would require him to give up guilt as the basis of his identity. Unable to receive what is offered, Francis leaves home after the family meal. On the street again, he comes to this preliminary insight into his own character.

> Yet after every admission that he was a lost and distorted soul, Francis asserted his own private wisdom and purpose: He had fled the folks because he was too profane a being to live among them; he had humbled himself willfully through the years to counter *a fearful pride in his own ability to manufacture the glory from which grace would flow*. What he was was, yes a warrior, protecting a belief that no man could ever articulate, especially himself; but somehow it involved protecting saints from sinners, protecting the living from the dead. And a warrior, he was certain, was not a victim. Never a victim.
>
> In the deepest part of himself that could draw an unutterable conclusion, he told himself: My guilt is all that I have left. If I lose it, I have stood for nothing, done nothing, been nothing. (Kennedy 1984, 216; emphasis added)

Francis's difficulty reflects the struggle between pagan and Christian aspects of his character; indeed, we could view Francis as a troubled pagan living in an ineffectual Christian culture. In him, the (alleged) freedom and vigor of the happy, pagan warrior are constrained by Christian sensitivities; he has been, as it were, corrupted by the residue of Christianity that informs his culture. Alternately, we might see him as a failed Christian, unable to submit himself to the healing ministrations that are available to him. The struggle between pagan and Christian sensibilities in Francis Phelan is, in part, a struggle about the source of grace. With apology for the alliteration, we could say that the struggle involves glory, guilt, and grace. Kennedy's "sensitive bum" (as the ragman Rosskam calls him) faces this dilemma: whether to try, a la the pagan warrior, to go forth into the world and by dint of his own prowess enact deeds glorious enough to establish himself as a sufficient self in the world, or whether, a la the repentant Christian pilgrim, to renounce the sufficiency of his own deeds and look beyond himself for grace commensurate with the terrible guilt he has incurred. From the perspective of a pagan warrior, the glory won by deed must equal the guilt that, in a Christian culture, seems invariably to accompany great deeds; from the perspective of a Christian, even a failed one, the attempt to establish oneself through glorious deeds perpetuates a vicious cycle of prideful overextension and disconsolate failure.

Without being able here to trace each step of Francis's journey, let me hasten to the end of the story, which is fraught with ambivalence in both novel and film. Any reading of the ending revolves around one issue: Does Francis Phelan stay on the freight train that is carrying him south to Florida, or does he jump off and re-

turn home to Annie? Does this story enact or subvert the homecoming mythologem? Does it console us by confirming our expectations, or does it disturb us
by working counter to them? In terms of the dichotomy just posed, does Francis
persist as a troubled pagan, or does he move toward a resolution akin to a Christian homecoming?

Kennedy and Babenco, in novel and film, attempt a difficult task: They attempt
to present two endings, two possibilities, with equal force. They want to hold in
delicate balance the suggestion that Francis goes his lonely way and the suggestion
that he will take up residence with Annie. Neither Babenco nor Kennedy, however,
is altogether successful in maintaining this balance. The film tilts the scale toward
Francis's not returning; the novel inclines toward his coming home. This difference in the ending accords with an overall difference between film and novel: The
film is bleaker, less consoling; the novel, although pained, is brighter, more hope-
ful. But despite this difference, both works, I venture, gain in stature and coherence if we see the final telos of each as the return of Francis Phelan to the house on
Pearl Street. Indeed, I would argue that the structure of the story requires the return, that the claim of the story on readers and viewers is greatly weakened without it.

In so setting the problem of the ending, we recall the remarks I made earlier
concerning the relationship between novel and film. In "reading" the ending of
the film, it makes an immense difference whether the film viewer has read the
novel. Those who go to the film with the novel as a part of their interpretative
equipment will, I think, be more apt to see and appreciate Babenco's subtle suggestion that Francis does return. Those who consider the film independent of the
novel will, conversely, be more likely to respond as did several early reviewers who
simply dismissed the film as a dismal portrayal of a fellow who begins and ends as
a bum. By placing the two works in complementary relation, we can discern more
clearly the fundamental inclination of William Kennedy's purgatorial sensibility,
which is toward restitution and return, recovery and reconciliation.

For an understanding of what happens to Francis Phelan, I take my clue from
these lines, which occur toward the close of the novel: "Francis walked to the
doorway of the freight car and threw the empty whiskey bottle at the moon, an
outshoot fading away into the rising sun. The bottle and the moon made music
like a soulful banjo when they moved through the heavens, divine harmonies that
impelled Francis to leap off the train and seek sanctuary under the holy Phelan
eaves" (Kennedy 1984, 225). So, moved by the purgatorial music, Francis heads
back home. Kennedy's lexicon is telling: *heavens, divine harmonies, seek sanctuary
under the holy Phelan eaves.* He is striving for the sublime; he wants to make this
season of Hallow's Eve, All Saints', and All Souls' Day a time for the recovery of
sanctity in a bum's life, a time for hallowing the everyday.

Like the homing pigeons that fly outside the attic window (in both novel and
film), Francis Phelan comes home to enjoy turkey sandwiches and Annie's tea and
quietly to receive the family's acceptance. Kennedy's prose—the tone of which

Babenco attempts to translate by use of amber light in the film—unmistakenly reminds us that we are dealing with serious, even spiritual, things. Nowhere is this more apparent than in the final paragraphs of the novel.

> The empyrean, which is not spatial at all, does not move and has no poles. It binds, with light and love, the primum mobile, the utmost and swiftest of the material heavens. Angels are manifested in the primum mobile.
>
> But if they [the cops] weren't on to him, then he'd mention it to Annie someday (she already had the thought, he could tell that) about setting up the cot down in Danny's room, when things got to be absolutely right, and straight.
>
> That room of Danny's had some space to it.
>
> And it got the morning light too.
>
> It was a mighty nice little room. (Kennedy 1984, 227)

The prose—the first two paragraphs here—takes us once again onto the Dantesque soulscape, but in the same phrase, the final three lines poetically place us in an ordinary house on Pearl Street in Albany, New York, in November 1938. We are not in the empyrean, which is the abode of the Holy One; we are, rather, in an attic room, which somehow, by some strange magic or inexplicable grace, is transposed into the primum mobile, the earthly paradise, the topmost level of the mountain of purgatory, the ninth and outermost concentric sphere of the Dantesque universe where angels are manifest. Here, the historical and the mythic intersect or coincide as in a sacramental mystery. Here, Annie is no Beatrice leading Francis to another world; she, rather, is a forgiving angel who ties him to such grace and goodness as are available in the present world, at home with the family on Pearl Street.

It is a mark of William Kennedy's power as a writer that the final line of *Ironweed*, novel and film, can credibly employ the word "nice" to evoke the depth of experience Francis Phelan has in coming home. Throughout both novel and screenplay, Kennedy retrieves and refreshes the word, thereby preparing us to accept the weight it carries at the end. Earlier, Francis comments on Annie's yard, "Damn, it's nice." To Peg's remembering that he likes plum pudding, Francis says, "It's nice you remembered that." About Billy, his son, Francis remarks, "Grew up nice, Billy did." So (in the novel), in the same narrative phrase with such august words as "empyrean" and "primum mobile," Kennedy credibly, without a trace of irony, uses the word to evoke the goodness of the ordinary, the paradise of an earthly home. Under the "holy Phelan eaves," a purged Francis Aloysius Phelan finds sanctuary in "a mighty nice little room."

4

The Christian Allegorical Structure of *Platoon*

AVENT CHILDRESS BECK

IN CRITICISM OF *Platoon* (1986), Oliver Stone's allegorical methods and sources have commonly been misunderstood. At best, the Christian motifs that distinguish Stone's narrative of war and personal growth are only passingly recognized. It is easily demonstrated that these borrowed motifs are not deeply hidden secrets that must be deduced or invented from vague hints. Indeed, Stone clearly indicates his reliance on the Bible, both in the film itself and in its published screenplay. We should not be surprised; Stone has said that for him the war was a "religious" experience.

Religious appreciations of war are common in American popular culture, perhaps no more so than with Civil War subjects, as Kevin Costner's revisionist *Dances with Wolves,* with its Major Dunbar riding as a crucified Christ between the opposing Union and Confederate forces, vividly reminds us. However, that this connection in *Platoon* takes place on a foreign field and contains within itself obvious spirits of mythic and political relativism complicates an appreciation of the matter as taking place within an especially *American mythic space.* I would suggest that this is only fair to history, that Stone has a fairly modern, cosmopolitan view of world affairs and looks back upon the war as hardly America's own: The United States is now one among many objects rather than the implied subject.

We note that Stone, in bringing allegorical methods to bear upon the Vietnam War, is in good company, as critics such as John Hellmann, Albert Auster, and Leonard Quart have shown, or as Michael Herr and Michael Cimino reveal in their screenplay notes and annotations to *Full Metal Jacket* and *The Deer Hunter.* Certainly, realism is important, and a historical fiction such as *Platoon* may rightly be lauded (or criticized) in terms of it. But realism is an uncertain concept and remains subordinate to storytelling or, in nonfiction settings, to the rationalized forms of historical narrative. For example, when among her praises for his powers of versimilitude Pauline Kael complains of Stone's literary pretensions—"too much filtered light, too much poetic license, and too damn much romanticized insanity" (1987, 95)—she understresses that *Platoon,* good or bad, likable or not, is necessarily popular art first, historical representation second. But a critique of the art in *Platoon,* as with any film, can easily fall prey to speculation and generalization; my primary purpose here is simply to document Stone's allegorical structure.

The film begins with a title snipped from Ecclesiastes 11:9, "Rejoice, o young man, in thy youth" (Stone 1987, 11). However, Samuel Barber's *Adagio for Strings,* stately and elegiac, immediately begins, setting an ironically contrasting tone. Stone does not complete the quoted verse, whose final clause is "for all these things God will bring thee into judgment." This is significant. Until this verse in its eleventh chapter, the Book of Ecclesiastes says nothing about judgment. Now, however, it resolves its well-known existentialism through a less often noticed orthodoxy of moral absolutes. The biblical voice says that not only does our dust return to the earth and our spirits return to God (Eccles. 12:7) but also directs us to "fear God, and keep his commandments: for this is the whole duty of man. For God shall bring every work into judgment, with every secret thing, whether it be good, or whether it be evil" (12:13–14). By not quoting these passages, Stone steers viewers away from expecting a story structured by moral absolutes. In the end, this silence has the effect of misleading viewers, for the film, in fact, retells the battle between good and evil, between the risen Christ and the beast.

The names of the characters are the clearest indicators that Stone has appropriated biblical models. "Chris" is usually a short form of Christopher or Christian, names that secondarily or directly refer to Christ. And indeed, Chris's character does ultimately constellate about Christ. But Chris has three other coordinating biblical parallels: with Elijah's disciple Elisha, with Jesus's principle disciple, Peter, and with a sweeping run from the two creation stories in Genesis to the Apocalypse that, among other things, recalls the legendary distinction of Christ as the second Adam. The persona of the "good" sergeant Elias reflects a similar coordination of allusory characters. Elias is the New Testament, or Greek, form of the Old Testament's Elijah, an equivalence Stone makes full use of, although most explicitly in the screenplay. Also, by some conflated identifications recorded in the gospels (e.g., Matt. 16:14), Stone legitimately borrows from John the Baptist and Jesus to help build "Elias." Moreover, allusions to events in Christ's story are correct chronologically but are staggered between Elias's and Chris's narratives. Finally, although Barnes is called "Captain Ahab" by Chris, the reference to Melville's nihilist hero is misleading. Aspects of Elijah's Baal-supportive opponent, King Ahab, lie behind both characters, but Barnes's more vivid ancestor, as we shall see, is the beast in Revelation 13. As the story unfolds, Barnes is revealed as evil incarnate, the appropriate opponent for the Christian savior-heroes, Elias and Chris.

The sets of allusions are purposefully interwoven, as tradition dictates they should be. Chris's movement from Genesis to Revelation associations is inseparable from the escalating moral contest between Elias and Barnes. Together, these narrative lines follow the basic, eschatological outline of Christian biblical "history." Stone does this in a clever way. When Elias, as both crucified Christ and Elijah, dies and leaves the narrative, the story's aspects of biblical expectation depart with him and leave only Chris-as-Christ, the transhistorical typos, to fulfill the climactic allegorical pattern. This is much the way Christian thought juxtaposes the Hebrew Bible and the New Testament, reducing the Hebrew Bible to the Old Testament and making the New Testament the fulfillment of intentional forecasts and prefigurations in the Judaic texts. Christ is there implicit at the beginning of time and there again at the end, as well as appearing in the flesh in between—as in the first verse of the Gospel of St. John. Similarly, Chris is there at the beginning and at the end of the movie, in between which moments he grows into his identification with Elias.

After the credits and the quotation from Ecclesiastes, the story begins in earliest Genesis, an arena of formlessness and creation. Disgorged from a transport's rear, Chris passes through clouds of yellow dust, innocent and shocked by the body bags and haggard figures he sees. Dangerously naive, he is called "new meat" and "fresh meat" (Stone 1987, 19, 20, 21, 27). The raw, sensual mystery washing over Chris's unseasoned character recalls the formless moment before creation when everything was still inchoate and without name. Immediately plunged into the jungle and put at point for the patrol with Barnes and Elias, he fails miserably. Barnes curses him and coldly walks on. Passing by, Elias stops to help him. In this fashion, Stone quickly sets out the duality of the story's conflict, who is dark and who is light.

Soon after, back at the company camp, the lieutenant and the noncommissioned officers plan a night patrol. The meeting finished, Elias walks away. Behind his back, Sgt. O'Neil complains, "Guy's in here three years and he thinks he's Jesus fucking Christ or something." Nothing has yet justified this association, but the rhetoric prepares us for the climactic allusion explicit in Elias's later death.

In the rain that night, alone on patrol watch, Chris squats in the undergrowth among the ruins of an overgrown temple, and a shadowy Buddha looms in the background much as God watched over his primeval garden (Gen. 3:8). In the solemn intonations of his voice-over letters, we listen to Chris's social conscience, his love for and identification with the common man, but also to his damnation of his parents' lifestyle and materialistic hopes for him. In contrast to the world he has left behind, he says, his fellow grunts are "the heart and soul," the downtrodden and unwanted, the kind of men to whom we imagine Jesus would have ministered. With his social conscience and structuring judgmental myths, Stone's Chris will imitate what Jesus liked to call himself, the "son of man." Then he adds, "I've found it finally, way down here in the mud—maybe from down here I can start up again and be something I can be proud of, without having to be a fake human being" (Stone 1987, 32). We hear the allusion to Adamic creation: "a mist went up from the earth and watered the whole face of the ground—then the LORD God formed man of dust from the ground" (Gen. 2:6–7). In the dripping, steaming, primal jungle, Chris sits soaking "way down here in the mud," despising his past and wanting to be re-created as a real person.

Through the firefight that follows, Stone leaves Genesis with a play on names and an open allusion to man's fall and exile from Eden. The other "new meat," we know, the hapless, innocent, aptly named Private Gardner, dies here. At first thought he is simply a victim of the timeworn maxim "you will die if you show a picture of your honey before entering battle." However, Gardner also showed a wallet photograph of Raquel Welch to Chris (Stone 1987, 29). Consequently, Stone has moved past the cliché to the effects of sin; by undermining his own innocence with this sexual curiosity, Gardner gets a hard boot out of what Stone calls a "garden of eden" (1987, 124). With his curious passing, this boy marks the story's entrance into the harsh, contested world of history and war, a violent, sinning world rooted in the exile from Eden (Gen. 3:14–23) and resolvable only by the Apocalypse.

Beginning with these passages of Old Testament introduction, Stone is moved by his Christian vision, or at least his Christian exegetical frame, to exercise strands of biblical narrative indicating the omnipresence of Christ throughout biblical history. As a consequence, his narrative gains a certain density from the complexity with which its mythic references intertwine with each other.

Slightly wounded in the neck during his baptism of fire, Chris thinks he is dying. On one level, the sequence is like Christian baptism, where the initiate first dies to the flesh then is reborn into the Spirit, able finally to enter the community of the faithful. On a second, narcotized level, the experience is analogous to Jesus's own baptismal vision of heaven and the Spirit of God (e.g., Matt. 3:16–17). The Spirit does not immediately fill Chris; first there is a trip to the hospital. Back at camp, King invites Chris to the "heads'" bunker, where Rhah presides over ritual and festivities. Chris is new to this fellowship, and Rhah does not understand his being there: "Watcha doing in the underworld, Taylor?" King answers for Chris: "This ain't Taylor. Taylor been shot. This man is Chris, he been resurrected" (Stone 1987, 45). Elias, in his John the Baptist mode, initiates Chris into the quasi-cult with the aid of spirit-enhancing narcotics. Blowing the sacramental smoke into the breech of a shotgun, Elias has Chris put his mouth over the muzzle and breath it in. He asks Chris if it is his first time. It is. "Then," says Elias, "the worm has definitely turned for you, man" (Stone 1987, 47).

Simultaneously, in the barrack of the "lifers, the juicers … the moron white element" (Stone 1987, 9), and the loners, O'Neil asks Barnes whether he thinks the lieutenant will live, and we learn that Barnes, in contrast to life-giving Elias, is intimately associated with death, if just teasingly right now. Also, O'Neil reveals that the weak, despised lieutenant is Jewish, a significant reference in light of Stone's Christian allegory. Puerile, treacherous, subservient to both Barnes and Captain

Harris, Wolfe lets Barnes run his murderous course. In the Gospel of St. Luke, Jesus calls Herod Antipas "that fox" (13:32), meaning to denigrate the secular Jewish ruler of Palestine who was responsible for John the Baptist's beheading, and who would be partially responsible for Jesus's crucifixion. A wolf and a fox are similar enough to make Stone's choice for the lieutenant's name a curious one. Jumping ahead for a moment to the frustrated prospect of a court-martial, we can speculate, too, about Captain Harris, whose role correspondingly echoes the figure of Roman authority, Pontius Pilate. If Wolfe and Harris are understood in these terms, then here Stone is beginning to align allusive referents for Barnes's later sermon on the "system."

From baptism and role clarification, *Platoon* moves into allusions to the temptation of Jesus in the wilderness and also to the moral struggle between God's prophet Elijah and the evil king Ahab. The next day, New Year's 1968, the platoon patrols along the Cambodian border, "walk[ing] through the jungle like ghosts in a landscape" (Stone 1987, 55). The platoon explores a North Vietnamese bunker complex, posting Chris and Manny as lookouts. As Chris waits tensely in the woods, a snake slides between his legs, and he is "frozen with dread" (Stone 1987, 57). Nothing happens, but the serpent's appearance is appropriate to the myth of Jesus's temptation, in which, as the satanic "tempter," it tries to lure Jesus into catastrophic sin (e.g., Matt. 4:1–11). Since Chris is about to be tempted into sharing Barnes's hotblooded rage, the snake's presence is not simply atmospheric. Immediately, a bomb kills two men, and soon after, Manny is found grotesquely slaughtered by the river as the platoon heads toward a village. Bent on revenge, the men proceed: "If [the villagers] had [known] they would have run. ... Barnes was at the eye of our rage—and through him, our Captain Ahab—we would set things right again. That day we loved him" (Stone 1987, 61). But this "love" bred of violence and soured brotherhood turns out to be short-lived.

In the sack of the village, a scene that reverberates with the My Lai massacre, Chris faces and overcomes temptation. Distraught with fear, horror, and the lethal opacity of the Vietnamese landscape, Chris nevertheless catches himself and pulls back from butchering a mother and her crippled son. Similarly, after his baptism by John, Jesus went into the wilderness and was tempted but did not succumb, instead returning "to the world" to begin his mission. Chris begins his own mission in the village by stopping a gang rape, although with unpolished eloquence.

> CHRIS: All you're fucking animals!
> TONY: Fucking A Fuck!
> CHRIS: You don't fucking get it man, you just do not fucking get it.
> (Stone 1987, 72–73)

The fight between Elias and Barnes, an interruption that keeps the sack of the village from becoming a virtual slaughter, completes the temptation moment and turns what were simply the differing styles of the two men into a mortal and morally clarifying opposition.

In the platoon's culture, divided as it is between liberal, drug-using spiritualists and lifer-alcoholic-demonics, the struggle between the two charismatic cult leaders splits the platoon, creating, as Chris says in the film, a "civil war." Although Stone may feel a sympathy between Barnes and Captain Ahab, it is a sympathy of character, not of narrative role. Rhetorically and structurally, the parallel is with the outrage and civil struggle between God's prophet and the cult of Baal maintained under King Ahab. King Ahab asks, "Art thou he that troubleth Israel?" Elijah answers, "I have not troubled Israel; but thou, and thy father's house, in that ye have forsaken the commandments of the LORD, and thou hast followed Ba'alim" (I Kings 18:17–18). In their brawling challenges echoing this biblical exchange, Barnes actively reveals his black soul and Elias his enlightened outrage, and what Stone calls the "narrowing drama" (1987, 67) propels the movie further and further into the confines of structural and symbolic allusion.

As the platoon leaves the burning village—which Stone describes as a "Bosch-like canvas" (1987, 74), equating his scene of moral conflict with the Flemish painter's phantasmagorias of temptation and judgement—the first allusion on the road to Elias's death and to Chris's spiritual inheritance is seen on Lerner's helmet. The word "GRACE" and a crucifix have been drawn on it with a magic marker, symbolically categorizing the revelation we have just witnessed and hinting at the destiny of the Elias-Christ figure. However, as Stone seems to know well, the prophet Elijah had his passing on, too. When Elias dies, Chris will inherit his principle role, much as the disciple Elisha was given his prophetic status by Elijah.

But first the narrative lines must be brought to their respective, conflating heads. Reporting to the company commander, Barnes and Wolfe contradict Elias about the events in the village. An investigation will have to wait, but Captain Harris is adamant: "I promise you if I find out there was an illegal killing, there will be a court martial." Prescient shades of My Lai, but with Wolfe and Harris typologically echoing specific Jewish and Roman authorities, the prospective court martial is also an allusion to the trials forced upon Jesus and Elijah. Complaining to his followers immediately after, Barnes calls Elias "a waterwalker" (Stone 1987, 75)—as was Jesus, we note.

At this point in the screenplay (Stone 1987, 76–78), in a scene absent from the film, Barnes's metaphorically phrased complaint is immediately balanced by the "heads'" ruminations on his demonism. He is said to come from Hell, figuratively, of course. Like the "beast" of Revelation 13, he remains indomitable although wounded seven times, a "fact" repeated later in the film. Rhah says, "Remember, the Devil does God's work too" (Stone 1987, 77), placing Barnes within the context of the fallen angel whose struggles with God are yet part of God's design. "LOVE" and "HATE" are tattooed on Rhah's knuckles (a detail, Lerner hints, borrowed from the preacher in Charles Laughton's nightmare fantasy *Night of the Hunter*); HATE is for Barnes, LOVE is for Elias, who came into the world "naturally"—like Jesus again, we note, and in obvious contrast to Barnes's demonic origin. Also, we find out about Elias's troubles with a "Jezebel," an open allusion to Elijah's own troubles in I Kings 19:2–4. Finally, we read, "You're fighting for your SOUL … if you'se a man, wrestle with that angel" (Stone 1987, 78), which, given the discussion's subject of heaven and hell, pointedly alludes to an individual's own "wrestle" with the "rulers of darkness" described in Ephesians 6:12 rather than to Jacob's "wrestle" with a heaven-sent angel in which Israel, not Jacob's soul, is the issue (Gen. 32:24–32). We can only wonder why the scene was dropped, although the number and tumbling, obvious natures of the allusions could have had something to do with it.

That evening, Elias and Chris sit alone together talking under the starry sky, a quiet scene suggestive of Jesus and Peter in the garden of Gethsemane or of Elijah and Elisha musing somewhere. In the movie's neutered version of the scene, Elias says, "I love this place at night. The stars … there's no right or wrong in them, they're just there." He goes on to say that he respects Barnes's commitment to the war. He once held it, too, but now thinks "what happened today's just the beginning. We're gonna lose this war. … It's time we got our own asses kicked." Then a shooting star crosses the sky, symbolically sanctioning the forecast.

This short, lean scene in the film is much longer and allusively rich in the screenplay, where, according to the descriptive notes, Elias "sermonize[s]" to Chris about moral life and the war, and they discuss death and reincarnation (Stone 1987, 79–81). The scene's allusions to the Last Supper, to Jesus's subsequent agony in the garden of Gethsemane, and to Elijah's sojourn in the wilderness are striking. At the Last Supper, Jesus calls the bread his body, the wine his blood, and their ingestion the absorption of his "new testament" (e.g., Matt. 26:26–29). As at Chris's "baptism," narcotics again have sacramental capacity. Their eucharistic faculty accompanying Elias's liberal testament is unmistakable—"like a power passed between 'em"—when Elias shares a joint with Chris and punches him once, saying, "You know it *till you die* … that's why the survivors remember. 'Cause the dead don't let 'em forget" (Stone 1987, 80; Stone's emphasis). Furthermore, when discussing reincarnation, Elias says, "Maybe a piece of me's in you now" (Stone 1987, 81), a conflation of the Eucharist with a foreshadowing of Chris as the risen Christ's "reincarnation" of the original incarnation, Elias. The jungle setting of this scene recalls the garden of Gethsemane, where, after the Last Supper and in the company of Peter, Jesus agonized over his fate. Aware of Barnes's hatred, Elias, Stone notes, covers "his own uncertainty" with a "certain bravado" (Stone 1987, 80), an echo of Jesus's "what, could ye not watch with me one hour? Watch and pray, that ye enter not into temptation; the spirit indeed is willing, but the flesh is weak" (Matt. 26:40–41).

The final and most interesting allusion within this scene is to Elijah, and it comes when Elias ponders his reincarnation. Threatened by Jezebel, Elijah fled into the wilderness, where the "Word of the Lord" came to him, saying, "Go forth, and stand upon the mount before the LORD. And, behold, the LORD passed by, and a great and strong wind rent the mountains … but the LORD was not in the wind: And after the wind an earthquake; but the LORD was not in the earthquake: And after the earthquake a fire; but the LORD was not in the fire: and after the fire a still small voice" (I Kings 19:11–13). Similarly, Elias tells Chris, "I'm gonna come back as ... as wind or fire—or a deer ... yeah, a deer" (Stone 1987, 85). Wind, fire, and a deer, and then the wish-fulfilling falling star. Wind, fire, blast, and a quietly grazing deer all appear near the end of both the screenplay and the movie: The bomb's blast is a fiery wind, and when Chris wakes up the next morning, a gentle deer is watching from the edge of the forest.

Stone skips a Judas kiss that night, and the day Elias dies begins with the platoon flying back into the forest. They land near the white ruins of a mission church—"a decaying French Catholic Church from the 19th Century," Stone writes, which he built for the movie (1987, 10, 81)—and after this symbolic reminder of the story's context, they walk into an ambush. Chris proves his combat mettle in the immediate crisis and goes with Elias, Rhah, and Crawford to head off an enemy-flanking movement by the river. Along the way, Elias leaves the three men to defend an intermediate position while he goes on solo. Chris wants to go with him. "No," says Elias with a grin, "I move faster alone" (Stone 1987, 91).

Treacherously shot by Barnes, Elias dies in the open as Chris and everyone else watch helplessly from the helicopters above, reversing the looking up at Jesus on the cross. Stone calls the mode of Elias's death "Elias crucified" (1987, 97). There is no mistaking the symbolic gesture when we see it ourselves—the torture, the arms outstretched, the martyrdom—and this is the one specific allusory moment most critics pick up on.

But another powerful allusory structure is being played out at this moment, whose conclusion, along with Elias's "crucifixion," leaves the mythic field free for Chris-as-Christ to lead us into Revelation. The time for Elias's namesake on earth is over: "And it came to pass, when the LORD would take up Elijah into heaven by a whirlwind" (II Kings 2:1). The prophet says to his disciple, "Elisha, Tarry here, I pray thee, for the LORD hath sent me to Bethel" (II Kings 2:2), but Elisha refuses and follows his master instead. This happens once again with Jericho the destination and, finally, with the Jordan River as the goal. After they cross the river, Elijah asks Elisha what he can do for his disciple before ascending. Elisha asks for a "double portion of thy spirit" (II Kings 2:9). Elijah agrees but adds that Elisha will get the gift only if he sees the ascension, which he, in fact, does see: "Behold, there appeared a chariot of fire, and horses of fire, and parted them both asunder; and Elijah went up by a whirlwind into heaven. And Elisha saw it" (II Kings 2:11–12).

In the movie, the break from this paradigmatic myth is that Chris not Elias, "ascends." The other elements are all there: The first destination of Elijah and Elisha was Bethel, meaning "house of God"; the platoon lands near the ruined church. Their second destination is Jericho, famous for its battle with Joshua; the platoon walks into the ambush. The third destination is the Jordan River; Elias, Chris, and the others head for the river. As well, we have the attempt to dissuade the disciple from following, the disciple watching the passage of the master, and the whirlwind of chariot and horses of fire (the "air cavalry" have insignia of a white wing crossed by lightning painted on their noses). The allusory pattern is followed precisely.

Chris's ascension in place of Elias—an exchange of Elijah's and Elisha's relative positions—makes sense in Stone's myth format. Although Chris ascends to safety, he nevertheless acquires Elias's mantle through a shared moment of horrific revelation. Stone uses Elias's death to draw together and close the several biblical strands Elias and Chris assumed: The Elijah strand is complete, so are the John the Baptist, the Elisha, the Peter, and the living Jesus strands. Only Chris is left, as a Christ figure resolving his righteous fury amid allusions to the New Testament apocalypse.

The passage of Christian history has its promised end in the Apocalypse, and this is the specific climax toward which Stone drives *Platoon*. Back at divisional camp, Chris works up a vengeful frenzy, but Rhah interrupts, saying, "Barnes been shot 7 times and he ain't dead, that tell you something? Barnes ain't meant to die. Only thing can get Barnes ... is Barnes!" (Stone 1987, 99). Stone confirms Barnes's enormous scar as fact in the Foreword to the screenplay (1987, 9), but Rhah's information also has a remarkable parallel in Revelation. The beast, the principal servant of the dragon (the Devil or Satan, Rev. 20:2), has seven heads, according to John of Patmos: "And I saw one of his heads as it were wounded to death; and his deadly wound was healed: and all the world wondered after the beast. ... Who is like unto the beast? Who is able to make war with him? (Rev. 13:3–4). The beast, which had the wound by a sword, and did live" (Rev. 13:14). Through Rhah's warning, Barnes's facial wound, and the peculiar use of "7 times," Stone is simply rhetorically partaking in Christian myth. The meaningful parallel to Revelation comes when Barnes intrudes upon Chris and Rhah and lectures them on the nature of society. "I AM reality. There's the way it oughta be and there's the way it is. 'Lias he was full of shit, 'Lias was a crusader—I got no fight with a man does what he's told but when he don't, the machine breaks down, and when the machine breaks down, WE break down ... and I ain't gonna allow that. From none of you. Not one" (Stone 1987, 99–100).

It is Barnes's turn to give a sermon, and we recognize his contrasting tone to Elias's earlier expressions of fairness and love. Associated with Barnes and death, the model for "machine" is the Antichrist's social order, which in Revelation immediately follows the passage on the beast's heads: "And he causeth all, both small and great, rich and poor, free and bond, to receive a mark in their right hand, or in their foreheads: And that no man might buy or sell, save he that had the mark, or the name of the beast, or the number of his name" (Rev. 13:16-17). This mark, name, or number is a symbolic token of an authoritarianism as foul and ordered as Barnes's machine. In Barnes's paraphrase of Revelation, society is beholden to the machine; the breakdown of the machine means the disintegration of reality. And this is the lie the Antichrist promulgates. But Elias and Chris think contrarily, as we have seen and as their typological models demand.

After the crucifixion, Stone moves quickly into the patterns of the Apocalypse. But there is a final play on the gospel story of Jesus's burial and resurrection. The next day, the platoon flies back over the church on its way to battalion camp. "I felt like we were returning to the scene of a crime," Chris says, echoing one interpretation of the crucifixion. Most significant, though, in an allusion to Christ's empty tomb and resurrection, we are shown the mission church and its cemetery but no body of Elias. A mysteriously vanished Elias actually makes narrative sense, since Revelation is propelled by a risen Christ, not simply a dead one. First narratively and now visually, Stone has cleared the deck for Chris's epochal transformation.

As evening approaches, Chris and King dig their foxhole on the battalion perimeter, preparing for the expected attack that night—the imminence of personified evil. Watching a patrol go out, King says, in words familiar from Barnes's apocalyptic persona, "Glad I ain't going with 'em. Somewhere out dere man is de Beast and he hungry tonight" (Stone 1987, 102). A "hungry" enemy appears again in the screenplay (Stone 1987, 110), but, more interestingly, the other instance of the beast in the screenplay designates the U. S. Army (Stone 1987, 82). Noting this, we understand more clearly Stone's dichotomy in which Barnes represents the omnipresent evil against which those who embrace "life"—the "heads"—must struggle. In other words, good and bad are not geopolitical entities in this Vietnam, nor, since the North Vietnamese Army is also the beast, is Stone involved in a simple denunciation of the United States.

All night the battalion struggles against a flood of NVA. But Chris comes into his own, or, more exactly, he grows into Elias's role of an ultimate warrior. With the camp overrun and falling, Captain Harris calls in an air strike. Just before the plane arrives, however, Chris and Barnes find each other in the flashing shadows of the perimeter. Barnes attacks Chris and is about to strike the fatal blow when the plane's silhouette fills the sky above his raging form. Significantly, in the screenplay Stone calls the airplane "a great white whale" (1987, 123); in the movie the plane is black, and it does not kill Barnes and destroy the battalion (or the platoon) as Moby Dick kills Ahab and sinks the *Pequod*. Having kept one eye on the Book of Revelation, we find the structural and symbolic forerunner to the plane and to Chris in the image of Christ as the "Word of God," whose "eyes were as a flame of fire" and who "was clothed with a vesture dipped in blood" (Rev. 19:1, 13). A bomb drops and knocks both Barnes and Chris unconscious. The battle-ending bombing strike resembles Christ's invincible flame of fire, and Chris's blood-soaked clothes, in which he wakes the next morning, emphatically evoke Christ's sanguine vesture.

Like a vengeful Christ crucified, conspicuously nursing his left hand and wearing an ankh crucifix we have not seen before, Chris staggers to his feet, picks up a rifle, finds Barnes and kills him. So in Revelation, the Word of God defeats the beast and the beast's army in the battle at Armageddon. We can tell that the battle in the movie is built from the penultimate rather than the final battle by the incongruous symbols that embellish Chris's rescuers: their armored personnel carrier has enormous shark teeth painted on it, and a Nazi flag flies from its radio antenna (Stone 1987, 125). Although Barnes is dead and Chris is alive, the metaphors of the machine live on.

Stone closes *Platoon* with Chris's ascension in the medi-vac helicopter, the red cross on its nose "now rising to meet God," as Stone writes in the screenplay (1987, 128), clearly indicating his imaginative frame. Down below, the bodies of the battle dead are heaved into bomb craters, perhaps recalling the "lake of fire" into which the beast and the "false prophet" were thrown after losing the next-to-last battle (Rev. 19:20). Finally, the screen whites out with the sun's light as Chris begins his concluding voice-over, the most sermon-like of them all, neatly terminating the mythic plot.

Using the trio of Chris, Elias, and Barnes, Stone plays out his story's moral conflict on idealized grounds that reveal the nondocumentary truth he is driving at, a sort of moral epiphany achieved in recent history's crucible. The story is Chris's, but the controlling figures are Elias and Barnes, charismatic personalities whose allusive characterizations stretch taut an oppositional duality that transcends their contemporary social differences. Chris's story is his choosing between them and then, having made his choice, his unequivocal emulation, defense, and fulfillment of Elias's christological implications.

To the credit of Stone's sense of history, he does not follow his allegorical model to its ultimate conclusion, a pure fiction by secular reckoning. The mythic narrative immediately dissipates when Chris leaves the battle scene, because post-Vietnam history is hardly the thousand years of blessed sovereignty that succeed Armageddon (Rev. 20:1–6). However, Stone's sudden recoil from the supporting myth is another waffling on the part of the director: Chris's closing sermon does not assert the absolutes we expect after the allegorical ride we have been on. As with his ironic use of Ecclesiastes in the first frames of the movie, Stone again disingenuously conceals his story's bedrock sense behind misdirecting words. Among other fair-minded bromides uttered during this voice-over, Chris equivocates about his role model, calling himself a son of both sergeants. This is an abortion of the sense Stone so strenuously fabricates during the active narrative.

Nevertheless, Oliver Stone's visionary statement on the Vietnam War is a powerfully constructive one, so unlike the absurdity of *The Green Berets* (1967) or the nihilism bred into *Apocalypse Now* (1979), *Coming Home* (1978), and their many sympathetic forerunners and imitators. As with Michael Cimino's equally Christian and mythic *The Deer Hunter* (1978) and Stanley Kubrick's Jungian *Full Metal Jacket* (1987), *Platoon* is a mythic reinvention of the war that displaces grand historical statement on the involvement of the United States with an assertion instead of the primacy of an individual's or a small group's religious or psychological experience of the war. This shift of perspectives could well be the natural reaction of these moviemakers (and their audiences, too?) to a painful inability to gather concordant historical sense from the war. And so, in dark theaters, at least, we are treated to balms of religious myth; in the case of *Platoon*, to the ordered familiarities and emotive comfort of the Christian narrative.

5

Hollywood and Armageddon: Apocalyptic Themes in Recent Cinematic Presentation

CONRAD E. OSTWALT JR.

A PREGNANT DEMI MOORE feverishly races to intercede in the chaotic events leading to the destruction of the world. A stolid Clint Eastwood emerges from snow-capped mountains, as the Pale Rider, to bring death and destruction to the forces of evil so the righteous might live in peace. And a militaristic Martin Sheen slowly inches into the inner recesses of Cambodia on a mission designed as a reign of terror in the "heart of darkness"—a mission that takes him to Armageddon itself. Each of these situations represents a recent cinematic interest in the apocalyptic drama and in apocalyptic themes. In the past twenty years or so, movie enthusiasts have witnessed a proliferation of apocalyptic films ranging from comedies and children's films to horror movies and nuclear disaster films. The box office constitutes a mass medium for the apocalyptic drama, which suggests the existence of a popular, apocalyptic imagination in contemporary society—an apocalyptic consciousness the movie industry has discovered and perhaps fostered. In any event, it is a safe bet that this apocalyptic consciousness will gain momentum as we move toward and beyond the end of this millennium.

In order to explore modernity's apocalyptic consciousness, in this chapter I attempt to isolate the basic themes of cinematic apocalyptic presentation in popular films rather than in classic ones. For the most part, the scope of this study encompasses U.S. box-office films released since the late 1970s. In particular, the criteria for inclusion of a film in this study are: (1) The film, although not necessarily about the end of time, must project apocalyptic themes and imagery; (2) the film should be relevant to contemporary popular audiences; (3) the movies should be from a variety of film types; and (4) the films, taken together, should be representative of the larger body of movies projecting apocalyptic imagery. Three films are particularly important for this chapter and represent a larger body of films that emphasize character, setting, or plot in terms of apocalyptic imagery: (1) A Clint Eastwood western, *Pale Rider,* emphasizes character; (2) the Vietnam War epic, *Apocalypse Now,* based on Joseph Conrad's *Heart of Darkness,* effectively presents the apocalyptic setting; and (3) the overtly apocalyptic film *The Seventh Sign* emphasizes plot. Through this examination of apocalyptic characters, settings, and plots, a consistent theme appears that characterizes a modern, cinematic apocalyptic consciousness. Although this twentieth-century apocalyptic imagination employs traditional apocalyptic characteristics, such as mystery, revelation, dualism, and imminent destruction,[1] it also departs from the traditional apocalypse to define the twentieth-century attitude toward the cosmic cataclysm that marks the end of the world.

Apocalyptic Heroes, Settings, and Plots

The western, as film type, is perhaps the best place to begin with such an investigation, for most westerns present the apocalyptic conflict between good and evil. In Clint Eastwood's *Pale Rider,* this dualism takes on an even more obvious apocalyptic sense through the film's incorporation of images from the Christian apocalypse, the Book of John's Revelation. The Pale Rider is a direct reference to Rev. 6:7, 8 and refers to the rider of the pale horse, whose name is Death. *Pale Rider* does not present an end-of-the-world scenario; however, this film incorporates apocalyptic imagery to introduce a complex, messianic character. Thus, *Pale Rider* represents a group of apocalyptic films dominated by character and character development (Greeley, 267–270).

The conflict in this story begins when a small, struggling mining community falls victim to a larger strip-mining company. The larger company intends to drive the community from its land claim and take over the canyon for its own use. The situation appears hopeless when a young girl in the community prays for a miracle; that day, as she reads aloud from Rev. 6:4–8 about the rider on a pale horse, Eastwood rides into the community on a pale horse. The girl knows he is the miracle—the one who has come to dispense judgment.

Eastwood apparently returns from the grave for retribution and for confrontation with evil: He wears a clerical collar; he is known as "Preacher"; and he soon befriends and supports Hull Barret, the unofficial leader of the community. The story line eventually pits Preacher against the hired guns of Coy LaHood, the owner of the strip-mining company; in the final battle, Preacher guns down six deputies and his old nemesis, Marshall Stockburn. At the end of the fight, the real hero emerges as Barret kills LaHood, saves Preacher, and eliminates the source of evil. If Preacher's struggle is a supernatural one of personal revenge against Stockburn, Barret's is a human and heroic struggle to deliver his community from the threat of LaHood. As the film ends, the apocalyptic figure, Preacher, mysteriously rides away (as he entered the story), and Barret stays behind to lead the small community in the life of peace and renewed wealth it had so long sought.

The overt apocalyptic images and implications come from the Book of Revelation, the dualistic battle represents the western version of Armageddon, evil is judged and defeated, and the community of the righteous is allowed to establish its own utopia. The interesting twist to apocalyptic themes in this film is seen in the complex, apocalyptic character Eastwood portrays. This figure is on the one hand a resurrected and demonic ghost who brings death with Hades on his heels; however, he is also a very human lover, fighter, hero, and apocalyptic preacher. He is without a doubt the defender of the righteous community, which is arrayed against the forces of evil; however, one still finds it difficult to picture this Eastwood character as a representative from the kingdom of God.

The classic western fell on hard times in the late 1970s and the 1980s, until the western, as film genre, made a limited comeback with the films *Silverado* and *Pale Rider*. However, in the lean years for westerns, science fiction provided an able substitute and continued the themes and conflicts normally reserved for westerns. Science fiction provides new frontiers, replacing the long-extinct western frontier, in which the apocalyptic drama can take place and the messianic hero can emerge. A few examples demonstrate how science fiction has become an extension of the western drama and a medium for presenting apocalyptic themes, especially in terms of the apocalyptic character. *Outland* reminds the viewer of a futuristic *High Noon* set in outer space. George Lucas's *Star Wars* trilogy provides both elements of the western and the presentation of the messianic hero through the classic confrontation between good and evil on a stellar level, and the famous intergalactic barroom scene reminds one of an old-West saloon. The movie adaptation of Frank Herbert's *Dune* presents Armageddon as a battle in which the planet Dune's existence and the survival of an empire are in the hands of the messianic Paul Atreides. *Star Trek: The Motion Picture* envisions a future scenario of destruction in which a returning twentieth-century space probe, *Voyager*, threatens to annihilate earth. Furthermore, in *Star Trek IV: The Voyage Home*, Captain Kirk and his crew must travel back in time to 1986 in order to save humanity and planet earth from future destruction. In each case, an apocalyptic hero or heroine emerges to avert the impending cataclysm. In fact, apocalyptic themes in most westerns and science-fiction movies seem to be dominated by this hero and, thus, by character rather than by plot or the actual movement of time toward the end.

Nevertheless, this dominance of the hero character in westerns and in science fiction is balanced by a fascination with the apocalyptic setting in other films. In particular, Vietnam War and nuclear disaster films provide some of the most effective settings for apocalyptic themes, because the terror and frustration of the war and the fear of nuclear annihilation have been part of the U.S. consciousness. *Apocalypse Now,* Francis Ford Coppola's adaptation of Joseph Conrad's *Heart of Darkness,* provides a surrealistic view of the apocalyptic setting in the jungles of

Vietnam and Cambodia—a setting that presents a terrifying view of the twenti-eth-century version of Armageddon.

The opening scene, which includes a view of the Vietnam jungle and the song "The End" by the Doors, sets the stage for the drama that takes the viewer to the end of sanity and civilization and beyond. Martin Sheen plays Captain Willard, whose mission is to penetrate the remote stronghold of Colonel Kurtz (Marlon Brando) and to eliminate his command. (It is interesting to note that around seven years later, Sheen's son Charlie plays a similar role by eliminating an evil command in the Vietnam classic, *Platoon*.) Kurtz has apparently gone mad and acts on his own authority, he has effectively severed the military's chain of com-mand, and he represents the dark side of humanity. The movie chronicles Willard's journey upriver toward Kurtz's renegade unit. As the journey proceeds, emotional intensity increases, and the setting becomes more and more threaten-ing until Willard finally reaches Kurtz's garrison, which is bizarre and hellish. Once Willard meets Kurtz, the apocalyptic imagery surrounding the destruction of evil is confused in and subsumed by, the turmoil and terror of the place—the apocalyptic setting effectively invites dread and horror. The drama finally comes to an end when Willard kills Kurtz and flees Kurtz's hell, meditating on "the hor-ror" of the place.

In *Apocalypse Now,* character development and the journey of a hero are impor-tant, as they are in the westerns and science-fiction films in question. However, this film provides another element, which makes it more effective in presenting the horror of the apocalyptic drama. The latter part of the film switches focus from the journey to the setting of Kurtz's command, and that setting invites the viewer to experience the madness and futility of Vietnam—of Armageddon. In fact, the purpose of the journey is to introduce Willard to settings that become more and more bizarre as he nears Kurtz, which tends to magnify the insanity of Kurtz, the desperation of Willard and his crew, and the horror of unrestricted ego, war, and evil. Cambodia, the forbidden zone, provides an atmosphere for the un-imaginable; the most remote and hostile jungle, eons from civilization, creates the appropriate setting for chaos; the otherness of the inner reaches of this alien envi-ronment makes this battleground Armageddon. At the end of the film, evil is de-stroyed in this setting, and the apocalyptic drama, no matter how unthinkable, becomes real because it is set in Vietnam—an unforgettable and very real place.

As in *Apocalypse Now,* war provides an effective setting for the presentation of apocalyptic themes in the nuclear age. The threat of nuclear destruction is a con-venient impetus for end-of-the-world scenarios, and a number of films have been concerned with the threat or reality of nuclear annihilation. These films illustrate effectively the ironies, dangers, and fears surrounding the end of time in the nu-clear age by focusing on a postnuclear setting. Movies such as *Def-Con 4* or *The Day After* present a grim, sobering view of familiar settings following nuclear Ar-mageddon. In addition, these films seem to operate on the premise that a nuclear doomsday is survivable if not avoidable—a notion that recalls the 1964 British, black comedy, *Dr. Strangelove: Or How I Learned to Stop Worrying and Love the Bomb.* Therefore, in many nuclear disaster and war films, the horror of a world (a setting) following nuclear holocaust breeds the desire to avoid such an Armageddon, and the idea of the end and its terror becomes secondary to the idea that world destruction can somehow be avoided.

This notion of avoiding the apocalypse provides the driving force behind many apocalyptic films that emphasize plot. We have seen how some apocalyptic films, such as *Pale Rider* and *Dune*, emphasize character (the hero), whereas others, such as *Apocalypse Now* and *The Day After,* emphasize the apocalyptic setting. Jim Henson's children's epic, *The Dark Crystal,* is dominated by plot and by the movement of time and events that push the story toward the end and toward the resolution of chaos. This film emphasizes the possibility of avoiding the apocalyptic cataclysm, and it is dominated by the movement of time toward the end of time. The film ends with the return of harmony, with a new genesis through renewal rather than destruction.

Renewal of the world, yet avoidance of the apocalyptic cataclysm, also describes the theme of *The Seventh Sign.* This film provides the most explicit example (from the films under consideration) of contemporary apocalyptic vision through a creative combination of Christian and Jewish apocalyptic imagery and folk tradition. *The Seventh Sign* opens with signs that forecast the beginning of the end. These signs are loose adaptations of the seven seals, signs, and bowls of judgment from John's Revelation—fish die in the waters of Haiti, a village freezes in the middle of the Negev Desert, and a river in a Nicaraguan jungle turns to blood. David (note the messianic name), the embodiment of a returned Jesus, dispenses the signs as a messenger from God—the messenger who once came as a lamb and is now returning as a lion. According to David, he represents God's wrath, God's grace is empty, the signs have begun, and the end is unavoidable. Nevertheless, Abby (played by Demi Moore) questions David about the inevitability of the end—could the end be stopped if one or more of the signs were stopped? David responds that perhaps the chain could be broken, but it would take hope, and hope is something the world does not have.

In addition to basing itself on the Christian apocalypse, *The Seventh Sign* borrows from the Jewish apocalyptic tradition. In particular, Abby finds a Hebrew scripture in David's apartment and with the help of a young Hebrew student, Avi, discovers that it is a passage from the Book of Joel: "Even upon the menservants and maidservants in those days, I will pour out my spirit. And I will give portents in the heavens and on the earth, blood and fire and columns of smoke. The sun shall be turned to darkness, and the moon to blood, before the great and terrible day of the Lord comes."[2]

In addition to these portents, David tells Abby a story about an ancient Hebrew legend and the final sign of the end, the Guf. Abby researches this legend and learns that the Guf is the hall of souls, a "seventh heaven" (Rappoport 1966, vol. 1, 20), a place where a finite number of souls are stored until they inhabit the bodies of newborn babies. According to Jewish myth and apocalyptic tradition,[3] the messiah, the son of David, will not come until the Guf is emptied—that is, until the first child is born without a soul. Abby suddenly realizes that her unborn child is to be the first child born without a soul, born dead, and that this birth will usher in the end of time—this is what David has come to oversee. In the meantime, Father Lucci enters the scene. Lucci is actually Kartaphilus, Pilate's gatekeeper at the Judgment Hall. According to Christian legend, Kartaphilus struck Jesus as he was forced from the Judgment Hall, and Jesus then cursed him to wander the earth until Jesus's return.[4] In the movie, Kartaphilus must wander until the end comes, and he takes on a demonic element to ensure that the apocalypse takes place. This version of the Legend of the Wandering Jew adds a dramatic element to the movie, because Lucci (Kartaphilus) is determined to see that Abby's baby is born without a soul, that the world ends, and that he is freed from his curse. However, Lucci's plan is spoiled as Abby and Avi team up to break the chain of events that will ultimately lead to the end.

Abby and Avi know the seventh and last sign will be the birth of Abby's baby without a soul, so they try to stop earlier signs to avert the final sign and the end of the world. In their attempt to stop the signs, Avi discovers from Revelation 6 that the sixth sign, from the sixth seal, will be the sun turning black, and Abby remembers that a solar eclipse is about to take place. Obviously, they cannot stop the sixth sign, so they back up one. The fifth seal mentions the death of the last martyr, and Abby suddenly remembers the scheduled execution of Jimmy, the Word-of-God killer, who murdered his incestuous parents because of God's command. Abby and Avi rush to the prison in a desperate attempt to stop the execution and, thus, the fifth sign. When Lucci realizes what is happening, he tries to kill Jimmy himself; he fatally wounds Jimmy, and he also shoots Abby.

With Jimmy, the last martyr, dead, events speed quickly toward the end as the last signs begin. Darkness and earthquakes provide drama as Abby is rushed to the hospital, fighting for her life and entering labor at the same time. Finally, her baby is born dead, apparently without a soul. However, Abby's willingness to sacrifice her life for his gives the baby life and the world hope. With a touch, Abby conveys her life force to the infant. The baby springs to life, Abby dies, and the catastrophes surrounding the end of time cease. As the movie ends, David comments that the hall of souls is full again because of the hope of one person, and he instructs Avi to record the events so others can learn from Abby's sacrifice. In *The Seventh Sign,* the cinematic presentation of the apocalypse avoids the catastrophic end of the world and provides humankind with one more chance—renewal without destruction.

Contemporary Apocalyptic Consciousness

With these examples in mind, we can isolate a few recurring themes in the apocalypse of the cinema that will, in turn, provide clues to contemporary understandings of the end of time. First, in those films dominated by character development, the strong character is usually a hero figure who rises to the occasion by preventing the end from coming or by defeating the forces of evil. Second, in those films that stress setting, the apocalyptic drama occurs in a familiar or an immediate setting that has been transformed into an terrifying Armageddon. Third, in those films dominated by plot, the emphasis is not on the end itself but on avoiding the end and on renewal without the necessity of cataclysmic destruction. When viewed together, these three elements create an apocalyptic vision in which the drama is usually played out in this world, not in an "other" or transcendent setting, and in which human beings can actually avert the end of time and avoid the destruction of the world.

It is at this point that the contemporary cinematic vision of the apocalypse varies from the familiar Judeo-Christian view of the end of time, a view upon which most of these films are grounded. And it is to this point that I will return in order to draw some conclusions. However, first, it is necessary to deal with the existence of the modern apocalypse and its functional role in terms of the twentieth-century imagination. This examination has only scratched the surface of movies that deal with the end of time, and we question why there is such a preponderance of apocalyptic themes in recent films. Perhaps the popularity of movies with apocalyptic themes represents a response to the desperate sense of crisis the twentieth century seems to foster; perhaps it typifies a response to such horrors as the holocaust or the possibility of nuclear annihilation. However, as Frank Kermode points out, surely the terrors of twentieth-century life are no less horrific than the first-century threat of legions and "armies in the sky" (1967, 95); therefore, our age, in terms of the threat of impending doom, probably differs little from previous ages. Perhaps the approaching end of a millennium has spawned this new apocalyptic interest (Kermode 1967, 9). Without a doubt, as the year 2000 draws closer, end-of-the-world predictions will increase; however, this in itself cannot account for the modern apocalyptic crisis. The importance of the contemporary apocalyptic imagination in cinema lies not in its causes but in its function, purpose, and difference from traditional apocalyptic literature.

The modern apocalypse functions as apocalyptic literature has always functioned: to provide meaning to chaotic existence. As Kermode says, "The paradigms of apocalypse continue to lie under our ways of making sense of the world" (1967, 28, 3–5). The apocalyptic model allows us to make sense of our lives by providing a means by which to order time. By placing the life drama in relation to a beginning, a middle, and an end, the apocalypse provides coherence and consonance—it makes time trustworthy, especially when plot points toward the future, as it does in the apocalypse.[5] The apocalypse allows "sense-making paradigms, relative to time," in much the same way we tend to organize time into "concords." For example, Kermode provides the illustration of the ticking clock. Human beings impose a tick-tock organization upon the constant tick-tick sound a clock makes. The tick-tock becomes a concord of time even though the time interval between the tock and the tick is the same as that between the tick and the tock. "Tick is a humble genesis, tock a feeble apocalypse" (1967, 44–46).

The need to organize time, to make sense of human time, gives rise to the modern apocalypse, and cinematic presentation of this apocalyptic drama is a natural medium for this ordering process, because the motion picture itself is nothing more than a meaningful arrangement of pictures.[6] However, the modern presentation of the apocalypse differs from the traditional Judeo-Christian apocalypse, which orders events between an "Eden ... and ... the New Jerusalem" (Scholes and Kellogg 1966, 224). It is to this point that I must return. The Jewish and Christian apocalypses "involve a transcendent eschatology that looks for retribution beyond the bounds of history" (Collins 1987, 9). Jewish and Christian eschatology (teachings about the final events), as recorded in apocalyptic literature, looks beyond time, world, and history to the dawning of the kingdom of God—to an "otherworldly revelation of a transcendent world and eschatological judgment" (Cohn 1980, 15). Furthermore, in traditional apocalyptic literature, this transcendent kingdom of God is usually ushered in by a messianic figure (Cohn 1980, 22); however, in the modern, cinematic apocalypse, it is often the messianic figure who prevents the dawning of the new age and the eschatological kingdom.

What is the significance of this shift in emphasis for the contemporary apocalypse? Why does the modern apocalypse avoid the end rather than seek it or welcome it? Perhaps Hollywood has unwittingly recaptured a form of the apocalyptic tradition implied in rabbinical literature in which renewal rather than destruction defines the apocalyptic drama.[7] However, I imagine something deeper is at work here—something that enlightens the viewer about the modern understanding of time and humanity's place in time and space. The traditional apocalypse assumes an imminent cosmic cataclysm in which God destroys the ruling powers of evil and raises the righteous to life in a messianic kingdom. The modern apocalypse keeps the notion of destroying evil; however, it loses the notion of world destruction by God's hand, and it transfers the messianic kingdom from a new-age heaven to a second-chance earth. It might seem that this modern apocalypse, through its negation of an end point and through its loss of eschatological consummation, destroys its own ability to order time into meaningful concords; however, the result actually magnifies the apocalyptic purpose for modernity by placing time completely in the control of humankind. The ultimate ordering of time, in order to overcome chaotic time, is granting humanity the ability to control the end. In other words, the modern apocalypse has replaced a sovereign God with a sovereign humanity, and instead of providing hope for an eschatological kingdom, the cinematic apocalypse attempts to provide hope for this world.

It seems no coincidence that the modern apocalyptic model has developed along with humanity's ability to initiate the apocalypse. For the first time in history, twentieth-century humankind sees in itself the ability to bring about the end of the world, and it is only natural that human beings also believe they can stop the end, even if this means forcing God's hand as in *The Seventh Sign*. So the modern apocalyptic imagination grants meaning in light of twentieth-century fears and egos. We might even say that Hollywood has captured and fostered the secularization of the apocalyptic tradition. The traditional apocalyptic model presented the end of time and history as an immanent, or at least an imminent, reality from God. The contemporary model of the apocalypse offers the notion that the end is avoidable altogether. In other words, the modern apocalyptic imagination removes the end of time from the sacred realm of the gods and places the apocalypse firmly in the grasp and control of humanity. It is this development that defines the cinematic presentation of the end of time, and it is this revision of the apocalypse that allows the apocalyptic message to remain meaningful for modern and secular society. Perhaps this is modernity's response to Yeats's "rough beast" in his poem "The Second Coming" (1957, 401–402), which, unbeknownst to the modern world, "slouches towards Bethlehem to be born."

PART TWO

MYTHOLOGICAL CRITICISM

What did people do, anyway, before there were movies?

By the rays of the sun or by wavering firelight they traced inked shapes. They sounded them in the air with their voices. They pulled strings to move puppets or spin tops. They draped rags over their heads and assumed the voices of kings or ghosts or serving maids. ...

The darkness was filled with names and rhymes, hoots and thumps, catechisms and soliloquies. By day due note was taken of scars and griefs and epitaphs. Somebody had once seen a play with a horse in it, or had been told of a battle. Extended reveries might be initiated by handling a remnant of someone else's life, a pipe, a candlestick, a bundle of letters. Dramas were buried in words ... and clothes. ... There was endless play in sticks, buttons, cracked roots, fallen trees. They hid. Shadows made rooms for them.

Then they made rooms for shadows.[1]

This is how Geoffrey O'Brien relates the medium of film to previous "media" of the human imagination. Our ancestors gathered to tell stories, sing songs, and play with images and shadows; we go to the movies. The movie theater serves as our collective dream space, the place where we moderns encounter images and narratives of superhuman beings, otherworldly creatures, heroic figures, and the full range of possible human destinies. In our need for such images and stories, we are like our ancestors, seeking deeper meanings and patterns. And yet, just as film represents a very different kind of medium from those earlier artistic forms, so we are very different from our ancestors.

The rise of film, after all, accompanies the decline of a certain kind of human religiousness. Specifically, during the same period in which film has risen in prominence, Europeans and Americans have shifted from a focus on the power of God toward one that emphasizes the power of humanity. Impressed with our own power, we may feel we need God less than we used to. Our ability to record things on film has probably contributed to this shift. Thanks to film, we can see things our ancestors never glimpsed: things that happen too fast or too slow to be perceived with the naked eye; things that occur inside living bodies, in space, under the seas; things that happened in other places and times but were recorded on film. Film has changed the way we perceive things and has given us access to experiences and knowledge our ancestors could not have attained.

But even if this means that film enhances human power and helps relativize God's power, it does not mean that film is antithetical to all religion. Theism, or belief in God, is only one part of human religiousness. Film could undermine theism while enhancing other dimensions of religion. O'Brien argues that this is precisely what has happened: "No previous medium having so vividly intimated the disappearance of God—there are sacred books but no sacred movies—it stood to reason that film would overcompensate by the systematic cultivation of visions, icons, exorcisms, martyrdoms, paradisiacal landscapes, and sacred rituals."[2] Indeed, the relationship of film and religion is fairly complex. Film affects human religiousness unevenly. In film we witness the simultaneous critique of some of the previous modes of religious imagination and greater fulfillment, perhaps, of others. If "God" has been given a smaller role, other religious themes and figures have gained greater prominence. If theistic theology has been called into question, archetypal myth thrives as never before, appearing on screens everywhere, reaching millions in major motion pictures.

Unlike theology, which supports a particularistic truth and tends to focus on the activities and purposes of the God of Judaism and Christianity, myth communicates universal truth. Through the millennia and across all cultures, myth has enabled human beings to connect with their psychological and religious depths, aspects of their world not normally accessible by the conscious mind. Myth puts people in touch with great foundational forces, powers that generate and govern the world. Sometimes these forces have a personal name—Shiva, Eshu, God, Jesus, Corn Mother—and sometimes they do not—destiny, nothingness, samsara, the tonal. Taking the form of stories about these world-constituting forces and finding expression in song, art, dance, ritual, and drama, myth provides human communities with grounding prototypes—eternal, exemplary models for life. By telling us who we are and why we are here, indeed, why anything is here, and why it is this way as opposed to some other way, these stories shape us profoundly.

Myth is essential to religion, for it is through myth that the worldview of a given religion is communicated to its participants. Through sacred stories, religious people learn how spiritual powers create, uphold, or destroy their worlds. Through sacred stories, people learn how to recognize and participate more fully in the cosmic drama unfolding around them. Through sacred stories, people communicate to new generations the traditions of the religion. Without such stories, religious people would be lost, their rituals deprived of much of their meaning, their gods reduced to actors without a script. In the history of religions, many particular gods have died, and religion has survived. However, if myth were ever to die, religion could exist no longer.[3]

Within Europe and North America, mythic narratives have been closely, but not exclusively, associated with religious institutions such as churches and synagogues. Such institutions rely upon sacred stories and rituals to legitimate and shape human life by placing the mundane events of human existence within a cosmic and sacred framework. Millions of Americans continue to find mythic meaning by participating in the worshiping communities of organized religion. Through their active involvement in such institutions, Christians, Jews, Muslims, Hindus, and many others help to make the United States seem like one of the most religious nations on earth.

Nevertheless, some sociologists of religion argue that traditional religious institutions are losing their ability to provide Americans with mythic meaning. Such scholars argue that a process they term *secularization* is taking place. Whether such a process is actually taking place is fiercely debated, as is the definition of the term itself. Generally, the term means that traditional religious institutions no longer exercise the degree of public power they once did.[4] For our purposes, we can distinguish between two versions of the secularization thesis. One version assumes that if traditional religious institutions no longer hold the social power they once did, this means religion itself is declining in power. The other version thinks that if traditional religious institutions have lost power, this says little about the fate of religion itself but may simply mean that people are "getting" their religion elsewhere. In our view, the first version is too simplistic. It defines religion far too narrowly by equating it strictly with what happens in a church or synagogue. On the other hand, the second version seems evasive. It risks downplaying the deep ways in which modernity challenges all religious orientations, not just specific religious institutions.

By defining religion broadly and taking modernity seriously, we hope to avoid either extreme. We think secularization is occurring, and we think religion is thriving. Many people, without necessarily participating in a traditional religious institution, are finding mythic meaning and orienting themselves toward something sacred. They are finding the key to the mysteries and spiritual longings of human life in a novel type of secular, religious imagination. On the one hand, this imagination is religious because it continues to present human beings in relation to awesome, nonhuman powers of creation and destruction and continues to grapple with classic religious questions. On the other, it is secular because this imagination does not elide the power of human beings living in a technological age.

This point was made in the previous section by Conrad Ostwalt in his discussion of apocalyptic films: "The traditional apocalyptic model presented the end of time and history as an immanent, or at least an imminent, reality from God. The modern model of the apocalypse offers the notion that the end is avoidable altogether. In other words, the modern apocalyptic imagination removes the end of time from the sacred realm of the gods and places the apocalypse firmly in the grasp and control of humanity." We continue to be fascinated with this possibility of a final apocalypse, but, unlike prior generations, we could actually produce one. Thus, our imagination of the end of time must be different from theirs. Whereas earlier generations only wondered how, where, and when God would bring closure to creation, we also have to keep an eye on ourselves. Only such a dual focus, only such a hybrid imagination, can fulfill our ancestral spiritual needs without violating our modern awareness of human power.

It should come as no surprise that the modern increase in humanity's power has led some theologians to argue for new metaphors to describe God.[5] God can no longer be viewed as absolute sovereign, says Sallie McFague, who argues that God should be described as "Friend, Lover, and Partner." Whether such metaphors will gain currency among Christians and Jews remains to be seen. It may well be that McFague is asking for too radical a transformation, that the biblical God and modernity cannot mix, and that people will identify more readily with the other gods, goddesses, and spirits of our nuclear, self-help age.

New wine, someone once said, requires new wineskins. It follows that we can expect that the deities of a hybrid secular, religious imagination will not be encountered first and foremost in traditional sacred institutions such as the church and synagogue but that they will manifest themselves most fully in modern, secular cultural formations. Could the movie theater be one of these secular institutions that provides modern Americans with a new mythology that is meaningful in our times? Perhaps so. Joseph Campbell, arguably the foremost scholar of mythology, suggested the idea. Campbell asserted that movies such as *Star Wars* function mythologically and religiously. Campbell talked about the ability of popular films such as *Star Wars* to perform the same function as ancient myth, which is to provide a means for human beings to experience and find meaning and significance in life.[6] Popular movies are cultural standard-bearers; they carry with them the values, beliefs, dreams, desires, longings, and needs of a society and, thus, can function mythologically. This view of film and culture should allow us to explore religious myths and patterns in popular film. In other words, film and religion intersect when films function mythically and provide access to universal truths.

The film critic who operates on the assumption that myth is a predominant component of any particular film wishes to illuminate those characteristics or elements of the film that tap into universal human feelings and reactions. To employ myth criticism is to assume that films have a distinct relationship to archetypes (universal symbols) in such a way as to communicate them to modern audiences in a meaningful way. In other words, we might examine certain films by employing the standards of myth criticism. Myths narrate an encounter with the mysterious unknown, with terrifying or awe-inspiring or enchanting otherness. They do so by describing a sacred space and time, by portraying the quest of a hero, and by probing universal problems of human existence and belief. Mythological films do the same.

Like myths, mythological films take people to places beyond the boundaries of the known world and require viewers to negotiate an encounter with "a world elsewhere,"[7] with a world that is "wholly other" and, therefore, sacred or religiously significant.[8] Through its encounters with sacred places, ordinary life is transvalued. Ordinary experience may become invested with mythological meaning; deeper levels of significance may become visible as a result of the encounter with the mystery. A film such as *Cocoon,* by taking us to a place where aging does not exist, makes us all the more aware of the fragility and value of human life. At a minimum, the mythological film may help us see our world more clearly because of the contrast produced by an encounter with an other world.

Many popular U.S. films create this type of world elsewhere, which functions to infuse the known world with transvaluing meaning. Some critics argue that science fiction is ideally suited to bring religion to secular audiences, because science fiction, like religion, is oriented toward the unknown. In his book on the genre, Mark Rose asserts that "one of science fiction's principal cultural functions appears to be to produce narratives that mediate between spiritualistic and materialistic world views."[9] His thesis finds support in our book. As the chapters in this section demonstrate, mythic themes appear in films such as *Star Wars, Starman,* and *Alien.*

This is not to say that science fiction alone exposes us to mythically charged settings. Many films have shown that earthly sites can be sacred as well. In scores of films, the West has been represented as a landscape of great mythic power, a place where nature is bigger and wilder and human inhabitants are naturally more free. In *A River Runs Through It,* the Montana wilderness, especially the Big Blackfoot River, symbolizes a vital, untamable force that timelessly regenerates those who respect its beauty. Paul, the character who is most in touch with the river, becomes a famous fisherman, but true to the type of the western hero, he cannot adapt to civilization like his father (a pastor) or intellectual brother (an academic). Free and wild, Paul is destined to die young but to be remembered and praised always as a man with a beautiful spirit.[10]

As we turn from the wilderness to the garden, it can be argued that the pastoral landscape in *Places in the Heart* or *Tender Mercies* carries mythic meaning on many levels. It evokes notions of human wholeness associated with Jeffersonian agrarianism. It functions as the stage on which Christian resurrections occur. But this landscape also has a power more properly associated with "pagan" religions. As in the religious myths of agricultural societies, dead things immersed in the soil come back to life. In each film, the lead character (Sally Field/Robert Duvall) has suffered a devastating loss (a husband/a wife). Each finds new meaning by engaging in the timeless activities of ploughing a field, planting, and harvesting a crop. The American heartland heals their wounded hearts. Indeed, the good earth has the power to bring together people otherwise divided by race or generation or death. Similar motifs appear in the film *Forrest Gump,* with its romantic vision of life in "sweet home Alabama."

In contrast, if the utopian fields of the American heartland reorient and heal people, the dystopian fields of battle disorient and tear people apart, literally and figuratively. Countless films, including *Birdy, Apocalypse Now, Coming Home, The Deer Hunter, Platoon,* and *Born on the Fourth of July,* have used the jungle setting of Vietnam to represent a mythic space where civilization and savagery blur and men lose their moral bearings. These films use the site of war to explore the meaning of suffering and to evoke a sense of evil. In such settings, if redemption comes, it occurs only with great pain.[11]

To the Western wilderness, the mid-American farm field, the southern home place, and the foreign field of battle, we must add the baseball field, another earthly mythic site beloved by Hollywood. In both *Field of Dreams* and *The Natural,* the baseball diamond becomes the transcendent setting on which dreams come true, where past meets present, bitterness dissolves into kindness, suffering and loss meet compassion, and faith conquers all. In each film, baseball is linked to pre-1960 America and rural wholesomeness, connections emphasized by musical scores inspired by Aaron Copland's *Appalachian Spring.* In *Field of Dreams,* nostalgia rules. The film provides access to an era that is beyond historical or linear time, that is cyclical and recoverable in nature. At the conclusion of the film, a son plays catch with his magically reincarnated father. In real life, the son and father had been estranged. On the mythic baseball diamond, they are reconciled. This scene comments on the chaotic experience of time in the modern world in which fathers and sons hardly relate. As such, *Field of Dreams* creates a sacred space and time of mythic proportions—a space and time that provide commentary on modern life. *The Natural* goes back even farther to evoke the Arthurian legend of the knight's quest for the Grail. Roy Hobbs brings a team (the Knights) and a city to life with his miraculous feats on the field of play. The rich, mythic resonances of the film have not gone unnoticed.[12]

If Hollywood films project a wide range of mythic spaces, they also create a great number of mythic heroes. The hero in myth is crucial. In most myths, the hero embarks upon a journey or a quest into another realm of reality, which requires some sort of struggle, often with monstrous guardians of the threshold dividing different worlds. Heroes are characters who try passionately to move toward greater insight and freedom or to better the condition of others. In many versions, the quest takes the hero from a state of "psychological dependency" to a condition "of psychological self-responsibility."[13] The hero makes the transition or reaches the goal only by confronting the things, forces, or persons that are most terrifying and oppressive (the belly of the whale, hell, a dragon, the wicked witch, a southern prison, urban crime, an endless repetition of Goundhog Days, Nurse Ratched, evil Bill and Ted, the Joker, Darth Vader, a psychotic played by Dennis Hopper). In these contests, the hero may either prevail or be defeated. The triumph of the hero provides hope to people undergoing a transition or experiencing a crisis; the defeat of the hero indicts the social forces that thwart human fulfillment, helping people name the obstacles that block their paths. In either case, the story of the hero provides people with a way to mythologize their lives, to make their own struggles coherent and purposeful. Modern films are filled with mythological heroes such as Dorothy, Cool Hand Luke, Randall P. McMurphy, Rocky, Batman, Luke Skywalker, Ripley, the children in *E.T.,* the good Bill and Ted, Forrest Gump.

In the following pages, authors explore the mythological functions and aspects of some modern U.S. films. Andrew Gordon explores the extent to which George Lucas has employed modern popular cultural symbols to construct Joseph Campbell's "monomyth." His insightful analysis demonstrates the extent to which Lucas's work is patterned after the mythic model, particularly when it comes to the hero's journey. Caron Schwartz Ellis focuses on movies dealing with humanoid alien visitors to earth. She identifies such figures with the mythic archetype of sky gods. Their cinematic advent brings modern viewers face-to-face with otherness, the sacred sphere, and, thus, presents the viewer with the mythological world. Finally, Janice Hocker Rushing reexamines the archetypal myth of the frontier in light of the feminine principle in *Alien* and *Aliens.* She thinks the old heroic myth of the frontier is detrimental to feminine consciousness and needs to be replaced by a myth that is more commensurate with the interdependence the infinite scene of outer space suggests. In each of these examinations, the author employs the principles of myth criticism to uncover the mythological potential of these films—the potential that allows "screening the sacred."

6

Star Wars: A Myth for Our Time

ANDREW GORDON

STAR WARS, George Lucas's lavish space opera, is truly a fantasy for our times, this generation's *Wizard of Oz*. Nevertheless, whereas Lucas's film has been almost universally praised for its costuming, sets, technical perfection, and wondrous special effects, its plot has been largely dismissed as corny or hokey, strictly kids' stuff. "The film's story is bad pulp, and so are the characters of hero Luke and heroine Leia," says Richard Corliss.[1] "I kept looking for an 'edge,' to peer around the corny, solemn comic-book strophes," writes Stanley Kauffmann.[2] And Molly Haskell sums up the critics' objections: "*Star Wars* is childish, even for a cartoon."[3]

If *Star Wars* is childish, then so are *The Wizard of Oz* and *The Lord of the Rings*. Like Tolkien's Middle Earth series,[4] *Star Wars* is a modern fairy tale, a pastiche that reworks a multitude of old stories and yet creates a complete and self-sufficient world of its own, one populated with intentionally flat, archetypal characters: reluctant young hero, warrior-wizard, brave and beautiful princess, and monstrous black villain. I would argue that the movie's fundamental appeal to both young and old lies precisely in its deliberately old-fashioned plot, which has its roots deep in American popular fantasy and deeper yet in the epic structure of what Joseph Campbell, in *The Hero with a Thousand Faces*, calls "the monomyth."

In an era in which Americans have lost heroes in whom to believe, Lucas has created a myth for our times, fashioned out of bits and pieces of twentieth-century U.S. popular mythology—old movies, science fiction, television, and comic books—but held together at its most basic level by the standard pattern of the adventures of a mythic hero. Star Wars is a masterpiece of synthesis, a triumph of American ingenuity and resourcefulness, demonstrating how the old may be made new again: Lucas has raided the junkyards of our popular culture and rigged

Reprinted, with revisions, from "Star Wars: A Myth for Our Time," *Literature/Film Quarterly* 6, no. 4 (Fall 1978): 314–326.

a working myth out of scrap. Like the hot rods in his film *American Graffiti, Star Wars* is an amalgam of pieces of mass culture customized and supercharged and run flat out. This chapter, therefore, has two parts: first, a look at the elements Lucas has lifted openly and lovingly from various popular culture genres; second, an analysis of how this pastiche is unified by the underlying structure of the monomyth.

Star Wars and Popular Culture

George Lucas, who both wrote and directed *Star Wars,* admits that his original models were the *Flash Gordon* movie serials and Edgar Rice Burroughs's *John Carter of Mars* series of books: "I wanted to make an action movie—a movie in outer space like *Flash Gordon* used to be. ... I wanted to make a movie about an old man and a kid. ... I also wanted the old man to be like a warrior. I wanted a princess, too, but I didn't want her to be a passive damsel in distress."[5] In other words, he wanted to return to the sense of wonder and adventure movies had given him as a child but to update that sense for modern tastes and take advantage of all the technological and cinematic innovations of the thirty years that had passed since *Flash Gordon.*

Thus, just like *American Graffiti, Star Wars* is simultaneously innovative and conservative, backward glancing and nostalgic. *Graffiti* takes a worn-out genre (the teenage beach party movies) and reanimates it; *Star Wars* gives new life to the space fantasy. "I didn't want to make a *2001*," says Lucas. "I wanted to make a space fantasy that was more in the genre of Edgar Rice Burroughs; that whole other end of space fantasy that was there before science took it over in the fifties. Once the atomic bomb came ... they forgot the fairy tales and the dragons and Tolkien and all the *real* heroes."[6] Both *Graffiti* and *Star Wars* express a yearning for prelapsarian eras: the former for the pre-Vietnam era and the latter for the innocence of the time before the bomb.

Although lamenting the dearth of classic adventure films and the consequent lack of a healthy fantasy life for contemporary youth, Lucas told an interviewer, "I had also done a study on ... the fairy tale or myth. It is a children's story in history and you go back to the *Odyssey* or the stories that are told for the kid in all of us."[7] "You just don't get them any more, and that's the best stuff in the world—adventures in far-off lands. ... I wanted to do a modern fairy tale, a myth."[8]

Much more labor went into fashioning the script than into making the final product.

> I began writing *Star Wars* in January 1973—eight hours a day, five days a week, from then until March 1976, when we began shooting. Even then I was busy doing various rewrites in the evenings after the day's work. In fact, I wrote four entirely different screenplays for *Star Wars,* searching for just the right ingredients, characters and storyline. ... What finally emerged through the many drafts of the script has obviously been influenced by science fiction and action adventure I've read and seen. And

I've seen a lot of it. I'm trying to make a classic sort of genre picture, a classic space fantasy in which all the influences are working together. There are certain traditional aspects of the genre I wanted to keep and help perpetuate in *Star Wars*.[9]

What exactly is heroic space fantasy, or, as it is often called, space opera, and what are the conventions of this genre Lucas wanted to revive? Perhaps the best definition of space opera is given by Brian Aldiss in his anthology of such stories. Aldiss calls it a "renegade sub-genre" of science fiction, "heady, escapist stuff. ... Essentially, space opera was born of the pulp magazines, flourished there, and died there."[10] Space opera is a formulaic genre, with certain rigidly fixed conventions that are its raison d'être. "One may either like or dislike those conventions," says Aldiss, "but they cannot be altered except at expense to the whole."

> Ideally, the Earth must be in peril, there must be a quest and a man to meet the mighty hour. That man must confront aliens and exotic creatures. Space must flow past the ports like wine from a pitcher. Blood must run down the palace steps, and ships launch out into the louring dark. There must be a woman fairer than the skies and a villain darker than the Black Hole. And all must come right in the end.[11]

Star Wars obviously fits this prescription: Not just the earth but the entire universe is in peril from the tyrannical Galactic Empire. The quest is to rescue the beautiful Princess Leia from the clutches of the villainous Darth Vader and transport to the rebel forces the secret plans of the *Death Star,* the Imperial spacefort that can smash whole planets with a single blow; the man of the hour is young Luke Skywalker (his name suggests his destiny), a farmboy whose father had been "the best starship pilot in the galaxy, and a cunning warrior"; there are aliens, robots, and exotic creatures aplenty; the action moves across the galaxy; rayguns blast, laser swords clash, and pitched battles explode in outer space; and the good guys save the universe at the last moment.

Science-fiction historian Sam J. Lundwall qualifies the Burroughs tales as pure entertainment, "immensely popular, despite the fact that every one of them on close scrutiny turns out to be rather old hat. ... The Burroughs adventure formula doesn't differ much from other action novels."[12] Of course not, since predictability is one of the formal reassurances pulp readers seek. What distinguishes Burroughs from the rest, according to Lundwall, is "the quick, breathtaking pace ... suspense ... from beginning to end, and in Heroic Fantasy, this is what counts."[13] In addition, good and evil are clearly differentiated: "His heroes and villains are painted in unmistakable terms of black and white." Thus, although Burroughs's heroes "kill like maniacs," they are still represented as clean.[14] In other words, Burroughs's lavish fantasies, no matter their unconscious content, are guilt-free for the reader; one can indulge oneself and still come away feeling innocent. All of these characteristics—old-fashioned adventure formulas, slambang action and suspense, and clear-cut good and evil, to the extent of dressing the hero and heroine all in white and the villain all in black—apply equally well to *Star Wars*.

If Burroughs provided the literary pattern, *Flash Gordon* established the cinematic conventions for space opera. Richard Corliss finds the influence of the *Flash* serials everywhere in *Star Wars*, "from the theme to the pacing (a climax every fifteen minutes) to the quick, dead readings by many of the movie's bit players, even to the visual 'punctuation' (wipes, fast dissolves, etc.)—and *Star Wars* begins smack in the middle of things, as if you'd just walked into Chapter Four of a Buster Crabbe cliff-hanger."[15] One might add that Ben Kenobi, Luke's white-haired mentor, fulfills the same role as Flash Gordon's Dr. Zarkov; that Princess Leia must be rescued from the villain's stronghold just like Flash's girlfriend, Dale Arden; and that Darth Vader wears the same black cape and speaks with the same sarcastic courtesy as Ming the Merciless.

But *Star Wars* is more than just an homage to Edgar Rice Burroughs and *Flash Gordon:* It also draws on elements common to other action-adventure and fantasy genres. As George Lucas (born in 1944) says, "It's the flotsam and jetsam from the period when I was twelve years old ... all the books and films and comics that I liked when I was a child."[16]

Forbidden Planet may be one of those sources. Released in 1956, when Lucas was twelve, it is the greatest of the color, special-effects, outer-space films before *2001*. I first saw the film at age twelve, and I can testify to its indelible impression on a youngster. For that matter, most hard-core science-fiction fans catch the bug with the onset of puberty. Certain key elements of *Forbidden Planet*—interstellar travel, a comic robot (Robbie), a damsel in distress, a mysterious "Force," and a vast machine civilization (the Krell), which explodes at the climax of the film—also figure prominently in *Star Wars*.

Another of those influences must have been the film *The Wizard of Oz*. As in the *Wizard*, we have a nice kid, an orphan who dreams of going "over the rainbow," who is tied to an isolated farm by an aunt and uncle but magically gets his wish. The crystal ball is represented by hologramed messages and the tornado by a spaceship. Munchkins are replaced by "Jawas," funny little creatures who live in caves and talk in a high-pitched gabble; the faithful little dog, Toto, is converted into the plucky little robot, R2-D2; the tin man into the humanoid robot, C3PO; the cowardly lion into an amusing, furry space creature named Chewbacca, who communicates by roaring; the wicked witch and her castle into Darth Vader and the *Death Star;* the good witch into Princess Leia; and the Wizard into Obi-wan Kenobi. Once again, the pure of heart are able to defeat the forces of wickedness: We even get the final awarding of medals to the heroes, as in the *Wizard*.

Yet another genre from which Lucas borrows is the western; as critics have pointed out, the scene in which Luke discovers his dead aunt and uncle is a reconstruction of a scene in John Ford's *The Searchers*, in which the hero returns home to find his parents massacred by Indians.[17] And straight out of the old West rides Luke's companion, Han Solo, a gun for hire, quick on the draw, dressed in the compulsory cowboy vest, boots, and tight pants, with pistol (now a raygun) slung low in a holster on his hip. Although Solo is a loner, as his name suggests, he has overtones of the good-guy Lone Ranger, with Chewbacca his Tonto. "The Wookies are more like the Indians," says Lucas, "more like noble savages."[18] As he told an interviewer, "One of the significant things that occurred to me is I saw the western die,"[19] and he is determined to revive the elements that constituted its basic appeal as adventure, even if the wide open spaces of the frontier are now in outer space.

In the tradition of Douglas Fairbanks and Errol Flynn, Solo is the bold and reckless captain of a pirate ship; instead of sailing the seven seas in search of adventure, he flies from one side of the galaxy to the other. Later in the film, Luke and the princess swing on a rope across a chasm in the *Death Star,* conjuring up Fairbanks and Flynn or, for that matter, Tarzan.

Japanese samurai films must have contributed to the conception of the half-religious, half-military order of the Jedi Knights. The laser sword battle between Ben and Vader is surely indebted to the stylized combat of such movies.

Lucas drew on footage from a series of old war movies to orchestrate the final dogfight in space,[20] and Darth Vader thus becomes the equivalent of the Red Baron or the leader of the Nazi *Luftwaffe* (Lucas even gives him a Nazi-style helmet). The fact that the sequence was filmed in England, so the rebel pilots speak with both English and American accents, could have been incongruous; instead, it adds to the effect. We have the Allies, the Royal Air Force, and the U.S. Air Force winning the war once again.

Time mentions Lucas's debt for some settings and concepts as being to such science-fiction writers as Frank Herbert, author of the epic *Dune* trilogy (the monstrous skeleton behind 3PO in one shot on the planet Tatooine resembles that of one of Herbert's desert sandworms), and to Robert Heinlein (*Starship Troopers*) and Samuel R. Delany (*Nova*).[21] In addition, many of the aliens, robots, sets, and costumes resemble those that have appeared for decades on the covers of science-fiction magazines and paperbacks, drawn by such artists as Ed Emshwiller and Frank Kelly Freas. From television's *Star Trek,* Lucas lifts the conventions of deflector shields and tractor beams.

Finally, we could cite the obvious influence of comic strips on the film, most notably *Flash Gordon, Buck Rogers, Terry and the Pirates,* and *Marvel Comics* (whose Dr. Doom bears an uncanny resemblance to Darth Vader). In fact, *Marvel* has issued a comic-book version of the movie, which easily translates back into that form. As Jack Kroll writes in his review of *Star Wars,* "The great comic strips were the fables and fairy tales of industrial society before television and science fiction wiped them out."[22] Lucas himself is a long-time fan who owns a comic-book store in New York. He claims comic-book art expresses "a certain cultural manifestation on a vaguely adolescent level but is much more pure because it is dealing with basic human drives that more sophisticated art sometimes obscures."[23] His remark could stand as a summary of his films.

Star Wars is, thus, a compendium of American pop and pulp culture, carefully crafted out of many and unabashed borrowings. As critic Roger Copeland pointed out, its debt to old movies alone is so great that "it could just as easily—and perhaps more accurately—have been called 'Genre Wars.'"[24] Film commentator Stephen Zito writes that "Lucas is most comfortable with what is known and familiar. ... *Star Wars* is literally constructed from bits and pieces of the usable past."[25] As Lucas says, the film is "a compilation. ... It's all the things that are great put together."[26]

Star Wars as Monomyth

Lucas's achievement is to construct a coherent myth out of his pastiche of pop culture. The multiple cross-references, the archetypal characters and situations give it both reinforcement and deep resonances for an audience that may not consciously recognize the sources but will still respond emotionally to the conventions. Moreover, at its most fundamental level, the plot partakes of the timeless elements of epic myth. According to Brian Aldiss, space operas say "a great deal about fundamental hopes and fears when confronted by the unknowns of distant frontiers, in a tradition stretching at least as far as *The Odyssey*. They are, in their way, abstracts of the same impulses that lie behind traditional fairy tales."[27]

If, as Lucas says, he has studied myth and deliberately attempted to construct a myth in his film, it would be useful to determine how successfully the work meets mythic criteria. In the remainder of this chapter, I examine *Star Wars* in the light of Joseph Campbell's thesis in *The Hero with a Thousand Faces*—that the hero of epic myth is a dream figure who stands in for the entire culture. According to Campbell, the hero must descend into the infantile unconscious, the realm of sleep: "All the ogres and secret helpers of our nursery are there, all the magic of childhood."[28] There the hero gives battle to "the nursery demons of his local culture" and "brings back from his adventure the means for the regeneration of the society as a whole."[29] Symbolically, he becomes a man by rescuing his mother and slaying his father. Despite the Oedipal nature of the conflict, he is finally accepted by the parent figures and, thus, discovers his true identity and attains his true powers, which he realizes were within him all the time. Campbell divides this monomyth into three main stages—departure, initiation, and return—each of which consists of various steps. I will trace the action of *Star Wars* to see how closely it corresponds to this traditional pattern of mythic adventure.

Typically, the hero is the orphaned son of royalty. Unaware of his true identity, he is consigned to a life of drudgery and exile. He is first called to adventure by a herald, signifying that "the time for the passing of a threshold is at hand."[30] The threshold represents a rebirth into adulthood; the hero or heroine must overcome the parents, who stand as threshold guardians. When we first meet Luke, we find him bored and restless for adventure, but he is kept on a farm on the remote planet Tatooine by his uncle, who fears the orphan may turn out like his father. Luke is curious about this father, who his uncle claims was the navigator on a space freighter. Later we find that Luke's father was actually a Jedi Knight and, in the words of Ben Kenobi, was "the best starship pilot in the galaxy, and a cunning warrior." The uncle, then, is the actual father—ordinary and repressive—and the knight is the idealized image of the father. At this point, the call to adventure arrives fortuitously for Luke: A little robot appears, carrying a hologramed plea for rescue from a beautiful princess. Symbolically, 3PO, R2's android companion, now refers deferentially to the boy as "Sir Luke." Like a Knight of the Round Table, he has been summoned to adventure.

The next step in this wish-fulfillment dream is the encounter with a protective figure, "some wizard, hermit, shepherd, or smith, who appears to supply the amulets and advice that the hero will require. ... The call, in fact, was the first announcement of the approach of this initiatory priest."[31] The wizard here is old Ben Kenobi, once a rebel general (Obi-wan) and a friend of Luke's father, now a hermit in the desert wastes of the planet; the princess's message had been a call for his help. Ben has supernatural powers: He first appears as a mysterious, hooded figure, uttering inhuman howls to frighten away the desert Sandpeople, who have attacked Luke. And he is indeed a priest, last of the Jedi Knights, a mystic religious order that worships the Force, the power that binds together the universe. Ben appears out of nowhere to save Luke, and he assumes the protective, paternal role he maintains throughout the film. Like Merlin, he tutors this rough-hewn country lad and hands him the sword his father willed him (in this case not Excalibur but the light-sword of the Jedi Knights).

Once he leaves the safe boundaries of the farm, Luke can never go back. As the attack of the Sandpeople shows him, the world is a desert place filled with danger, but only by abandoning the security he had known, leaving the womb of his childhood, can he enter the adult world. Luke at first refuses the call to adventure, but he joins Ben when he discovers that, in his absence, Darth Vader's storm troopers have burned the farm and killed his aunt and uncle.

Of course, nothing in mythic plots adheres to the conventions of realism; it is all guided to fulfill the hero's "destiny." And what is destiny but a supernatural "Force" that arranges for things to happen. It is another word for the belief in the magical omnipotence of thought. For example, why does a chain of circumstances detour the little robot to Luke's farm? This is not chance—it was evidently predestined for Luke's sake. And why is Ben living as a hermit near Luke's farm? Obviously, so he could be there when Luke needed him. For that matter, the death of Luke's aunt and uncle is arranged conveniently.

"Destiny" also helps to make Luke seem blameless: He does not seek out Ben but merely tries to return the wandering R2 unit to the farm; still loyal to his uncle, he refuses the call to adventure until he is left no choice. It has all been magically manipulated for Luke: His wish for adventure materialized, and the obstacles (uncle and aunt) were conveniently removed.

At the same time, our blameless hero is provided with a ready-made excuse for rebellion in the political situation and the slaughter of his father, aunt, and uncle by Vader or his minions. As Otto Rank notes in *The Myth of the Birth of the Hero,*

"The myth throughout reveals an endeavor to get rid of the parents," particularly the father; yet the hero, like Hamlet, sees himself not as the persecutor but as "the avenger of the murdered father."[32] In fact, Luke has a careless habit of losing father figures: First the knight, then his uncle, and then Ben fall to the demonic Darth Vader (whose name suggests "dark" or "death invader" or even "death father").

According to Campbell, the mythic hero, once he has stepped beyond the safe bounds of his everyday routine, sallies forth with the Wizard, "the personification of his destiny to guide and aid him." Now he must confront a dangerous ogre, a "threshold guardian."[33] Here we have a series of threshold guardians: first, the marauding Sandpeople; next, a storm trooper guarding the entrance to the spaceport; and, finally, a foul-looking alien in the spaceport bar. In each case Luke is saved by Ben, who uses either the Force or the power of his light saber.

The next stage of the adventure, says Campbell, is the passage into "the belly of the whale";[34] in *Star Wars* the heroes are sucked into the enemy space fortress by a tractor beam. Here the hero dies symbolically and is reborn in the second phase, or initiation.

The initiation consists of a series of miraculous tests and ordeals: "The hero is covertly aided by the advice, amulets, and secret agents of the supernatural helper."[35] In Campbell's scheme, the endless corridors of the *Death Star* would represent for Luke "the crooked lanes of his own spiritual labyrinth," and his perils would represent the type we encounter nightly in our dreams.[36] Interestingly, among the typical dream perils, Campbell mentions two in particular: "Themistocles dreamed that a snake wound itself around his body, then crept up to his neck" (an obvious phallic symbol), and "the dreamer is absolutely abandoned … in a deep hole of a cellar. The walls of his room keep getting narrower and narrower, so that he cannot stir. In this image are combined the ideas of mother womb, imprisonment, cell, and grave."[37] Luke encounters these two perils after his plunge into the inferno of the garbage room. Meanwhile, he is aided by his various helpers: Ben unlocks the tractor beam to release their captive ship, and he fights Vader; the robots stop the walls from crushing them; and Solo and Chewbacca help the group shoot its way out. But Luke has passed his initiation; whereas previously he had relied passively on Ben, he now initiates and carries out the rescue of the princess and the escape from the *Death Star*.

At the center of the journey are "the Meeting with the Goddess" and "the Atonement with the Father," both symbolic stages in working out the Oedipal crisis. The rescue of the princess represents the former stage, and the death of Ben represents the latter. Luke's guardian, having fulfilled his function, seems to will his own destruction and is cut down by Vader; nevertheless, he does not die so much as he disappears in order to be subsumed into the Force. He persists as a voice that guides Luke at critical moments, like the superego, which Freud posited as nothing more than the internalized voice of the parents. Once they are safely aboard Solo's ship, Luke mourns Ben and is comforted by the princess, who maternally puts a blanket over his shoulders and tells him he is not to blame; there is nothing he could have done. Ben had similarly exculpated him after Luke found his aunt and uncle dead.

We see here again how Lucas attempts to make this essentially Oedipal fable guilt-free. If myth is dreamlike, then all the characters are merely extensions of the wishes of the central character. Vader as destructive devil acts out Luke's patricidal desires, yet Ben, his good side, still forgives him and blesses him, as we all wish our parents to do. Solo, the apparently amoral loner, acts out Luke's antisocial desires for total independence; Luke himself is presented as dutiful and dependent. The ambivalence of love yet hate toward authority is, thus, successfully contained by parceling it out among separate characters. Finally, the Oedipal desires toward the mother figure are also kept in check by the inability of the princess to decide between the two rivals, Luke and Solo.

Having symbolically met his mother and made his peace with his father, the hero, according to Campbell, has reached the stage of apotheosis. He is now the possessor of the grace of the gods, "the Ultimate Boon" that can restore his culture. This boon is, of course, the Force. As Campbell writes, "Briefly formulated, the universal doctrine teaches that all the visible structures of the world—all things and beings—are the effects of a ubiquitous power out of which they arise, which supports them and fills them during the period of their manifestation, and back into which they must ultimately dissolve. ... Its manifestation in the cosmos is the structure and flux of the universe itself."[38] This ur-religion is a basic element of all myth; the hero becomes the possessor of this ubiquitous power, or "Force," when he achieves adulthood.

Thus, the mystical elements of *Star Wars* begin to make sense; they are indispensable to the mythic structure. Moreover, this Force, as Campbell explains, is not simply a religious power; it is also the power of the libido, and "its guardians dare release it only to the duly proven."[39] Luke, having won through his trials and proven himself to his guardian, can now enter manhood. The father dies for his sake, freeing Luke's libido; as Ben tells him, "The Force will be with you always."

The departure and the initiation completed, the hero now begins the third and final stage—the return: "The full round, the norm of the monomyth, requires that the hero shall now begin the labor of bringing the runes of Wisdom, the Golden Fleece, or his sleeping princess, back into the kingdom of humanity, where the boon may redound to the renewing of the community, the nation, the planet, or the ten thousand worlds."[40] Luke, accompanied by the princess, escapes with the plans of the battle station in Solo's ship out of the *Death Star*, out of the belly of the whale. He now undergoes what Campbell calls "the Magic Flight";[41] he is chased by symbolic "demons" out of the *Death Star* but manages, with the aid of Solo, to destroy the pursuing ships and reach the rebel base—significantly, a lush, green, light-filled planet.

Having crossed the threshold from "the world of light" into "the world of darkness" and returned alive, Luke is now "master of the Two Worlds."[42] He has the power to move at will between the two worlds, which he proves by returning at the risk of his life to the *Death Star* in order to destroy it. In combat Luke now assumes his true identity, which is that of the ideal father: Jedi Knight, starship pilot, and cunning warrior. Guided by the Force, he naturally succeeds in his task, dropping some proton torpedoes down a symbolically suggestive narrow chute. The *Death Star* goes up in an orgasmic explosion of fireworks.

According to Campbell, "The work of the hero is to slay the tenacious aspect of the father (dragon, tester, ogre king) and release from its ban the vital energies that will feed the universe."[43] His job, in other words, is to destroy the status quo in order to permit renewal and restoration, and this is the task Luke—ordinary boy raised to the status of mythic hero—successfully perfoms.

It is this sense of renewal that makes *Star Wars* so appealing. In the absence of any shared contemporary myths, Lucas has constructed out of the usable past, out of bits of American pop culture, a new mythology that can satisfy the emotional needs of both children and adults.[44] The passion for *Star Wars* is akin to the fervor of a religious revival.

The fact is that each generation must create its own myths and heroes or regenerate those of the past. We are in a period in which the heroes have been cast down through such national catastrophes as Vietnam and Watergate, when the lines between good and evil grow cloudy, and when sexual identities have been redefined by the women's movement. Meanwhile, we have created a machine world for ourselves, a world that seems drained of spiritual values, a world in which we feel impotent and alien. We desperately need a renewal of faith in ourselves as Americans, as good guys on the world scene, as men and women, as human beings who count, and so we return temporarily to the simpler patterns of the past. The old superheroes rise again—*Wonder Woman* and *Superman*—and we get old-fashioned genre films such as *Rocky* and *Star Wars.*

Such fantasies give voice to our deepest longings and speak to our hopes about the future of our society and ourselves. For example, in opposition to the dehumanizing uses of technology, *Star Wars* shows the triumph of good technology over evil machinery[45]—an updated version of the triumph of white magic over black magic in *The Wizard of Oz.* Viewers recognize that *Star Wars* has no direct relation to external reality, but it does relate to our dreams of how we would *like* reality to be. As reviewer Jack Kroll says about the film, "It's the last chance for kids to have fun before they grow up to be Oedipus. And we hollow-eyed Oedipuses can, if we try, go back and enjoy the fun of our pre-guilt stage."[46] "Kids' stuff," after all, is the stuff that dreams are made of.

7

With Eyes Uplifted:
Space Aliens as Sky Gods

CARON SCHWARTZ ELLIS

Keep watching the skies!

— from *The Thing*

FROM THE ALARMING "carnivorous carrot" in *The Thing* (Christian Nyby/Howard Hawks 1951) to Steve McQueen's getting "slimed" by *The Blob* (Irvin S. Yeaworth Jr. 1958) to Richard Dreyfuss's *Close Encounters of the Third Kind* (Steven Spielberg 1977) to the downright cuddly *E.T.: The Extra-Terrestrial* (Steven Spielberg 1982), science-fiction films have been bringing alien life into American movie theaters, drive-ins, televisions, and VCRs for nearly forty years.[1] This fascination with aliens reveals much about Americans' deepest fears. During the 1950s, cinematic aliens clearly reflected Cold War fear[2] of "penetration, invasion, and colonization by an alien Other."[3] One thinks of films such as the aptly named *Red Planet Mars* (Harry Horner 1952) and the emotionless, faith-free pod people of *Invasion of the Body Snatchers* (Don Siegel 1956), both representing what life under communism would be like. During the 1960s, space aliens descended less frequently to earthly screens. Film scholar Vivian Sobchack posits that this shift away from overt representation of otherness may be the result of a new focus on the domestic "Other" in the form of the proud Black, the liberated woman, or the alienated and rebellious youth.[4] During the 1970s, real space aliens returned, this time, however, in much less threatening forms. In this chapter I focus on these kinder, gentler aliens, arguing that their appearance addressed our deep fears about technology and answered spiritual questions about our destiny.

The space alien dramatically reentered earth's atmosphere in 1976 with the release of Nicholas Roeg's *The Man Who Fell to Earth*. Importantly, Thomas Jerome

Newton appears entirely human. He is neither a repulsive blob nor a mechanized robot nor a blank-faced automaton nor a horribly deformed creature. He is an entirely recognizable human being.

In the decade that followed, humanoid aliens, markedly different from the classic Cold War aliens, were frequent visitors. This is not to say that nonhuman aliens stopped dropping by as well. *Close Encounters, E.T., The Terminator* (James Cameron 1984), and *The Abyss* (James Cameron 1989) are but a few of the popular movies that deal with extraterrestrial visitors that are not humanoid. The focus of this chapter, however, is on aliens who are unmistakably humanoid. Why has Hollywood begun to make aliens in our own image?[5]

This chapter examines, along with *The Man Who Fell to Earth,* three other spaceman movies of the 1970s and 1980s: *The Brother from Another Planet* (John Sayles 1984), *Starman* (John Carpenter 1984), and *Man Facing Southeast* (Eliseo Subiela 1986). Each of these films centers around an intentional visitation. Some visitors come for purely selfish reasons: Newton (David Bowie) is on a quest for water for his drought-ridden planet, and the Brother (Joe Morton) is seeking asylum from galactic slavery. Starman (Jeff Bridges) seems to have simply responded to the invitation broadcast by Voyager II. The visitor in *Man Facing Southeast* claims pure altruism; Rantes (Hugo Soto) wants to alleviate the suffering of the poor and helpless.

Each visitor, despite his familiarly human, nonthreatening appearance, is regarded with awe and fear—as a holy person and a fiend, a highly evolved superman creature, and a charlatan. The earth person's reaction toward the alien seems ambiguous and confused. The spaceman, seeming to burst out of nowhere into the everyday world, may be regarded as a hierophany, a manifestation of the sacred.[6] And the ambivalent earthling response of attraction and dread, fascination and fear, love and disgust reflects the visitor's numinous, or sacred, quality.[7] The alien is, quite simply, Other, not one of us. He may resemble us, but he is different.

Why do the aliens seem so mysterious, awesome, and extraordinarily powerful? Why are the visitors always described as more highly evolved, more civilized, more intelligent, more technologically advanced than the people who make and watch the films? The fact that we can identify a virtual genre of films depicting such aliens suggests that these visitors are important to us. As film scholars such as Stuart Kaminsky argue, "The more popular a film (the more people who see it), the more attention it deserves as a genre manifestation. If a film is popular, it is a result of the fact that the film or series of films corresponds to an interest—perhaps even a need—of the viewing public."[8] He continues, "Genre analysis can involve an attempt to understand the milieu and background of the work through its relationship with religion, mythology, the social sciences, psychology, and anthropology. The roots of genre are … in the fabric of existence itself. … The very persistence of genre films argues that they must be dealing with basic aspects of existence and social/psychological interaction, or they could not continue to be made."[9] Since these basic aspects of existence are also the prime subject matter and concern of myth, I would argue that generic films can act as powerful purvey-ors of myth.[10] These films serve as repositories and reminders of our deepest con-cerns.

Many would argue that in the twentieth century our central concern is technol-ogy. We modern Westerners regard ourselves as rational beings who understand creation through science. Our cosmogony has nothing to with gods, not with the spoken word of the Hebrews' Yahweh nor the cosmic dismemberment of the Hin-dus' Purusha, but with a chemical reaction. We believe all matter was created ini-tially by a "primeval fireball."[11] After the Big Bang, hydrogen and helium co-alesced into stars. That is our creation story. We and everything we know are essentially "stardust."[12]

Although we understand our creation story rationally through the hard sci-ences—physics, chemistry, mathematics—we enjoy experiencing our science in the form of fiction, especially at the movies. Science-fiction films project a world at once familiar and other. Space travel happens in NASA-like space ships, num-bers and lights flash on computer screens just like our comfortable and conve-nient personal computers, characters wear shiny uniforms and use multisyllabic words. As scientifically oriented people, it is as if we want to act as though we are not involved in myth. We resist admitting that we are like all other human com-munities, in need of orienting myths and transcendent values. Science fiction en-ables us to have our cake and eat it too, to experience a world centered on technol-ogy that nonetheless allows for an encounter with cosmic otherness. Consider this: We are fascinated with space aliens, with familiar-looking men who *fall to earth* because this genre tells us of our beginnings. By coming into contact with people who are *closer to the stars* than we are, we are doing nothing other than par-ticipating in a mythic experience; through watching space alien films, we are get-ting in touch with our roots, exploring the secret, sacred dimension of our scien-tific worldview. And, as Vivian Sobchack points out, "The great force of the genre film is that it depicts truth without contemplating it, that it dramatizes our deepest conflicts in such a way that they are apprehended indirectly, painlessly."[13] We receive the message in a nondidactic way, as entertainment. We are "indirectly, painlessly" seeing the deeper meaning of our cosmogonic myth enacted on the screen.

In order to understand their innate Otherness, let us examine the numinous quality of each spaceman. Each alien is regarded with awe and fear, as a manifesta-tion of *mysterium tremendum et fascinans.*[14] Ambiguity is the key. *The Man Who Fell to Earth,* Tommy Newton, is strangely androgynous. When he first meets Oli-ver Farnsworth (Buck Henry), Newton's dark hat is dipped over one eye, and he refuses (or does not know how) to shake hands. His physical features and actions are such that his gender is nearly undeterminable. The diminutive Mary-Lou (Candy Clark) carries him out of the elevator. In this context, the fact that she is more able-bodied than he underscores Newton's uncertain gender. Androgyny is an ancient attribute of the gods. "Universal bisexuality" is revealed in cults of a bearded Aphrodite and a bald Venus, in the androgynous nature of many vegetation and fertility gods, and in the Talmudic midrashim (commentaries) depicting Adam and Eve as sharing one body.[15] The significance of this divine "totalization" is that it forms a simultaneity of cosmos and chaos, "a reintegration of opposites, a regression to the primordial and homogeneous. It is a symbolic restoration of 'Chaos,' of the undifferentiated unity that preceded the Creation."[16] Newton's physical "undifferentiated unity" is a manifestation of his numinosity.

In *The Brother from Another Planet,* everyone seems to like the Brother, but most are somewhat disturbed by him as well. This is revealed best in the early scene in Odell's bar. Each of the "regulars" has his own territory: Odell (Steve James) is comfortably in charge behind the bar, Smokey (Leonard Jackson) is seated at the bar, Walter (Bill Cobbs) slouches at a table, Fly (Darryl Edwards) mans the video game. As a group of four, they seem to represent order and stability, even though they also seem to be in their own worlds. When the Brother wanders in, the fifth wheel, he disturbs the easy equilibrium. The normally aloof men are forced to interact, even though, like themselves, the Brother sits by himself. When unable to engage the Brother in conversation, the men are frustrated, but they do not shun him. Smokey pops a bag behind his head to test him for deafness and tempts him with whiskey "to find out if he's crazy." Later, Sam (Tom Wright) arrives, evening up the number of men in the bar and restoring a sense of order. He sits with the Brother, finds him a job and a place to live. The men acknowledge that he is a little strange, yet they are attracted to him as another, somewhat alienated Black man adrift in Harlem.

Jenny's (Karen Allen) reaction to the *Starman* is one of fear and attraction. When she awakens to find a clone of her dead husband in her living room, she approaches, calling him by her husband's name. She is attracted to him because of the uncanny resemblance yet faints of fright when he approaches her. She dresses him in her husband's clothes, which shows her attraction. But when he puts on his cap she is repulsed because it is too weirdly familiar. Jenny nearly abandons him at a truck stop but changes her mind when she witnesses him reviving a recently slaughtered deer. Her emotions flip back and forth throughout the film as she tries to respond to an inexplicable, ineffable situation. National Security is also of two minds toward the visitor. George Fox (Robert Jaeckel), the businesslike professional man in charge, feels he should be captured and investigated and calls the chase "a combat mission." In contrast, Mark Shermin (Charles Martin Smith), the informal free-lance scientist, wants to get to know him as an individual.

Rantes, the *Man Facing Southeast,* remains an enigmatic character. He is loved by his fellow inmates in the asylum, who accompany him on his daily vigils when he faces southeast "receiving and transmitting information." Yet Dr. Julio Denis (Lorenzo Quintero), despite his obvious affection for the man, never believes his celestial origin and continues to try to cure his "neurosis." Rantes's ambiguity climaxes in the scene at an outdoor concert when he displaces the conductor and leads the orchestra in a rousing Beethoven's *Ninth Symphony,* stirring the patients to march to the park. The movements of the patients are choreographed to the music, as are the swinging billy clubs of the police, lending an air of strange other-worldliness to the situation. Although it is possible to believe that the patients could have found their way to the park, it seems improbable that they would march there in time to the music. The police ultimately lead Rantes away. Is he criminal or savior? Is he a troublemaker or a problemsolver? Is he extraterrestrial or insane? We are never quite sure where to place him. He remains the Other, characterized by Rudolf Otto as "that which is quite beyond the sphere of the usual, the intelligible, and the familiar, which therefore falls quite outside the limits of the 'canny.' The contrast between the Other and the familiar fills the mind with blank wonder and astonishment."[17]

Like all sacred beings, each alien has extraordinary power. Newton is an extremely gifted electronics engineer whose nine basic patents can, as his business partner Farnsworth exclaims, "take on RCA, Eastman Kodak, and Dupont, for starters." This power is revealed on the screen primarily through monetary accomplishments. His lover, Mary-Lou, is at first a uniformed housekeeper in a hotel, supporting him in a crowded studio apartment. Soon she is wearing designer outfits and extravagant wigs and enjoying the expensive toys he lavishes on her including, ironically, a telescope.[18] Newton does not seem particularly gifted, either physically or psychically. Driving forty-five miles per hour makes him dizzy, and he faints in elevators. Yet, his power is manifest in his agelessness. At the end of the movie Mary-Lou and Nathan Bryce (Rip Torn) are paunchy and gray, indicating the passage of many years, whereas Newton remains slim and redheaded. His only "inexplicable" act is to appear to Bryce, before they have actually met, as a ghostly apparition, dressed in black with a hood over his head, his face a white spot in the darkness,[19] saying "don't be suspicious." The next day when they do meet, Newton self-consciously repeats his plea, revealing that Bryce did not imagine their encounter.

The Brother demonstrates his power in several ways. He can fix things. When he first arrives at Ellis Island, he heals his own mangled leg with his glowing hand. The video machines in Odell's bar and Hector's (Jaime Tirelli) "video graveyard" all respond to the power in his hand, as do Little Earl's (Herbert Newsome) scraped knee and broken television. As he works his magic, his face shines with a beatific glow. The Brother is also supersensitive to the pain of others. In the immigration center he can sense those who have arrived before him; when he touches a pillar or sits on a bench, cries and voices leap out at him. In Odell's bar he violently recoils from "the death seat," because by simply approaching it he "hears" the scream of the man who was shot there. He experiences a heroin high by injecting himself with the empty syringe of an overdosed junkie. Moreover, the Brother can see more than ordinary people, having the remarkable ability to remove an eyeball and have it "film" things he is unable to witness himself. These out-of-body visions are in slow motion and are jerky, as if to emphasize their uncanny nature.

Except for his ability to start a car, rig a slot machine in Las Vegas with his fingertip, and impregnate the infertile Jenny, the Starman's main source of power seems to be small, mirrored marbles.[20] It is as if the energy of the stars has been solidified, to be used as needed. With the help of these marbles, the Starman sends an emergency transmission to his planet, prints a map of the United States on a car windshield, heats up a lug wrench, and survives a car crash. The Starman is also a miraculous healer, able to resuscitate the dead. First, we see him bring a deer back to life. The camera remains in the truck stop with Jenny, viewing him through a plate-glass window across a parking lot. He does not have to touch the deer, he merely stands before it holding a glowing marble aloft. Because the camera, and, thus, the audience, remains at a distance, we are reminded of the taboo in most religions that is associated with extraordinary power, the injunction to approach the holy with great care.[21] Also, with his back toward us we are unable to witness how he works his miracle; we see only its results, making it seem all the more mysterious and uncanny. Later, the Starman revives Jenny. He kneels beside her, holding his uncannily potent nugget. Again, we view him from behind and are not privy to his healing knowledge, as the glow from his power source lights up the entire mobile home in which they are traveling.

Rantes's power is demonstrated mainly by his intense stare. If the eyes are the seat of the soul, this metaphor is a striking indicator of the potentiality of Rantes's soul. With his eyes he can not only move items, such as plates of food to a poor family in a restaurant, he can also move his fellow inmates at the asylum. His healing power is subtle; no one is "cured," but the men seem to get better. He touches the forehead of a catatonic man and places his jacket around his shoulders, to which the man warmly responds. Rantes claims to have no feelings, and his unblinking, luminous eyes rarely betray emotion. His blank face may seem to reveal feelings, but often it is simply the actions and looks of those around him that impart emotion to his face.[22] He says he is merely "programmed" to respond to stimuli, explaining to Dr. Denis, "I'm more rational than you. I respond rationally to stimulus. If someone suffers I console him. If someone needs my help I give it." Rantes is also a brilliant organist, and Beatriz (Ines Vernengo) reveals that he can deliver babies and is building a computer out of discarded electronic components. Yet it is only in his eyes that his extraordinary intelligence and compassion are revealed.

The films under investigation all begin with descent from the sky: Newton plunges in a humanoid-shaped stream of white light, crashing into a lake in New Mexico; the Starman arrives in a beam of light that crashes into the Wisconsin wilderness; the Brother is portrayed in his spacecraft before he tumbles into New York Harbor. Rantes, however, describes rather than demonstrates his descent from above.[23] But there is no question that these beings originate in the sky, evoking the archetypal symbolism of the sky and the figure of the sky god.

As Mircea Eliade observed, "Simple contemplation of the celestial vault already provokes a religious experience. ... The 'most high' is a dimension inaccessible to man as man; it belongs to superhuman forces and beings."[24] These forces and beings include a wide range of spiritual beings, depending upon which religious tradition is consulted. Sky gods are characterized as those who have come to earth to participate in the creation and then withdraw to become *dei otosi,* absent gods.[25] Unlike angels, who are not originally from earth but return there frequently to help individuals, sky gods are mysterious and remote beings whose earthly appearances are associated with times of cosmic creation or collective crisis. It is the archetypal pattern of the sky god that can be traced in the careers of our cinematic aliens. Each of these aliens, despite tarrying on earth, remains remote. Unlike the angel Clarence in *It's a Wonderful Life* (Frank Capra 1946), they cannot really relax and enjoy human company. Newton, for instance, dreams of his celestial home and family and begins to withdraw into television and alcohol addiction. But when he reveals his "true nature" to Mary-Lou, perhaps in an effort to renew intimacy, this leads to an increased sense of alienation. In a spectacularly bizarre sequence, filmed in low light and with unusual camera angles, he emerges from the bathroom as a hairless, nippleless, cat-eyed creature. Mary-Lou shrieks and drops her glass, repulsed by the sight of her tender lover transformed into a "monster." She tries to make love with him, to accept him as he is, but Newton does not seem to be there. He daydreams: The scene is intercut with shots of coitus on his planet, two glowing creatures embracing and exuding a gleaming liquid. When he reaches out, leaving his luminous bodily fluid on Mary-Lou's skin, she runs from him, screaming, and crouches trembling as a wide-angle lens distorts her almost beyond recognition. His innate distance combined with her knowledge of his ineffable otherness destroys their intimacy. The once inseparable couple must part.

The Brother's alienation is evident in his inability to speak. Although he is able to communicate using hand and body language, his distance is apparent because he is often spoken to without an expectation of a response. Randy Sue (Caroline Aaron), who gives him room and board, drones on and on about her absent husband. Hector gabbles at him in Spanish. Ace (Liane Curtis), the video junkie, never taking her eyes from the blips on the screen to even acknowledge his presence, complains in a monotone of her dissatisfaction with slow video games. A rookie, white police officer talks confidently of his delight at working in Harlem; his crouched, self-protective posture, however, reveals his actual discomfort. Malverne Davis (Dee Dee Bridgewater), removing her false eyelashes in another room, blithely reminisces about her past. Although he appears to be accepted by those around him, the Brother, in truth and in silence, remains apart.[26]

The Starman's separation is demonstrated primarily—and effectively—by plot device. He simply must leave again. His comrades are returning for him in three days[27] regardless of whether he falls in love with Jenny. He cannot survive long on earth even with the relationship.

Rantes's separation from humankind is manifest in his blank face and his claim to feel no emotions. Despite his exceptional compassion for others, he avoids getting involved. Even with his fellow "agent" Beatriz, he remains aloof. They sit on opposite sides of the hard, wooden table when she visits him. The camera remains distant, thus making the viewer see them from afar and increasing the sense of Rantes's alienation. As they dance at the outdoor concert, they hold each other not as intimates but in response to the uplifting music.[28] When Dr. Denis discovers a photograph of Rantes and Beatriz, it is torn, and the piece that should have shown another person standing next to Rantes is missing. The doctor speculates on whether that person was one of his parents. Dr. Denis sadly acknowledges Rantes's supreme aloneness, and so does the audience. Space aliens cannot make themselves too much at home on earth, for they are true to the archetype of the sky god.

It is typical of sky gods to leave a son or representative to complete their work,[29] and these filmic aliens all leave a legacy of some sort. Newton makes a record album that tells his story, hoping that one day his wife will hear it on the radio. The Brother eludes his evil slave-trading pursuers, and they, in embarrassment and frustration, self-destruct. He has, at least temporarily, vanquished evil. The Starman leaves Jenny pregnant with their son, who, he declares, "will know everything I know and when he grows to manhood, he will be a teacher." Rantes has forever changed the lives of the mental patients. Dr. Denis says, "The patients didn't accept Rantes's death. They said he had gone but that he would return in a spaceship. They would be there, waiting."[30]

What is the significance of our fascination with space aliens? I suggest that it is part of our pursuit of origins. We have faith in a cosmic Big Bang creation myth that explains natural and supernatural phenomena—how the world came to be, why things are the way they are, what will happen next. Our perfect beginning involves the fallout from exploding stars. Cinematic space aliens appear to irrupt *from the stars,* becoming literal, visual representations of our origins. This is where I see the significance of their *human* appearance. The ancient sky god of the West spoke his desire to "make man in our own image" (Gen. 1:26), and this statement has often been taken literally in our Sistine Chapelesque (which also requires uplifted eyes) imaginings of a white-bearded human, heavenly Father.[31] We are simply more comfortable with recognizably human-looking gods. In seeing the familiar-looking people of the stars, we witness our stardust beginnings.

Their significance does not end with creation: "The cosmogony is the exemplary model for every creative situation: Whatever man does is in some way a repetition of the pre-eminent 'deed,' the archetypal gesture of the Creator God, the Creation of the World."[32] In the movies discussed here, each alien, in one way or another, is a model for correct action. Although the aliens recall sacred beginnings, they are acting in profane time and are actively demonstrating that moral perfection can extend into ordinary existence. In this way they point in the direction of positive social action.

The man who fell to earth fell for one reason: to search for solutions to environmental problems on his home planet, where a severe drought rages. Although Newton does not warn earth of impending doom if its environmental problems are not addressed, I think the implication is clear. He hires Bryce to work on fuel conservation. The conservation of nonrenewable resources is a problem we earthlings have been grappling with for some time. However, Newton's ultimate goal is to develop a fuel-efficient spaceship to enable him to return to his family. He has been forced to leave his wife and family in search of water; overuse of natural resources on earth may eventually cause similar familial breakups. Many of the products of his company, World Enterprises, appeal to the family—for instance, superior sound equipment and a self-developing camera. In his concern with nonrenewable natural resources—water, fuel, and family—Newton appears as a role model for correct living.

The Brother's plight as an escaped slave opens the possibility for commentary on bigotry of all sorts, manifested in a wide variety of prejudicial comments. Potshots are hurled relentlessly at many races and minorities. Walter, sitting alone at his table in Odell's bar, rambles on about Haitian and Polynesian "diseases." When Bernice (Ren Woods) suggests Szechuan food to Odell, he proclaims he "won't eat anything he can't pronounce." Sam is ridiculed by his buddies because he comes from New Jersey. Mr. Lowe (Michael Albert Mantel), owner of the video parlor, comments, "They're clever with their hands, the colored, but they forget things," and "They give you a good day's work, the Spanish, but they have no sense of time." Smokey, after encountering the Men in Black (John Sayles and David Strathairn), mumbles in bewilderment, "White people get stranger all the time." These prejudicial attitudes are never resolved, but their unrelenting frequency during the film leads the viewer to an awareness of our casual intolerance.

The Starman makes it clear that he comes from a more "humane" civilization. He protests the needless slaughter of animals, asking when he sees the slain deer, "Do deer eat people?" He describes his planet this way: "There is only one language, one law, one people. And there is no war, no hunger. The strong do not victimize the helpless." As he speaks he is driving through the Arizona desert with a golden sunrise haloing his head, as if to emphasize his purity. He seems a totally responsible, mature humanitarian—a good example for earth people to emulate. The Starman has not written off the earth race but is fascinated and troubled by it. When Shermin asks him why he has visited, he replies, "We are interested in your species. … You are a strange species, unlike any other. Bright, intelligent, but savage. … You are at your very best when things are worst." Humans may be unpredictable, he implies, but at least they are able to cope with reality. He goes on to admit that his is not a perfect world: "We are very civilized but we have lost something. You are all so much alive, all so different." The implication is that perhaps superior technology can lead to impersonalization and mindless conformity.

Rantes states rather plainly that his mission is to assist the helpless, which is why he has lived contentedly in the asylum and worked with the poor in the surrounding area. When Dr. Denis asks about his collection of newspaper clippings of natural and manmade disasters, Rantes explains, "We are preparing the rescue of those who cannot survive amidst the terror, those who are without hope …

here." Rantes exhibits many characteristics of Christ, the Western sky god known for extraordinary compassion toward the meek. He sits quietly hearing "confession," as a long line of dejected men wait to see him. A "last supper" is played out as Rantes, surrounded by men at a long, wooden table, hands out food to them from his own plate. Indeed, Dr. Denis refers to Rantes as the "Cybernetic Christ." He says, "Since Rantes was becoming more Christ-like, his end would be the same." The doctor refers to himself as Pilate for following the institute director's order to forcibly sedate Rantes, which leads to his deterioration and death. Rantes's final words are the plaintive cry, "Doctor, doctor, why have you forsaken me?"

What, finally, explains the recent movie trend toward beneficent heavenly Otherness? These beings from outer space, living where other mythological sky gods live, are our celestial divine beings. They are numinous and awesome, technologically advanced creator gods who attract those of us who are fascinated with the myth of science. They are the *dei otisi* of stardust who until now have seemed inaccessible and withdrawn. We go to space alien movies to look up and "worship." Although we would like to look to the sky for revelation and redemption, the sky today is not always pleasant to regard. Sometimes all we see are palpable clouds of air pollution. Poisonous acid rain pours down from above. The diminished ozone layer permits dangerous levels of ultraviolet rays to penetrate the atmosphere.

But even more dramatic a concern is the fact that the sky may also be regarded as a "corridor for chaos,"[33] the place from which nuclear weapons fall. G. Simon Harak posits that the Strategic Defense Initiative (SDI, or "Star Wars") was an effort to reinstate the benevolence of the sky. Since historically the United States has considered itself invulnerable to attack because it is surrounded by two oceans, "the most apt solution [to nuclear invasion] is … to treat *the sky* as a 'third *ocean*' and make it, by technology, impenetrable."[34] SDI, in effect, was a modern, rationalistic, scientific prayer to the ancient sky gods, pleading with them to protect humanity from above. In a similar vein, Ira Chernus has written that our relationship with the bomb is marked by the ambiguity inherent in the numinous. Perhaps we look to the sky to actually call upon the ultimately destructive, yet somehow fascinating, nuclear weapons because they, *irrupting from the sky,* have come to represent our absent gods. This is no doubt a horrifying thought—that the bomb, because of its heavenly realm, may actually be regarded as a savior.[35]

Technologically superior modern sky gods have been returning to earth in the technologically advanced art form of the movies for around forty years. Beginning in the 1970s, kinder, gentler aliens began appearing. Perhaps their appearance coincides with years that seemed more fraught with technological peril. Because of the remarkably swift advancement of science (as evidenced by myriad nuclear capabilities), Americans sought compensatory fulfillment through human-looking, extraordinarily powerful and compassionate gods who understand and use technology in nonthreatening ways. In viewing our gods, in hearing our mythic stories, in sitting around the brightly lit screen in the darkened room, in seeing *actors* depicting mystery and Otherness, we are participating in one of the oldest human activities—the telling of the stories of the gods. Film scholar Darrol Bryant articulates this well when he writes, "Film [is] a response to the ambition of a technological civilization to discover the alchemical formula that could wed the machine to the transmutation of nature and the deification of human culture. In a word, as we sit and watch a film, we are participating in a central ritual of our technological civilization."[36] Our spacemen are important to us: They give us hope in a world in which our vision of the stars is obscured by pollution and the potential for nuclear holocaust.

8

Evolution of "The New Frontier" in *Alien* and *Aliens:* Patriarchal Co-optation of the Feminine Archetype

JANICE HOCKER RUSHING

FROM EARLY PILGRIMS to recent progress, the myth of the frontier has inspired U.S. literature and rhetoric, reflecting its self-concept and molding its personality.[1] The frontier has always been a patriarchal myth in which women were overwhelmingly dominated by men. Although necessary to life on the real frontier, women were rarely the center of action in the myth; those heroines who did appear were usually caricatures, masculine personalities in female bodies.[2] Ever present in the background as helpmates, mothers, captives of the Indians, schoolmarms, and saloon girls, women were nevertheless primarily supplements.

Despite the relegation of women to the periphery, however, the frontier myth has never lacked for rich imagery of the feminine. As Annette Kolodny points out, the land in the frontier myth has typically been imagined metaphorically as female. In *The Lay of the Land,* she documents the connection between the two in male frontier literature, concluding that "the American landscape has not been experienced as something similar to, or merely comparable to, but as the female principle of gratification itself, comprising all the qualities that Mother, Mistress, and Virgin traditionally represent for men."[3] American literature was uniquely able to revive the dead conventions of European pastoral literature because, unlike Europe, America held "the promise of fantasy as daily reality." This fantasy was one of "harmony between man and nature," with the land as "the total female principle of gratification—enclosing the individual in an environment of receptivity, repose, and painless integral satisfaction."[4]

Reprinted, with revisions, from *Quarterly Journal of Speech,* February 1, 1989, vol. 75, no. 1, pp. 1–24. Used by permission of the Speech Communication Association.

As with most stories with such an abiding grip on the public imagination, however, the American frontier myth has evolved. Before the land, the frontier locus was the sea, and after a short-lived and rather unsuccessful stint in the city, the myth, which showed signs of decay, has recently been revived in the scene of space.[5] In an article that examines films that characterize the myth's development, I argue that the evolution of the frontier must be understood as a cultural variant of a larger evolution of the archetypes inherent in the myth. For example, the latest scenic transition into space has produced, at least in some cases, a new kind of hero; as the concept of "frontier" shifts from finite land to infinite space, the action turns from conquest to coexistence, from exploitation to conservation. The hubris of the old western patriarchal hero recedes, and the new frontier hero eventually ceases to dominate the scene and vanquish the enemy.[6]

Although Kolodny does trace shifts in the frontier hero's relationship to the feminine/land over time, she does not place these changes within the context of archetypal evolution. If feminine symbolism in the frontier myth is reinterpreted as an evolving cultural manifestation of an archetypal process that is itself developing, a more complete, historically grounded understanding of the emerging role of the feminine within the myth can be constructed. To this end, I first develop an archetypal view of the evolution of feminine consciousness that overcomes a partiality in Kolodny's view of feminine symbolism in the myth. I then use this perspective as a critical frame to analyze two contemporary extensions of the frontier myth into space—the films *Alien* (1979) and *Aliens* (1986). The analysis also functions as a counterpoint to existing feminist readings of these films.

Evolution of the Archetypal Feminine

My understanding of myths begins with the conviction that they are central to the meaning of life; as Alasdair MacIntyre says, "The unity of a human life is the unity of a narrative quest."[7] Thus, myths are not simply aesthetic fictions nor perpetrators of false consciousness. Myths that endure over time and place have both archetypal and rhetorical aspects. The archetypal imagery of a myth expresses what Carl Jung calls a universal psychic truth; it is addressed to what Joseph Campbell terms "ultimate questions"; and it includes, but is not reducible to, a biological drive or a psychological function.[8] Its purpose is not unconscious wish fulfillment but the expression of spiritual meaning. Although archetypes are sometimes conceptualized as static Platonic forms, they are more properly conceived as changing over time, co-varying with the development of human consciousness.[9]

As stories that are told and retold, myths are also consciously shaped by their particular communities.[10] As Richard Slotkin puts it, "The success of the myth in answering these [archetypal] questions for a people depends upon the creation of a distinct cultural tradition in the selection and use of metaphor."[11] The cultural expression of a myth responds to historical and political contingencies and may appropriate archetypal imagery, consciously or unconsciously, for rhetorical means—that is, to further the ends of a particular person or group of people or to advise a general course of action.[12] Thus, the important myths of a society are complex blends of archetypal and rhetorical elements, which are sometimes in concert and other times in tension with one another. Myths are neither constructive nor destructive per se, as Edward Whitmont explains: "They may be either, depending upon how they are fitted into the life of the community or of the individual and how they are lived in terms of the here and now. If they are consciously related to and reconciled with ethical requirements they will be constructive because they are the elements through which life receives its impulse."[13] It is when myths are unconsciously lived that they lean to regressive wish fulfillment or take on a sinister cast.

The archetype of relevance to questions of the feminine in the frontier is that of the Great Goddess, also called the Great Mother. Comparative mythology reveals the evolution of the feminine from early times through its critical turning points to its contemporary condition. In viewing the archetype from this broad evolutionary framework, it is possible to extend our understanding of the feminine principle in the land-based frontier myth, as well as to interpret its reemergence in the spaced-based new frontier.

The Undivided Goddess

As Kolodny discusses it, feminine imagery in the frontier is grounded in the principle of gratification. Appearing as Mother, Virgin, and Mistress, the feminine is, thus, defined in relation to masculine needs and desires and also in terms of mutually exclusive roles. Although it is possible to be both Mother and Mistress simultaneously, it is not possible, by contemporary standards, to be Mother and Virgin or Mistress and Virgin. But ancient mythology reveals numerous instances of goddesses whose identities were not established by their relationships to men and for whom the various roles were not contradictory. The archaic goddess, according to Esther Harding, was typically "virgin" in the original sense of being "one-in-herself."

> Her instinct is not used to capture or possess the man whom she attracts. She does not reserve herself for the chosen man who must repay her by his devotion, nor is her instinct used to gain for herself the security of husband, home and family. She remains virgin, even while being goddess of love. She is essentially one-in-herself. She is not merely the feminine counterpart of a male god with similar characteristics and functions, modified to suit her feminine form. On the contrary she has a role to play that is her own, her characteristics do not duplicate those of any of the gods, she is the Ancient and Eternal, the Mother of God.[14]

This goddess, then, could be Virgin, Lover, and Mother simultaneously without loss of her independent identity. Sylvia Perera finds the Sumerian Inanna to be an example of this all-encompassing goddess, who represents "a wholeness pattern, of the feminine beyond the merely maternal. ... She combines earth and sky, matter and spirit, vessel and light, earthly bounty and heavenly guidance."[15] Inanna was not a settled and domestic wife or mother under the patriarchy; she was independent and magnetic. She was also not originally a mother-lover to sons—a role that is probably an invention of the patriarchy, "when women were depotentiated and lived their potential in projection on envied and beloved male offspring."[16]

Not only does Kolodny's static view of the feminine archetype lead to a restricted definition, but it also excludes other dimensions of the archetype—ones imputed almost exclusively to the masculine in contemporary times. A little-understood aspect of the ancient Great Goddess, for example, was her association with warfare and destruction. Whitmont reminds us of the oldest deities of war in various countries: In addition to Inanna in Sumer, there was Anath in Canaan, Ishtar in Mesopotamia, Sekhmet in Egypt, the Morrigan in Eire, Kali in India, Pallas in Greece, and Bellona in Rome. These archaic goddesses ruled over both love and war and were chaste and promiscuous, nurturing and bloodthirsty. "But," Whitmont explains, "they were not at all concerned with conquest and territorial expansion. Those were male obsessions. Rather, these goddesses monitored the life cycle throughout its phases: birth, growth, love, death, and rebirth."[17] These ancient female divinities could have dominion over love and destructiveness simultaneously because they were associated with the experience of nature as a whole, of life and death as interdependent processes in the Great Round. Inanna, for example, "is not the feminine as night," Perera writes, "but rather she symbolizes consciousness of transition and borders, places of intersection and crossing over that imply creativity and change and all the joys and doubts that go with a human consciousness that is flexible, playful, never certain for long."[18] Death, decay, even active dismemberment of life forms were required so that life could be born anew.

Although the Goddess was not unrelated to the masculine, male gods were subordinate to her in ancient times. Because of her association with the inconstancy of the earth's cycles, she could not have a single, immortal partner; her consort was a mortal man-god, such as the year-king, who embodied the life-death polarity of the never-ending process of change.[19] Most often her lover was a "lunar consort," since both he and the moon forever disappeared, only to be resurrected. The Goddess's sacred consort is known to us through the Greek myth of Dionysus (Azazel in Sumer, Bacchus in Rome), the ever dying and ever reborn god who was always accompanied by women. "The Dionysian rites were first and foremost women's rites," Whitmont says.[20] As is well-known from Euripides's *The Bacchae*, these rituals were often ecstatic, drunken, mad revelries, expressing the paradoxes of joy and fear and the celebration and destruction of life. As an earthly deity, Dionysus was the god of both the vine and violence. The Dionysian cults existed in part as a sanctioned arena for the ritual expression of human desires, including violent aggression, which can be seen as a necessary aspect of the Goddess—the impulse to destroy form so it may be reconstituted, to kill the old so the new may arise. Obviously, this urge can result in undisciplined and needless brutality. But in honoring rather than condemning the impulse, the Dionysian rites served also to inhibit its expression in other, literally destructive ways. The rituals, thus, allowed the participation of each individual in the seasonal cycles of the earth and expressed the tendency to accept what is rather than to mandate what should be— that is, to receive the will of nature rather than to achieve a will of one's own.[21]

Since the American frontier myth developed long after the demise of the ancient Goddess as a prominent deity, Kolodny's confinement of the feminine to that which receives its identity in relation to men seems largely correct. Even so, however, there are cultural traces of the original undivided archetype in the frontier myth—particularly when the locus of the frontier was the sea and later as it moved out on the range. The Goddess's realm was the earth as a whole, not just the land. Since the archaic Goddess was associated with the moon, she was often linked to the sea (both the moon and the womb run the same fluctuating cycle of oceanic tides).[22] Goddess shrines were typically found near wells, springs, lakes, or seas.[23] So, too, the ocean as the vast expanse separating the old world from the new was generally imagined in precolonial literature as feminine—more like the original Great Goddess than the Nurturing Mother—wild, unpredictable, and free; seductive but unable to be possessed. In the "western," which began in the late nineteenth century, the hero left the alternately threatening and comforting forested enclosures of the East and South, and the cowboy replaced the hunter and the yeoman farmer.[24] In many screen westerns, the open land was depicted at first as infinite and awe inspiring to the hero, much as the ocean had been for the early explorers.[25] It even defeated him occasionally (as in, for example, *Jeremiah Johnson*). Both the sea and the land have, then, from time to time provided fitting challenges in the guise of the Great Goddess for the frontier hero.

The Divided Goddess

The classical myths and fairy tales that are better known today are probably revised from the earlier Goddess myths to reflect a later patriarchal bias that coincided with the heroic, war-torn Iron Age.[26] The new hero was the masculine ego, which set itself against nature and the feminine, creating the initial dualism upon which the rational mind is based. Whereas nature and the Goddess were inconstant and metamorphic, forcing humans to submit to a greater law, the heroic ego attempted its own immortality. As Whitmont puts it, "Ego strength is measured by the capacity to assert one's will over nature, forcing it to serve ego's striving for permanence, comfort, and avoidance of pain, and by the capacity to control one's urges, needs, and desires. Existence is perceived as limited to the world of space; hence it is irrevocably terminated by death and decay of the space-visible body."[27] The ego can now operate on the earth (and the body); indeed, its existence is predicated on this ability, and our language expresses the development.[28] Intellectually, we can "stand on a premise," "lay the groundwork," or "knock down the arguments." The hero's task is to divide himself from the earthly plane.

In order to ensure his continued existence, the ego-hero fought the Mother/ Goddess. Kolodny is correct insofar as the feminine principle includes a maternal aspect that wishes to retain its hold over the emerging ego; the Great Mother will not release the ego without a battle. But to the heroic impulse, this aspect ceases to be nurturing and comfortable and appears as devouring and smothering—the horrible dragon monster that must be slain so the hero may be free. Mythological examples of this archetypal contest include Perseus severing the Medusa's head, Apollo shooting the Python, and St. George conquering the dragon. The hero ultimately won, of course, and whereas his prize includes the achievement of rational thought, the price was the severing of the feminine into its upper-world, acceptable forms and its underworld, repulsive ones.

The maternal element, or Great Mother, was thus divided into the Good Mother, who was retained in consciousness, and the Bad Mother, who was relegated to the unconscious and for whom a hostile animal was substituted. As Erich Neumann explains, "The figure of the Great Mother splits into a negative half, represented by an animal, and a positive half having human form."[29] The Great Goddess, although a more encompassing figure than the Mother, was severed along with the Mother, and her fate was similar.[30] The original creatress deity was differentiated, broken up into different aspects. Inanna, for example, became two goddesses: Inanna was her upper-world, light aspect, and Ereshkigal, sometimes called her dark sister, was carried off into the kur (the netherworld, or desert wilderness).[31] Furthermore, in the patriarchal system, "'virgo' came to mean 'virgo intacta': a chaste or celibate woman. Intact means 'untouched by anything that harms or defiles, uninjured, unimpaired.' In order to be suitable and limited to continuing a patriarchal family lineage a 'good' woman had to be a 'good breeder' and limit the 'use' of her body to her lord whose property she was to be."[32]

The good virgin, then, represented in Christian cultures as the Virgin Mary, is an unspoiled but much diminished version of the original Goddess who was one-in-herself. The promiscuous virgin, because she refused a property relationship with any man, became a harlot—the whore as the shadow of the madonna—and was relegated to the underworld or the fringes of society. The feminine principle, once whole, looks like this in patriarchal cultures:

upperworld	=	pure virgin
conscious		Good Mother
underworld	=	harlot
unconscious		Devouring Mother

Furthermore, the Dionysian figure was exiled along with the Goddess, for he represented irrepressible urges and the destruction of matter; with the later development of the patriarchal hero into the ideal of the One God (Jehovah, for example), such uncontrolled frenetic transience had to be repressed. Jehovah was the "'I am that I am' (Exodus 3:14) who condemns graven images [the animal and Goddess icons of the previous eras], issues commandments, and sets up tribal laws of communal taboo. Eventually the laws expand into an ethic which claims universal validity. ... The newly discovered personal I may now obey or disobey divine commandments under the risk of penalty for disobedience. Evil is no longer an external misfortune, but a human act of disobedience."[33] Control of aggression and desire—reconsidered as evils to be conquered rather than essential parts of nature to be accepted—became a matter for law, ethics, and exercise of the individual will, not for ecstatic revelry. Dionysus, once the great goat-god, turned into the horned and hooved Satan, the scapegoat, who was banished (as the escape-goat) and later sacrificially burned (holocausted). The victimization of Dionysus, or of any suitable scapegoated substitute, allowed the aggressive urge to retain its outlet, but the urge was now regulated by law and limited to males in the service of the group.[34]

If the hero is understood archetypally as the patriarchal ego, which fought for its existence by conquering the Devouring Mother (in the process, also splitting the Goddess in two), it is possible to reinterpret what Kolodny sees as the central "inevitable paradox" facing the frontiersman—infantile containment in the land versus active penetration of it. Kolodny argues that "the success of settlement depended on the ability to master the land, transforming the territories into something else—a farm, a village, a road, a canal, a railway, a mine, a factory, a city, and finally, an urban nation."[35] But those who had responded eagerly to the invitations of a feminine landscape eventually found themselves either shrinking in guilt at their own depredations—that is, at their transformation of the land from Virgin to Mistress—or succumbing to a life of infantile regression by accepting the land as all-embracing Mother. As each new paradise became stained with blood, the settlers continued to move westward, always invoking maternal and sexual imagery simultaneously, with incestuous results.[36] The precarious balance between passive childishness and active penetration finally proved impossible for the frontiersman to maintain, and the ideal of paradise eventually gave way to the reality of mastery as the United States entered its adolescence in the nineteenth century, "leaving behind (except, perhaps, in the South) the configuration of the Mother and making of the landscape, instead, a field for exercising sexual mastery and assertive independence, its conquering hero captured in the legendary figure of John Henry, the steel-driving man."[37] The closing of the frontier signaled that there were no more landscapes to fulfill the pastoral impulse, and men's frustrations were expressed in anger at the land that eventually defeated its own promises. "What appears today as the single-minded destruction and pollution of the continent," writes Kolodny, "is just one of the ways we have continued to express that anger."[38]

But if to be heroic in an archetypal sense means to leave behind the Nurturing Mother (paradise) and to defeat the Devouring Mother (the threatening forests and their beasts), to move past both regression (the son) and incestuous desire (love of the Mother), then the true hero is angry at the Mother when she makes it difficult for him to go, not to stay. His concern is for his own ego independence, not for easy comforts, which would ruin his heroic status. He despoils and rapes the land, then, because of ego inflation, or hubris, the attempt to ensure his own immortality against the disintegrating impermanence of the earth. As the hero perfects his ego through various agencies (horses, guns, and force), he learns once again to conquer the infinite spaces, to stand over the land rather than allow himself to be dwarfed by it. As the finitude of the land becomes apparent (or, archetypally, as the Goddess and Mother are subdued), the scene ceases to dominate, and the hero stands out.[39] Property exerts its primary magnetism before it is used, and just as a conquering hero might discard the virgin he defiled for the excitement of a new and unspoiled one, the frontier hero tends to press on to virgin land as the old is "used up," participating in a continual dialectic between himself and the land as master. It is a contest, of course, that the hero finally won.

Also central to the heroic mastery of the feminine/land was the projection of the Dionysian element onto the Native Americans. Kolodny points out that the Indians were often inextricably linked to the landscape in the mythic imagination.[40] Slotkin notes their connection with Dionysus and with Moira (the maternal world of the unconscious and need gratification), who in all archetypal myths is in tension with Themis (the paternal world of conscious rationality and responsibility).

> Although Moira ceases to dominate the gods, she or her avatars retain a subordinate position under Zeus and periodically assert their primordial power against paternal authority. Bacchus or Zagreus—or the drunken "Indian Joes" of American literature—are their children, embodiments of the childish and primitive impulses of the unconscious: hunger for food, power, pleasure, dissolution of the self in passionate love, and cruelty. These qualities make the children of Moira a perpetual source of disorder, inciters of female or youthful violence against paternal agents of order like the king of Thebes and the artist Orpheus.[41]

Although the frontier myth retained a fascination with these "red devils," at times linking them with the infinite Goddess of the untamed landscape and at other times with the pure virgin (as in the "noble savage" motif), they were foils for the heroic mentality, as was the feminine/land. Ultimately, their libidinous and creative-destructive qualities were emphasized more than their pure ones—that is, they were linked to the underworld evil qualities of the feminine—and had to be purged, as all scapegoats for the patriarchal impulse toward violence must be.

Search for the Lost Goddess

Psychological energy, like physical energy, may be displaced but not destroyed, and there is considerable evidence in mythology that the human psyche (and community) yearns for the return of that which has been exiled. This desire for wholeness is present both in masculine myths, in which the male hero searches for the feminine he himself has expelled, and in feminine myths, in which the Goddess strives to reunite herself with her lost half.

The male version of the search is typically expressed as a quest. Paul Zweig observes that in the archetypal adventure story, "At the darkest end of his [the adventurer's] episodic travels, the mysteries which he encounters, which are the source of the stories he brings back to tell, are more often than not profoundly feminine."[42] The medieval Arthurian grail myth, probably the best and most elaborate example of the quest, may be seen as the journey of the knight away from his kingdom, which has degenerated into a wasteland. The earth is withholding its fruitfulness and the king is mortally wounded because the social order is patterned by authority rather than by the natural flow of life. The knight enters a grim and joyless yonder where the insulted feminine is hidden away. He renews himself by risking combat with her terrible horned companion (the Dionysian character), and through reverence for and acceptance of the Goddess in both her repellant and beautiful guises, he receives her boon and drinks the waters of the feminine from the grail, which has been in her keeping. He neither defeats nor owns the Goddess; he marries her. This kind of search (but not conquest and possession) is an expression of the urge to understand the complementary equality of the masculine and feminine principles.[43]

The female version of the search is not as familiar as the quest theme, for patriarchal cultures prefer the heroic, and the feminine motif does not fit the conventional requirements. The Goddess's task is one of reunification of the upper and lower parts of herself; thus, it typically involves her initiatory descent. Examples include the Japanese Izanami, the Greek Demeter and Kore-Persephone, the Roman Psyche, the Sumerian Inanna and Ereshkigal, and the fairy-tale maidens who go to Mother Hulda or Baba Yaga or the gingerbread house witch.[44] By the time of most written tales, the Goddess had already been divided and sent underground. "Thus there was a necessity," Perera explains, "to traverse both regions to restore a sense of creative wholeness and to comprehend the rhythmic interplay of life."[45]

The upper-world Goddess descends into the underworld, or into a tunnel, belly, womb, or mountain, or through a mirror.[46] There she meets her dark counterpart, who symbolizes raw instinctuality—need and aggression split off from consciousness—and suffers what typically feels like total dismemberment or disintegration. When Inanna goes down into the underworld, for example, Ereshkigal is furious at the invasion and sends her gatekeeper, a male, to defend her. Ereshkigal then kills Inanna and turns her into a piece of rotting meat hung from a peg. The dark Goddess symbolizes not only active destruction but also the kind of metamorphosis wrought only through the slow and deliberate organic process of decay and gestation, which may even work on the initiate invasively and against her will. This unconscious part of the Goddess pitilessly devours her lighter counterpart but also incubates her and eventually gives birth to her as a transformed being. Contrary to the way she is often understood, Perera explains, the dark Goddess is not automatically antagonistic to the masculine.

> The forces and modalities of the Great Round do not wish to rule, or even to resist, hierarchical, progress-oriented, Logos modes. They do require reverence and respect, however. Ereshkigal rages when she is not met with respect. She is proud, but she does not mount an offensive, nor does she transgress her own boundaries. ... Rather, it is the defensive fear inherent in hierarchical, heroic consciousness that turns from the flow of change and its own split-off "infantile" impulses. Projecting these onto the

mother, it sees her as enemy and refuses to recognize her own kind of wisdom, which is necessary to life as its own.[47]

When the upper-world Goddess actively and consciously accepts her underworld half (or when the feminine part of the masculine psyche does the same), she is transformed and made whole.

If the patriarchalized feminine (and masculine) remains unconscious to the lost Goddess, however, or descends and greets her with disrespect or with a conquering attitude, the Goddess rages as the Furies, the maternal aspect whose motive is revenge for the rejection of the feminine image.[48] The Furies emerge from the caves to which they have been relegated to punish crimes of matricide (such as in the Oresteian trilogy)—the ultimate sin against the feminine.[49] As long as the Goddess is split, half of her repressed into the unconscious and the other half oppressed in a false consciousness defined by the patriarchy, the feminine will tend to force her entry into consciousness demonically "through disguised, painful, symptomatic, pathological and morbid forms."[50] "Gods banished from the high altar have a tendency to creep in through seamy back streets."[51] As we shall see, this fact has not been lost on Hollywood.

Although neither the archetypal quest nor the descent themes have thus far been prominent in the land-based frontier myth, there are reasons to expect that the tyranny of patriarchy will begin to unravel in the new scene of space and that the quest and descent myths will consequently reappear. Unlike land, for example, space has no literal characteristics; because it cannot be sensed or acted upon, it is not amenable to the projection of gender. Thus, we do not speak of "virgin space," of "the motherspace," or of "raping space." Furthermore, unlike the land, space is not a frontier that at first seems infinite and unknown but eventually becomes finite and familiar. As actually infinite, it cannot ultimately be dominated.[52]

But perhaps the most significant potential of space as the New Frontier is to perspectivize the planet we call home. From the vantage point of outer space, the earth does not look flat to the human eye—it does not stretch out in front of the astronauts (or of us lesser beings who must view the earth in their photographs) as a horizontal landscape. The geographic line has historically beckoned men to spread out, to seek dominion over, to conquer—or, in Kolodny's implied sexual pun, to lay. By contrast, the globe is associated archetypally with the transcendental, the infinite, the eternal; it is a symbol of the whole—both of the individual self and of the cosmos and of their ultimate interdependence.[53] The sphere symbolically invites a reimagining of earth as an undivided totality that is a part of the greater whole of the universe. Thus, the "Whole Earth" has become a symbol of the ecology movement, as in, for example, *The Whole Earth Catalogue*. We have not ceased to speak of the earth as feminine, but many of the ecologically minded now demonstrate their reorientation by referring to the planet as "Gaia," the Greek word for the Oldest of Divinities—the ancient Mother Earth before her shrines were co-opted by the patriarchal Olympian gods under Zeus.[54]

If it is the case that the spatial scene of the New Frontier tends to reperspectivize the feminine as whole, it is reasonable to expect that both quest and descent themes would begin to emerge in mythic New Frontier texts. We might also expect that such advances would occur in fits and starts, for patriarchal repression has sedimented over centuries and is not easy to dislodge. I next offer an analysis of *Alien* and *Aliens*. When considered together, these films constitute one fledgling form in which the archetypal descent myth has entered into a rhetorical text in the new frontier.

The Feminine in the New Frontier: *Alien* and *Aliens*

Critics have responded diversely to feminist implications in both *Alien* and *Aliens*. To some, the *Alien/s* story, with its strong central female character (Sigourney Weaver as Ripley), seems to project an impressive demonstration of feminine energy. Rebecca Bell-Metereau finds Ripley in *Alien* to be the ideal androgynous heroine: "Ripley's ultimate survival is a subtle hurrah for the human race, and for womankind at that."[55] *Aliens'* producer, Gale Anne Hurd, regards the movie as a feminist document and enthuses over its reception: "I really appreciate the way audiences respond. They buy it. We don't get people, even rednecks, leaving the theatre saying, 'That was stupid. No woman would do that.' You don't have to be a liberal or ERA supporter to root for Ripley."[56] *Ms.* magazine's Ari Korpivaara proclaims that *Aliens'* "Ripley, nurturer and adventurer, is a role model for all of us humans."[57] And David Edelstein of *Rolling Stone* praises *Aliens* for celebrating motherhood.[58]

Others find one or both films to be offensive to women. Ruth Prigozy refutes Hurd's feminist claim, pronouncing *Aliens* "nothing less than a disaster" for its depiction of women.[59] Edelstein's generally favorable review belies an uncomfortable ambiguity as he notes that neither film is exactly a "woman's movie" and that director James Cameron may be mocking the gung-ho marine aesthetic in *Aliens*, "but he's also embracing its essence; this is the chomp-down-on-your-cigar-and-shoot school of filmmaking."[60] And Barbara Creed applies Julia Kristeva's theory of horror as abjection to demonstrate how *Alien* equates archaic mother symbolism with the horrific, thus reaffirming patriarchy's fear of, and disgust with, the feminine.[61]

If the two films are placed within a combined archetypal and cultural framework, we can see that both views have merit but are incomplete. If the symbols of the repressed feminine are interpreted within the archetypal context of descent and the cultural context of the frontier, it becomes evident that the surface feminist appearance of the film is not the whole story. My claim is that the dominant text of *Alien/s* subverts patriarchal consciousness (as represented by the military, the bureaucracy, and frontier exploitation), introduces the feminine descent and revenge motif into the New Frontier, and provides an appealing heroine; thus, it appears to reaffirm the feminine principle. A close examination of the subtext, however, discloses that the story mixes the feminine descent and revenge motifs with the more familiar ego-hero myth. In fact, the schism in the Goddess is not healed, for the patriarchy has induced the feminine to fight itself; thus, the undercurrents reveal that the feminine is actually subverted. This is, then, a "hybrid" New Frontier story: The scene is space, and the feminine is much more prominent than in the Old Frontier, but traditional patriarchal values are ultimately reaffirmed.[62]

Symbols of the Repressed Feminine

From the title, we enter the theater expecting the tone of *Alien* to be ominous. Even so, there is something bizarre and ill fitting about the opening scene, for we feel we have been here before—but not like this. A spaceship journeys home. But are not scenes of space travel supposed to be high tech, lyrical, awe inspiring, light filled, uplifting, and expansive? This noisy craft rumbles along like the outmoded ore barge that it is, heavy and creaky, sooty and dark—it seems to be going more in than out, more down than up. The crew members can hardly be called astronauts; they are in deep sleep while a computer named Mother controls the voyage. No Strauss waltzes or John Williams in the background; the sound track is more like a funeral dirge, and this general sense of foreboding proceeds to materialize into "a genuinely invasive work—a cold, brilliant act of cinematic rape."[63] Indeed, the film moves from outer space to claustrophobic craft, from latent gloom to nascent in-the-body demon.

Filmgoers get no relief from *Aliens*, which begins in similar ominous tones. But the significance of this dark theme, a sort of flip side to the light-motif of the usual space exploration story, does start to slowly dawn, even if day does not. In a synecdoche for both films, *Aliens'* first scene follows company explorers laser cutting a crude opening so they may enter the womblike sleep chamber of the last movie's heroine. Ripley (Ripley van Winkle?) has had a long nap—fifty-seven years, to be exact—and it is pure luck that she is found. Ripley's unconscious mind has been invaded against her will; it seems that back in a recovery hospital on earth, her dreams are infested with the stomach-wrenching reptile that claimed her unfortunate crewmate in the original.

NURSE: Bad dreams again? Want something to help you sleep?
RIPLEY: No! I've slept enough.

Although Ripley appears to be waking to her sleep's urgent messages, everyone else is "asleep" while awake. Her horror stories of almost six decades ago are ignored, as she is chastised for destroying the multimillion-dollar spacecraft and is stripped of her flight officer's license. She is horrified to learn that the bureaucracy has set up a colony on the planet she remembers too well. At first, however, she wants nothing to do with her company's next mission—to send marines to inves-

tigate the colony with which they have lost contact (investments must be pro-
tected) and to conquer the "monster" no one but she is taking seriously. "You
don't need me, I'm not a soldier," she says, battling her own demons. But the facts
of her situation change her mind. She is an outsider in a time-world she does not
know; she has been demoted from a flight captain to a cargo loader; a company
representative, Burke, assures her that this time they will destroy the monster and
not bring it back as a weapon of war; and her dreams continue to be nightmares.
Reluctantly, she acquiesces, knowing what they all must face.

Once again the entrepreneurs strike out for a distant land, this time with marines as a modern cavalry. Once again, as the spaceship lurches upward, our
moods sink downward. The crew members wake up from their deep sleep, crabby
and scuzzy. Although the marines are outwardly derisive about the chances of
meeting "Ripley's monster," they do appear vaguely aware that they are sinking
into danger. As an advance guard takes a shuttle craft from the mother ship to the
colony, one of the marines says gloomily, "I've got a bad feeling about this drop."
Looking around at the drizzling, atmospherically processed rain and the absence
of light in what is supposed to be day, another says, "We're on an express elevator
to Hell. Going down!" This is more to the point, for these ill-prepared rovers,
upon waking from their travel sleep, are entering a world very much like an archetypal dream or myth of descent.

What is this mythic hell into which the space probers descend? Partly because
the new frontier contains no more objectively verifiable occupant-enemies to
serve as scapegoats, and partly because the exploration of outer space tends to coincide with the exploration of inner space, the voyagers in both films look in as
well as out.[64] What they find is the darkness of their unconscious psyches, where
the contents are their own repressions. As three crew members in the first film
leave their spaceship to investigate a crashed craft, a full moon appears over the
area and slowly changes into a thin, silver crescent, as if to warn them that this is
the abode of the Goddess and her mutating lunar consorts. Barbara Creed notes
that the crew members "enter the body of the unknown space-ship through a
'vaginal' opening: The ship is shaped like a horseshoe, its curved sides like two
long legs spread apart at the entrance."[65] Although the Mother herself does not
appear in the entire film, her presence is amply in evidence in many scenes, such
as the images of birth, the gestating eggs, and the womb-like, winding tunnels
leading to her chambers.[66]

Although Creed does not link feminine imagery to the land, her concept of the
feminine in *Alien* is similar to Kolodny's concept of the feminine in the frontier.
That is, both see the feminine in their texts as represented in relation to masculine
desires and fears. Unlike Kolodny, however, Creed incorporates a more evolutionary view on the archetypal level, recognizing an "archaic mother" from ancient
mythology, who, like the Great Goddess, "does not depend for her definition on a
concept of the masculine," and who is the subject, not the object, of narrativity.
This archaic mother is symbolized by the womb, which is its own point of refer-

ence, and not by the female genitals, which can be constructed as the "lack" of the penis.[67] By contrast, the pre-Oedipal mother, as conceptualized by Freud, Lacan, and Kristeva, is "a figure always in relation to the father, the representative of the phallus." The father relies on her "lack" of a penis to define himself: "Without her 'lack,' he cannot signify its opposite—lack of a lack or presence."[68] The pre-Oedipal mother (the underworld Devouring Mother) must be repudiated by the son (the hero) so he can assume his appropriate place in the patriarchy. Creed argues that the archaic mother is much more threatening to the male symbolic order than is the pre-Oedipal mother, for she could swallow him back up and return him to his predifferentiated, maternal source. Thus, many horror films, including *Alien,* depict the archaic mother as a negative force, or the "abject," that which must be rejected and escaped from in order to reaffirm the centrality of the patriarchy. Creed claims that "what is common to all of these images of horror is the voracious maw, the mysterious black hole which signifies female genitalia as a monstrous sign which threatens to give birth to equally horrific offspring as well as threatening to incorporate everything in its path. This is the generative archaic mother, constructed within patriarchal ideology as the primeval 'black hole.'"[69] When the archaic mother is imaged as monstrous, the separate ontological status of the mother is denied, and she is objectified as a projection of male desire and fear.

Whereas it is true that *Alien* (and *Aliens*) presents "the miracle of birth" as the disgust of filth, wallowing more than it needs to in the abjectness of the maternal functions, this monster cannot be adequately understood only as a projection of patriarchal fear of the archaic mother. For if the monster is viewed merely as a projection, the relevance of both the scenic context and a dominant theme in both films becomes problematic. *Alien* and *Aliens* are not just horror movies; they occur in space, and the motive for the adventure in each is frontier exploitation. It is significant, for example, that *Aliens'* space colonists are called "terra-formers"— literally, "those who shape the earth," for this land is not the earth but is still treated as if it is. Bell-Metereau recognizes that the name of the explorer ship in *Alien* (*Nostromo*) finds its literary origins in Joseph Conrad's novels, in which greed, commercial exploitation, the baseness of bureaucratic motives, and the essential aloneness of the individual are underlying themes. *Alien* "doesn't deal with man's glorious quest for self-knowledge or understanding of the unknown. It treats the Company's grimy search for profit at any cost."[70] They work for a company that extracts mineral ore from distant planets; thus, the terra-formers carry on the long tradition of forcing nature to yield up her gifts, disclose her mysteries, and service her conquerors before they move on to virgin soil. The investigators in *Alien* and the colonists and marines who come to save them in *Aliens* extend the work of the ego-hero to inappropriate regions. They still divide and conquer, treating the indigenous inhabitants as satanic scapegoats to be purged rather than as parts of themselves to be accepted. The Goddess of the dark world they invade may be horrible in part because she represents male fears of reabsorption, but she is also angry at the ravaging of her domain and at the conquerors' lack of respect. She does not transgress her own territory, but she wants revenge, and that is why she is showing her nasty side—her incarnation as the Furies.

Like Ereshkigal in the myth of Inanna's descent, the raging Goddess (only implicitly present in *Alien*) first sends her male counterpart to defend her. As *Alien*'s crew member, Kane, pokes into a gestating egg, an octopus-like demon bursts forth and implants a tentacle in Kane's mouth in a repulsive scene of oral-phallic impregnation. Against Ripley's orders, the science officer, Ash, opens the doors of the spacecraft to let Kane and the other crew members in. Having done his reproductive duty, the spidery fellow falls off Kane's face and "dies," only to be reborn (just as the crew is celebrating Kane's recovery) by exploding through the stomach wall of his unwilling benefactor. The new screeching, phallic monster is unspeakably more horrible than the first; it grows at an alarming rate and proceeds to haunt the ship, eventually killing all the crew members, one by one, except for Ripley and her cat.

Creed sees this scene as another part of the ideological project of *Alien*—the archaic mother, represented by the egg/womb, is collapsed into the more familiar figure of the pre-Oedipal mother, symbolized by the phallic monster who explodes from the egg. In her view, the monster is the patriarchal notion of female fetish objects as "what women want"; that is, women's desire for a phallus to substitute for their supposed castration is represented as horrific—something to be repudiated. The chameleon nature of the alien makes sense if interpreted as a form of double, or multiplication, of the phallus, "pointing to the mother's desire to stave off her castration." It is also coded as a "toothed vagina," says Creed, "the monstrous-feminine as the cannibalistic mother."[71]

But whereas *Alien*'s monster, as well as his counterparts in *Aliens,* is obviously phallic, interpreting him as a patriarchal projection and repudiation of what women desire cannot explain several of the facts of his existence. He is both the "son" of the mother (he emerges from her egg) and her "consort" (he presumably mates with her later so that other eggs can be laid). He "dies" after fertilizing his victim, only to be "reborn" in a scene that leaves no doubt as to his victory over death. And he serves the submerged Mother as her protective gatekeeper. He is, indeed, related to the feminine but not as a male projection of a female fantasy. Rather, he is an odious, bloodthirsty Dionysus—the ever dying, ever reborn god who went underground with the Goddess and who also erupts with rage when repressed for too long.

Whereas her existence is only implied in *Alien,* the Mother makes her entrance in *Aliens.* The marines discover that the colonized planet is still infested, not only with one monster but with many and also with the eggs from which they are hatched. The Mother Monster is located by crawling through numerous dark and oozing womb-like passages; she lives, as we note when Ripley takes the elevator down to rescue Newt, the seven-year-old sole survivor of the colony, on Sublevel 2. The animalized Mother, as well as the Furies, are associated in myth with dark, underground swampy districts because these are symbolic of the repressed unconscious.[72] This ogre is more than just Creed's "archaic mother"—she is Virgin, Mistress, and Mother simultaneously. She is not a virgin in the patriarchal sense but in the sense that she is unrelated to and independent of any one male figure. Her consorts are drones, aiding her in her reproductive process and protecting her and her eggs from attack. Shaped like a hulking pelvis with fangs, she is also a frightening open womb, the Devouring Mother at her horrendous best. She traps her intruders in a spidery web (the spider is a Mother symbol, for she ensnares the unwary male). Finally, like Ereshkigal and the Furies, she is "an enchantress who confuses the senses and drives men out of their minds. ... Madness is a dismemberment of the individual, just as the dismemberment of the body in fertility magic symbolizes dissolution of the personality."[73] Indeed, the marines are confused and disoriented when they try to track her down; many of their battle scenes with her brood are violently disorienting to the audience as well. One soldier's (Hudson) personality disintegrates into that of a whining prepubescent. And in the end, all the marines except one are massacred.

Although this monster shares many characteristics with her earlier prototypes, she has developed a few perverse contemporary twists, indicating that the long-repressed feminine has evolved into the modern age. For although she lives in a wet and sunless underworld, it is no longer that of the "earth." Rather, she has made the factory her lair. She has forced her way into the instruments of industrial exploitation; she has slimed the sacred places of the patriarchal era. What is more, she and her descendants have metal-eating acid for blood—which means they are more potent in death than humans are in life. And in a vengeful inversion of the Golden Rule, she turns the one talent for which she has been valued by the frontiersman into a weapon against him. She heartlessly uses each trapped colonist and explorer as a breeding ground that, once it has served its function (rendered up its "virginity"), is abandoned for unspoiled turf. The whole Caesarean-from-within motif, perhaps the scenes that have most made *Alien/s* famous, seems a macabre parody on the exploitative, rape-and-ruin habits of the old West. The motif is also an angry perversion of the gestation function of the dark Goddess; since she is Fury-ous with revenge, she incubates her intruders for the birth of her own kind and not for the explorers' ultimate resurrection.

On one level, then, *Alien/s* appears to be a rhetorical warning: If the modern conquering hero is too infused with hubris to recognize the Goddess's regency, she will burglarize his temples and defoul his shrines, eating away their core until they collapse with decay. More pointedly, if the contemporary ego persists in raping space the way it has the earth, she will, with the aid of her Bacchanalian counterparts, destroy it from within. Ken Wilber puts it well: "The mythology of sex and murder, which began in the mythic-membership period, is now retained, intensified, and compounded due to its repression—it explodes with a compulsive vengeance in (dissociated) egoic times. The obsession with sex and violence is still with us to this day because the dissociated ego is still with us."[74]

But warnings against exploitation are generally ignored and trivialized by those who come to conquer. According to Neumann, Western man emphasizes the conscious ego in order to denigrate and defame the unconscious forces of which he is afraid: "This form of apotropaic defense-magic invariably attempts to explain away and exorcise anything dangerous with a glib 'nothing but' or 'it's not half so bad as you think.'"[75] The company workers in *Alien*, for example, are much more concerned about their paychecks than they are about the dangers they could encounter. And although the marines in *Aliens* may harbor a diffuse sense of foreboding when they see the deserted colony, director James Cameron has them treat their operation at the outset more like comic-book camp than mission impossible. The cigar-chomping sergeant greets his "few good men" (who also include a few good women) with mock toughness as they wake from deep sleep: "Another glorious day in the Corps. A day in the Marine Corps is like a day on the farm. Every meal is a banquet, every paycheck a fortune, every formation a parade. I love the Corps!" As they get dressed, they compare muscles and machismo and exchange lewd put-downs and comebacks. At breakfast they joke about the "poontang" they'll probably score at this outpost. When one marine asks what their mission is (apparently, he had not bothered to find out before), another answers, "There's some juicy colonists' daughters we're supposed to rescue from their virginity." When they are preparing for landing, Sergeant Apone, classically tough but completely out of touch with the potential of the subrational monster to upset orderly strategy, barks out, "Now I want this to go smooth and by the numbers!" When Apone asks if there are any questions, one marine says, "Yeah, how do I get out of this chicken shit outfit?" As the investigative unit flies to the space outpost and the gloom-monger shares his bad feeling, another recruit brushes him off with "you always say that, you always say, 'I've got a bad feeling about this drop.'" Sergeant Hicks does not even bother to stay awake. Upon completing the drop, Apone orders, "All right, I want a nice, clean dispersal this time," as military drumbeats roll in the background.

Even after disastrous contact with the monster's "family," the military-industrial representatives do not seem to comprehend fully the power and significance of the aliens. In response to Ripley's suggestion (after the first go-round with the horde) that they take off in the ship and nuke the site from space, Burke reminds them that "there's a substantial dollar value attached to this!" Hudson, more in touch with the realities than Burke, whimpers, "Maybe you haven't been keeping up on current events, man, but we just got our asses kicked!" Yet even he refuses to recognize that the monster is kin. As the handful of survivors plot their strategy inside the factory, the lights go out.

RIPLEY: They cut the power.

HUDSON: How could they cut the power, man, they're animals!

Burke is woefully wrong, not to mention evil, to think he could bring the monster (or at least one of her consorts) back to ego-land without dire consequences.

Through much of *Aliens* the men are not conscious of what the title subtly insists: The enemy has multiplied.

The Illusion of Victory

Only the women seem fully alive to the monsters' import; they are more aware than the men because the monster is their "other half." (This does not hold for the female marines in *Aliens,* who have become so totally masculinized that their sergeant does not bother to make a gender distinction, which seems all right with them.) In *Alien,* company employee Parker worries aloud one too many times whether he will get a bonus for the additional tasks the crew is ordered to undertake. Ripley retorts condescendingly, "I'm sure you'll get what's coming to you." In marked contrast to the men, the other female crew member seems aware at the outset of the investigation of the significance of their adversary. In *Aliens,* Ripley and the young girl, Newt, are the ones whose sleep is bothered by the dragon, and their "possession" makes them more awake to her presence. In one of the all-time understated acknowledgments of the fact of fantasy, Ripley tries to put Newt to bed on a factory bunk. She attempts to calm Newt's fear of nightmares by looking inside her doll's head and declaring it to be free of ogres. "Ripley," replies Newt positivistically, "Casey doesn't have nightmares because she's just a piece of plastic." Newt completes her reality check with Ripley:

NEWT: My mommy said there aren't any monsters, but there are.
RIPLEY: Yes, there are, aren't there?

Perhaps because of their heightened awareness of the monster's significance, both Ripley and Newt are more resourceful than the others in planning a way out of her labyrinth. In descent myths, it is common for the initiate to make some plan for escape ahead of time. Inanna, for example, instructed her handmaid, Ninshubur, to come after her if she did not reappear from her journey into the underworld after three days. "Psychologically," Perera explains, "she [Ninshubur] seems to embody that small part of us that stays above ground while the soul descends, the still conscious and functioning aspect of the psyche which can witness the events below and above and feel concern for the fate of the soul."[76] When Ripley goes back to rescue Newt from the aliens' lair, she drops flares in her path so she can retrace her steps. Like Ninshubur, Ariadne, Hansel and Gretel, and Danny Torrance of *The Shining,* Ripley rightly intuits that she might not emerge from the traps of the unconscious without a measured, rational plan for escape.

Aliens' story not only aptly depicts the circumstances of the submerged and demonic Great Goddess but reveals the maternal side of Ripley as well. Her mothering instincts were latent in *Alien,* although they almost got her killed as she searched for her lost cat. When Ripley discovers Newt, however, she begins to transform from the accidental heroine of the first film into the Good Mother in the second. When the marines get no response to their interrogations of the shell-shocked little girl, Ripley substitutes nourishment (hot chocolate) for questions. It is then that Rebecca (her real name) tells Ripley she goes by "Newt." From that moment on, they adopt each other. We sense the quiet power of their feminine bond (and perhaps also the bond they share with their foe) as Ripley holds Newt in her arms while they watch the space shuttle that was supposed to take them away from further carnage crash in flames. A full moon shines behind them, casting a silvery-blue glow over the desolate landscape. Ripley soon makes a promise, cross her beleaguered heart and hope to die, never to abandon Newt. Ripley's promise is put to the test, of course; her determination to rescue Newt from the clutches of the monster recalls Demeter's rage at Hades for the theft of Persephone. Unlike Demeter and more like Osiris, she actually returns to the underworld and defies its deities in order to bring her adopted daughter back to the land of the living. This cinematic episode becomes, then, a celebration of the mother-daughter bond, which, unlike any other parent-child relationship, has been almost entirely neglected in Western mythology except in the Demeter story.[77] The juxtaposition of Ripley with the monster also accurately portrays the Good Mother–Devouring Mother division of the Goddess in patriarchal cultures today.

Ripley is more than a nurturing mother, however, and Newt is more than a loyal daughter. Both have assimilated several classic heroic traits—they are smart, competent, moral, and courageous. A newt is a semiaquatic salamander, and the little girl has, in fact, become quite facile at slithering through dripping subterranean tunnels. In mythology, a salamander is a symbol for that which is unscathed by fire; it is the promise of new life after fiery destruction. Not only has Newt survived alone in her hell for many weeks, but she is more stoic in battle than many of the marines. In *Alien,* Ripley is the one who tries to prevent the crew from bringing the contaminated Kane into the ship; she finally deciphers correctly the signal from the planet they visit as a warning, not an sos; she interprets the computer data that inform her of the company's hostile intentions toward the crew; she rightly mistrusts the robot, Ash, and confronts him at risk of her own life; she is the only one with enough strength and wit to survive the monster. In *Aliens,* she surprises the marines by operating heavy industrial equipment onboard the ship; she figures out that the ammunition will set off the nuclear reactor inside the atmospheric processing factory and advises the lieutenant to order the marines not to fire; she drives a modern tank to aid the trapped investigative unit when the lieutenant in charge clutches; she reads a blueprint of the factory to plan strategies for sealing off air vents; she surmises in a second the chain of command when the lieutenant is wounded and the sergeant killed; she values life more than property and suggests bombing the planet as they take off in space "to make sure."

In the message that "women can play, too" and that they can exhibit heroic qualities without sacrificing their nurturing ones and especially in the fact that Ripley survives, this gutsy story, with a brave and attractive female heroine and strong supporting female characters, certainly affirms women's equality with men on some levels.[78] If, as Carol Pearson argues, women need to expand beyond the martyr archetype, in which they are often stuck, and learn the warrior role—at least the part of it that demands self-assertion and confrontation in order to protect their values and their people—then Ripley does indeed provide a welcome role model.[79]

The Reality of Defeat

On its face, the *Alien/s* story appears to grow increasingly antipatriarchal from the first film to the second. The bureaucracy, for instance, is more odious in *Aliens* than in *Alien*. In *Alien* it is represented by the products of technology—the robot and the computer—which attempt to carry out the directives of the unseen company. No human bureaucrats are on board. In *Aliens* the authorities are pictured in a classic smoky boardroom after Ripley's return, woodenly refusing to accept the heroine's supernatural encounter ("normal" citizens never believe such stories) and worrying more about their financial than their human losses. This time the company agent, Burke, sets up the next mission knowing the dangers and is revealed, after the aliens have scored a few impressive victories, to be as carnivorous in his own right as the monsters themselves. (He wants to bring one home by letting it "impregnate" either Ripley or Newt and sell it to the military for biological warfare.) "You don't see them [the aliens] fucking each other over for a god-damned percentage," Ripley snarls at Burke after she survives his murderous plan. Moreover, the military (the warrior aspect of the patriarchy) makes its entrance only in *Aliens* and is made to look disorganized and impotent.

As the feminine foil to patriarchy, Ripley is suspicious all along of the ego-inflated bureaucratic-military mode. When a knife accidentally pricks Bishop's skin and his milky blood reveals him to be a "synthetic person," Ripley is furious and distrustful—recalling, no doubt, the villainous Ash from her previous voyage. As the narrative unravels, however, we see that she is wrong about Bishop; indeed, he becomes her bravest and most loyal ally, volunteering for danger in order to summon a rescue ship and saving Newt from oblivion. In her initial wariness of the technocracy's impressive achievement, Ripley is fooled, and so are we. When she comes to rely on it for her very life, our own heedfulness of its treachery is likely to have receded.

When the going gets tough, the tough get masculine. Ripley is fully initiated into the male-military-technological way by Corporal Hicks (with whom there is a small spark of attraction, consummated more in the energy of battle than the union of flesh). Saying "I wanna introduce you to a personal friend of mine," he teaches her to use an M41A pulse rifle, and when he balks at instructing her on the grenade-launching attachment, she urges him on by reminding him, "You started this." With her penchant for cosmic double entendres, Ripley again calls the situation correctly, for Hicks represents what did start this sort of frontierism. But from now on, Ripley is a convert. In her harrowing battle with the mother monster, she operates a "loader"—a gargantuan hunk of steel armor used for moving industrial supplies—to fight the "bitch" in a colossal clash of metal with extraterrestrial flesh and bones. She is in this moment of glory an embodiment of the military-industrial complex; she is inside this gestalt and has become a "fighting machine."

By this time, the audience has been gradually prepared for Ripley's role as hero, so that when she does arm herself to fight like a man, it seems almost natural. The narrative follows the archetypal structure of any ego-hero story; its surface details, because this is an American film, synthesize the western and the war-action genres (which, as stars such as John Wayne and Clint Eastwood have illustrated, are easily fused). Like the classic westerner, for example, Ripley is in but not of the community.[80] Since at the beginning of *Aliens* she is returned to a time with which she is not familiar, she is an outsider on earth, and she is not indigenous to the space colony she comes to save. From the little we see of it, she practices an ascetic lifestyle; she does not seek adventure but reluctantly accepts her task only when it is clear that her services are needed. (Burke also appeals condescendingly to her pride by telling her she must not be defeated by a little setback—she's got to "get back on the horse" and give it another shot.) Once she accepts her task, she is fully devoted and unflinchingly forthright. When she is inevitably isolated from all human help in the showdown with the villain, she is a "single combat warrior"; like David against Goliath (or Gary Cooper against the outlaws), she is the bravest young warrior the community has to offer, sent out to fight the best the enemy can supply.[81] In the final scenes of *Aliens*, when Ripley takes up a machine gun and blasts her way into the mother monster's nest to rescue her captive, she would make Rambo proud. (Sigourney Weaver has referred to her role in *Aliens* as "Rambolina.")

In her victorious fight with the mother monster, Ripley delivers a stunning defeat to the reemergence of the feminine principle. The publicity poster for *Aliens* bears the caption "There Are Some Places in the Universe You Don't Go Alone." If Ripley were a mythic Great Goddess rather than a conquering mother/hero, this phrase would have omitted the Alone, for the Goddess does not sanction exploitative entrepreneurship in an occupied land.[82] Rather than assist her co-combatants in accepting the Bad Mother as a part of us all—as the mythic counterpart to herself in dire need of reintegration—she perpetuates the division. Martha Solomon's cogent analysis of Phyllis Schlaffly's success in pitting the archetypal Good Mother (the STOP ERA supporter) against the Bad Mother (the women's liberationist) indicates that women sometimes participate willingly—even strenuously—in preserving this cleft in present-day feminine consciousness.[83] By allowing herself to be co-opted, *Alien/s'* heroine helps male consciousness to fight off its fear of absorption in the Devouring Mother of the unconscious. For her male companions, then, this is "Let's You and Her Fight."[84] Masculine consciousness has gained an ally.

Although by the end of the second film the monster has literally ripped technology asunder (in the form of poor Bishop), the audience is given the illusion that the heroine is now in control. Ripley casts her nemesis into the black void, pieces Bishop together again as best she can, and frees our dreams of the horrid thing.

> NEWT: Are we going to sleep all the way home?
> RIPLEY: Yes.
> NEWT: Can I dream?
> RIPLEY: Yes, honey, I think we both can.
> NEWT: Affirmative.

The young girl, too, is now a budding military recruit, and the audience can go home "knowing" its sleep will be serene.

Conclusion

In this chapter I have traced the evolution of the feminine in both its archetypal and American rhetorical forms and have argued that the land-based frontier myth represents a middle stage in which a once-whole feminine was split by the development of the patriarchy. An analysis of *Alien* and *Aliens* demonstrates that the frontier is again evolving but only into a hybrid of the old and new myths, in which the lost feminine is encountered, is found to be vengeful at the exploitation of her domain, and is then killed by a patriarchalized heroine.

It is possible that *Alien/s* is a portent of things to come—in the New Frontier or even in the old—for, as Thomas Farrell observes, rhetorical propositions are always open to reappraisal.[85] Insofar as the land-based frontier myth remains rhetorical, it is open to revision based on the new perspectives acquired in the scene of space. If this hybrid of the egoic hero and the descent to the Goddess is influential either in revising the telling of the old myth or in developing the direction of the new, this will not bode well for the acceptance of the feminine principle into the consciousness of the culture. Searching for the lost Goddess is a necessary task, but treating her as "alien" and then killing her helps to ensure that the Furies will wreak vengeance again. As William Barrett warns, "It would be the final error of reason—the point at which it succumbs to its own hubris and passes over into its demoniacal opposite, unreason—to deny that the Furies exist, or to strive to manipulate them out of existence. … We may, of course, be able to buy off the Furies for a while; being of the earth and ancient, they have been around much longer than the rational consciousness that would entirely supplant them, and so they can afford to wait. And when they strike, more likely than not it will be through the offending faculty itself."[86] And we might speculate that when the matricide is perpetrated by a woman, such as Ripley, the Furies' wrath would intensify, for the woman kills her own kind. Irene de Castillejo summarizes the dilemma: "A woman today lives in perpetual conflict. She cannot slay the dragon of the unconscious without severing her own essential contact with it; without in fact destroying her feminine strength and becoming a mere pseudo-man."[87] Indeed, it is she who will suffer the most when the Furies strike back, for she will remain divided against herself and haunted by the half that will not stay buried.

We might ask, then, whether there are any narrative alternatives for the heroine (or hero) who seeks the submerged feminine but finds her to be threateningly demonic. A clue can perhaps be derived by looking at the best-known literary text in which the Furies ascend—Aeschylus's *Oresteia*—for full-blown contemporary problems are often prophesied in the first dim light of "progress." The myth Aeschylus relates originated in a time when the new patriarchal gods were not certain about what to do with the feminine—should it be exiled as a threat to the new order or honored as its parent? Of most interest here, in *The Eumenides* Orestes is haunted by guilt and hounded by the Furies for his crime of matricide in *The Libation Bearers*. He seeks sanctuary at Delphi with Apollo, who speaks to the Furies harshly: "Freaks like you should make their hole/ deep in some blood-beslobbered lion's den/ and not come rubbing off their filth/ on those beside these sacred mantic spots."[88] But Apollo, as the new patriarchal god of reason, can only put the Furies to sleep; he cannot drive them away. He sends Orestes to Athens to appeal to Pallas Athena, who calls a jury of citizens to try Orestes. The jury produces a tie, and Athena breaks it in favor of Orestes. The enraged Furies utter horrible threats to Athena, promising to poison all the crops and to bring disease and misery to all. But Athena, the symbol of masculine courage and understanding united with feminine feeling and instinctive wisdom, serves as a mediator between Apollo and the Furies. Although she votes to acquit Orestes, thus favoring the law over the blood feud, she also recognizes that "if civilized justice and reason become identified with the Apollonian values as the only good, the destructiveness of the ancient mother goddesses will erupt in untold evil for mankind."[89]

In her wisdom, Athena faces the terrible power of the wounded goddesses and speaks kindly to them, recognizing that "these women have a work we cannot slight."[90] At first the Furies' anger will not abate. As Athena continues to show her respect, however, they are gradually persuaded, withdraw their threats, and even promise blessings on the people. Athena renames them "the Eumenides," which means "the Gentle Ones," and they are led with honor and dignity to their shrines under the earth. William Barrett suggests that this solution may not be as frightening as we might imagine, since "in giving the Furies their place, we may come to recognize that they are not such alien presences as we think in our moments of evading them. In fact, far from being alien, they are part of ourselves, like all gods and demons."[91]

One could object at this point that once Ripley embarked on her journeys, she had two choices in both *Alien* and *Aliens*—kill or be killed—and that expecting her to face down the monsters and speak kindly to them is both naive and absurd. Within the context of the action as it is scripted in this story, soft words from Ripley would, indeed, turn the drama into farce. In these films the characters' purpose, even before they board the first spaceship, is commercial exploitation; thus, anything that gets in the way must be eliminated. It is a perfect situation for an ego-hero; patriarchal purpose, that is, calls for a masculinized agent. If Athena's wisdom is to be recalled in contemporary times, the purpose of the story will have to be different from the beginning.

The old heroic myth, once essential and glorious, has run its course. In the new context of interdependence suggested by the infinite spatial scene, its continuation is dangerous, and, as we have seen, it cannot accommodate feminine consciousness without corrupting it. The new myth for humankind needs to be a quest, not a conquest; its purpose must be to search rather than to search and destroy. Projections of an inner to an outer other must be withdrawn. In the United States we seem to have finally dispensed with transforming the Dionysian god into an Indian devil (although, tragically, too late for the benefit of Native American culture). But other targets have been found and can always be found as long as we do not wrestle with the horned demon gatekeeper inside. Only when we are ready to accept this challenge will we find what has been lost, face the Goddess in all her radiance and wrath, and decide what to do.

PART THREE

IDEOLOGICAL CRITICISM

When Marx and Engels first developed a critique of ideology, the Anglo-European popular classes were largely illiterate agricultural or first-generation urban workers, there was no universal public education or political suffrage, no technology of mass entertainment, and one social institution—religion—that influenced every cultural practice and offered everyone—in discourses, rituals and images—an explanation/justification of the world and society. Thus, the first Marxist attempt to understand ideology ... tended to conflate a critique of ideology with a criticism of idealism. ... We now understand ... ideology is less tenacious as "a set of ideas" than as a system of representations, perceptions, and images that precisely encourages men and women to "see" their specific place in a historically peculiar social formation as inevitable, natural, a necessary function of the "real" itself. This "seeing" precedes and underlies any ways in which social subjects "think about" social reality, and this "seeing" is as likely to be shaped through a relaxed fascination with the page or the screen as through any serious attention to [ideas].[1]

Thus, James H. Kavanagh articulates how the critical study of ideology has changed since the time of Marx and Engels. From a narrow focus on ideas and religious beliefs, ideological critics have turned to consider all kinds of symbolic representations and a wide range of social apparatuses. Writing theoretically informed works on matters of race, class, and gender, they have contributed significantly to the emergence of the interdisciplinary field of cultural studies. Among the many topics they have treated are the family, schools, TV, MTV, sports, literary genres, Elvis, Banana Republic catalogs, national parks, taxidermy, the weather, and Hollywood film. Such efforts have done much to expand our conception of the range and power of ideology.

This new scholarship challenges the assumption held by the mass media and by perhaps the greater part of the U.S. public that it is possible to live without ideology. In the media's view, only radicals such as Fidel Castro, Milton Friedman, and

Robert Bork "have" an ideology. Such individuals are termed *ideologues*. Because they are committed to a "coherent and rigidly held system of political ideas," ideologues cannot think freely or openly.[2] They are unable to see the world clearly, so their access to power needs to be restricted.[3]

The new scholarship has adopted a different, far less pejorative definition. It holds that ideology is not excessive or optional but is a necessary part of the process through which human beings come to know their social worlds. Not everyone is an ideologue, but everyone has an ideology. In the view of the French philosopher Louis Althusser, "Ideology is not an aberration or a contingent excrescence of History: It is a structure essential to the historical life of societies."[4] For Althusser, ideology connects individuals to socioeconomic reality by providing them with a way of "thinking about the social world," about themselves, and about their role within that world.[5] Ideology does this through representations. Indeed, Althusser identifies ideology as a "system (possessing its own logic and rigor) of representation (images, myths, ideas or concepts as the case may be) existing and having a historical role within a given society."[6] The system of representations, or "picture," addresses not just rational interests but also stimulates, manipulates, and mollifies unconscious fears and desires. Ideology touches people on a fundamental level, moving them toward a particular vision of "reality" and their relation to it.[7]

As mentioned at the beginning of this book, Althusser's understanding of ideology has influenced many film critics. Interpreting film as a system of representations, they ask how films and film genres shape social subjects and reveal how the ideologies of social subjects shape films and their interpretation. This type of inquiry is fairly advanced in the area of gender analysis of film and is impressively developed in the areas of class and race analysis.[8] Unfortunately, this inquiry is rather weak in the analysis of religion. Indeed, with the great expansion of the range of ideological analysis, the relative attention given to religion has declined. From being a primary focus of ideological criticism in the nineteenth century, religion has become simply one possible topic of inquiry and, in fact, not a particularly important one.

Although this trend is ironic, considering the significant attention given to religion in earlier forms of ideological analysis, it does not seem to disturb contemporary critics such as Kavanagh. They seem to assume that religion has declined in importance in the modern age of advanced capitalism, that the critical action is elsewhere—with Madonna, not *the* Madonna—and that religion no longer holds the power it once did to perform ideologically. Such assumptions, although commonly held, are called into question by this collection. The chapters in this book show us that religion, thanks in part to the cinema, is reaching more people than ever. As viewers look toward the screen, they are "seeing" religious themes, theologies, morals, myths, and archetypes represented in a visually compelling medium their ancestors never experienced. For this reason, we consider naive the critical trend toward ignoring or discounting religion and its study. More than ever, ideological analysis needs to take religion seriously. Far from being confined to churches or limited to a precapitalist era, religious symbols and values are diffused throughout popular culture and continue to shape contemporary subjects. Because religion remains powerful, critics need to examine how it interacts with ideology in the cinema.

In this section, Joel W. Martin's chapter is influenced by the type of ideological analysis developed by Fredric Jameson, Douglas Kellner, and Michael Ryan.[9] In the words of Ryan and Kellner, "Ideology needs to be seen as an attempt to placate social tensions and to respond to social forces in such a way that they cease to be dangerous to the social system of inequality. Ideology carries out this task through cultural representations which, like mental representations in relation to the psyche, orient thought and behavior in a manner that maintains order and establishes boundaries on proper action."[10] This view emphasizes the necessity for ideological texts to address those forces that might call into question the system of inequalities supported by the particular ideology. In a capitalist system, this means that the suffering of working-class whites has to be acknowledged, even if the purpose of doing so is to reaffirm the system of unequal rewards that causes such suffering in the first place.

Focusing on the contest between the Italian American contender Rocky Balboa and the African American champion Apollo Creed, Martin examines *Rocky* as an ideological text. He argues that this film neutralizes white, working-class resentment by directing it away from capitalism per se and toward a spurious culprit, the African American population. This reliance upon race baiting was noticed by other ideological critics.[11] What was not noticed was how the ideological power of the film depended to a great extent upon the screening of a scapegoating ritual. Tapping the scholarship of religious studies, Martin shows us the importance of taking religious myth, symbols, and rituals seriously.

Influenced more strongly by Althusser's perspective is Elizabeth McLemore's chapter on the film *Blue Velvet*. In her reading, the film highlights the representational processes through which male subjectivity is constructed. She writes: "With the gaze as the structuring, organizing principle in the [male] subject's symbolic, woman becomes the symbol of a biological lack that symbolically poses the threat of castration for the male. Faced with this threat, the male unconscious ... has only two alternatives: voyeurism/sadism ... and fetishistic scopophilia." Both of these alternatives are depicted in David Lynch's gripping, disturbing film.

Yet, as McLemore argues, the film also comments on the contrived character of the very processes of subjection it depicts. It does this primarily by employing in a self-conscious way the conventions of a mix of established film genres, particularly those associated with the detective story and pornography—genres closely tied to voyeurism and male sexuality. Because of the way the film appropriates older genres, McLemore does not hesitate to label *Blue Velvet* a "postmodern" film.

Whatever else the term postmodern may mean,[12] it signals that our connection to the past has become enormously complicated in an age of simultaneous electronic communication, unprecedented visual media, and global multinational commerce. This problematic relation to the past threatens traditional religion, because traditional religion typically locates its authority in the primordial past, particularly in archetypal narratives. McLemore calls attention to the gap postmodernity introduces between such narratives and contemporary culture. She notes that *Blue Velvet* has been read by some critics as a morality play in which purity prevails over evil. Using an allegorical approach, these critics link characters and events from the film with biblical characters and events, so that the young man, Jeffrey, for instance, becomes Adam in the garden. McLemore understands this type of reading but refuses to give it a privileged status, since any allegorical reading is but one of many possible interpretations of the film. If we insist on elevating a religious reading of this work of pastiche, McLemore thinks it is because we desire a unifying history, look toward the past with nostalgia, and rely upon religion to guide our interpretations. Rather than invoke religious allegories, McLemore wants us to face the failure of interpretation produced by this postmodern work, to acknowledge the crisis in our representational order, and to expose the problems in our reigning ideology of gender.

Gender identity and religion are key concerns of Irena Makaruska as well. Her chapter analyzes *Nine and a Half Weeks,* a film that on the surface appears to have little to do with religion. She finds religion within the film, however, because she defines it in a way that does not focus on specific contents but, rather, emphasizes its general function. She does not equate religion with denominationalism or belief with adherence to a set of specific faith claims, prescriptive laws, rituals, and practices. Rather, she identifies religion as the creative processes performed by individuals and communities to make life meaningful. Religious processes occur whenever people grapple with ultimate questions such as, Who am I? Where did I come from? Where am I going? What is the significance of the journey? These processes might occur in a church or synagogue, and they might not. They might involve traditional religious themes and images, and they might not. They could, for instance, involve sexual exploration and center on the struggle of a young woman to become an autonomous individual. Employing this approach to religion, Makaruska "reads" *Nine and a Half Weeks* as a religious "text" that reveals our current cultural assumptions about women, creation, freedom, and identity.[13]

What makes Makaruska's chapter a good example of ideological criticism is the way it focuses on a religious quest but simultaneously illumines the social and political contexts of that search. Specifically, Makaruska calls attention to pervasive patterns of gender inequality. "Reading" through a feminist lens, she considers carefully the cost of creating a meaningful life in a culture in which women and men do not have equal access to power and authority. Her work enables viewers/readers to gain a critical perspective on the dominant values that structure our world.

Rocky, Blue Velvet, and *Nine and a Half Weeks* are films that elicit very strong re-actions from audiences and critics. Their relevance to matters of race, class, and gender makes them ideal foci for ideological analysis. And yet, as these chapters show, these three films are also in dialogue with religion in vital ways. Appreciat-ing the richness of this dialogue helps us to better understand these films. It en-ables us to consider critically the use of a scapegoat ritual pattern in *Rocky,* to weigh carefully the influence of Christian allegory on *Blue Velvet,* to identify the protagonist's quest for meaning in *Nine and a Half Weeks.* As these chapters sug-gest, greater sensitivity to religious themes, symbols, rites, narratives, and values will not undermine but, rather, will enhance ideological criticism. By studying the interaction of religion and ideology in film, we can understand more fully how movies move audiences so deeply by "screening the sacred."

9

Redeeming America:
Rocky as Ritual Racial Drama

JOEL W. MARTIN

ROCKY (1976), THE FILM that made Sylvester Stallone a star, is deceptively simple. Shot on a relatively low budget in the streets of Philadelphia, the film tells the story of a palooka from the neighborhood who gets an unexpected chance to contend for the world boxing championship. The story is told in a straightforward, linear fashion; there is nothing aesthetically original about the film. Yet despite its conventionality, *Rocky* deserves critical attention because it conveys powerful ideological and mythological meanings. The film promotes conservative, even reactionary, social values. To illumine the ideological dimensions, I draw upon neo-Marxist film theory and Michael Riffaterre's theory of fiction production. To probe the mythic dimensions, I turn to the history of Christian theology and Rene Girard's theory of ritual violence.

The film's title prepares the viewer for a forthright film, an earthy story of hard realities. From the outset, *Rocky* exerts great pains to establish itself as a truthful representation of reality. Through an explanatory title, we are told explicitly that the action occurs in Philadelphia and that it begins on a specific day: November 25, 1975. The use of this title gives the film the feel of a documentary, as if it will simply report the straight, undoctored facts. This initial claim of documentary verisimilitude is steadily reinforced throughout the film with images of gritty streets, caged dogs, loud television sets, and seedy bars. A cameo appearance by Joe Frazier as himself underscores the film's authenticity.

This topos of "authenticity" provides the hard stage for the central narrative: the story of one man's painful rise from squalor, minutely detailed and told in strict chronological order, push-up by push-up. Here, however, we must attend to other levels of the film. Additional narratives with broader implications bind themselves inseparably to the progress of our muscular pilgrim. Most important, Rocky's story is tied to a larger narrative of patriotic nationalism. This narrative surfaces most obviously in all of the hoopla concerning the U.S. Bicentennial. The country is eagerly anticipating the dawn of the year 1976. Rocky, a second-rate boxer, gains a shot at the championship solely because his Italian immigrant heritage ties him to the myth of new world opportunity. His ethnicity, not his ability as a boxer, makes him a fitting participant in a Bicentennial fight. The fight is staged as a Bicentennial gala, and the reigning champion masquerades first as George Washington and then as Uncle Sam.

Ironically, this Bicentennial color camouflages the film's specific design for national rejuvenation. The Bicentennial is really "just a show," and the civil religion portrayed here is one projected through a very conservative lens. Beneath the hoopla, the film develops a much more nasty and ideologically powerful program for the United States. Among other things, this New Right vision includes an attack on the civil rights movement, glimpses of a race war, and a call for the resubjugation of African Americans.

These claims may at first seem harsh or ill-advised. On the one hand, it seems inappropriate to label this a "New Right" film, since the film predates the Reagan revolution by several years. On the other hand, it seems inappropriate to call the film conservative, because it does offer some socially progressive images. It features, for instance, an attractive, articulate, and successful African American businessman/boxer (Apollo Creed). In order to argue that this is a conservative film, we must first account for the apparent anachronism and then discount the liberal images it projects. These kinds of issues are addressed in the critical theory of film developed by Michael Ryan and Douglas Kellner. Although their theory must be modified with insights from religious studies and the study of myth, it may be used to explain how films can anticipate politics and turn liberal images to conservative ends.

In their book *Camera Politica: The Politics and Ideology of Contemporary Hollywood Film,* Ryan and Kellner argue that films (and other forms of representation) often foreshadow political developments, shape individual identities, and steer collective projects. They claim that one of the essential ways contemporary Americans learn their politics, values, and roles is through exposure to cinematic narratives, stories in film. Films transcode or translate the social order into images and narratives, teaching us through screen representations which boundaries we must honor and which we may be able to transgress. Many films, for instance, transcode into mundane visual stories the discourse of male dominance and its sacralization of traditional gender roles. Such films teach men to expect to exercise control and women to accept subordination.[1]

Ryan and Kellner argue that the stability of any set of representations depends upon the stability of the social order. When the social order is stable, the dominant discourses, value systems, and accompanying symbolic systems are also secure. When the social order is in crisis, a simultaneous crisis occurs in the realm of representations. In the latter case, the cinema becomes the site of contested representations; new kinds of stories appear, including stories that violate old boundaries. For example, *Desperately Seeking Susan* (1984) does not support the traditional order of patriarchy; rather, it shows women succeeding in the world without men and women bonding with each other. This film is an example of a cultural representation that attempts to draw new lines. According to Ryan and Kellner, in times of crisis, conservative films that reinforce old patterns of inequality will also appear.

This recuperative project became urgent after the 1960s. The 1960s introduced major challenges to the existing system of representations, challenging racial and sexual hierarchies. The U.S. defeat in Vietnam, Watergate, and the economic recession of 1973 called into question fundamental American values. Accordingly, Ryan and Kellner argue that Americans have had no choice but to engage in a massive cultural and political struggle over the social order. This struggle has surfaced spectacularly in popular religion and politics, in the New Right "return to traditional values," and in the Reagan call for "a great national recovery." This intense contest also inscribed itself in the realm of popular culture, especially in the films of post-1960s U.S. cinema. This brings us back to *Rocky* or, more broadly, to the major films of Sylvester Stallone. His films symbolically resolved the crises of the 1960s and helped bolster key cultural and ideological preconditions of the Reagan era.

Stallone is most closely associated with two extraordinarily successful series of films: the Rocky and Rambo cycles. Film criticism usually treats the two cycles separately, relating Rocky to movies about fighters (*Rocco and His Brothers* [1960], *Raging Bull* [1980]) and linking Rambo to other films depicting the return of the Vietnam veteran to the United States (*Coming Home* [1978], *The Deer Hunter* [1978]). Although such a critical route is valid and productive, it does not thematize or analyze the relationships between the Rocky and Rambo cycles.[2] Rather than divide these cycles by genre or theme, we might learn something equally important by paying attention to powerful linkages between them. The films share a common star and are united at deeper levels as well.

First, let us look closely at the name of the star and treat it, "Sylvester Stallone," as a text in its own right. This may seem a rather strange tack to take, but it is in accord with recent insights into the production of fiction, and it produces some striking observations. According to Michael Riffaterre's analysis of fiction, textual production often begins with a kernel word, a word that evokes "a web of metonyms and … stereotypes." Metonymns and stereotypes consists of all of the ideas, things, values, and symbols usually associated with a particular word or phrase. The word *king*, for instance, might bring to mind an object such as a crown, the idea of sovereignty, and the historical figure of Henry VIII. According to Riffaterre, textual production happens when the web of associations of a kernel word is unraveled through a meandering process of amplification, which produces description. Finally, the unfolding system of description "needs only to be given a sequential structure and a temporal dimension to become narrative."[3] Thus, a story is born.

One of the ways Riffaterre explicates his view is to examine a scene in the novel *Pickwick Papers*. At a picnic, Mr. Pickwick drinks too much. He ends up being carted about in a wheelbarrow pushed by his manservant. Several ironic encounters with various classes of people lead ultimately to Pickwick's arrest as a drunk and a trespasser. Working backward from the narrative to seek the germ of the story, Riffaterre recalls the eighteenth-century English saying "drunk as a wheelbarrow." Although nonsensical, the words would catch a writer's fancy. The saying "proffers a link between drunkenness and wheelbarrow; it does not make sense, but it has authority of usage, however ludic. ... A whole story [may be] concocted to bring about a pun or a punch line. ... Dickens' chapter was born that way." In Riffaterre's highly original and provocative model, description is elevated; description is not supplemental or "subordinate to narrative" but is the "womb of narrative."[4] I propose to borrow Riffaterre's theory and apply it to the films of Sylvester Stallone, and more precisely, to the very name Sylvester Stallone.

To do this may seem ill-advised or even far-fetched. Riffaterre's theory, after all, was created to describe literary production by individual authors such as Dickens. Filmmaking uses a different medium of expression and involves a very different type of production process that requires the labors of many more individuals. It is unlikely that any "kernel word" could be as important in the making of a film as it might be in the writing of a story. Nevertheless, on the good chance that the theory may have something to teach us, I shall plunge ahead.

Functioning as kernel words, *Sylvester* and *Stallone* evoke a range of stereotypes and metonyms that describe the characters of Rambo and Rocky, respectively. These stereotypes and metonyms can then become the basis for filmic unpacking through narrativization. Let us begin with the word *Sylvester*. When thinking about this word, an English speaker will likely think of something sylvan: trees, the forest, the woods. Someone familiar with Latin or European folklore will think of the figure known as the *silvestre*. The *silvestre*, in Latin and early modern European thought, was the wild man, the human who had withdrawn from civilization and become one with the forest. Living at the margins of thought and society, the *silvestre* incarnated chaotic unconscious energies that threatened ordinary codes of behavior and reason. As far-fetched or coincidental as it may seem, Sylvester Stallone played a character who embodied in nearly perfect fashion the characteristics of the *silvestre*. In *First Blood* (1982), Sylvester Stallone as John Rambo portrays a wild man at home in a primordial Pacific Northwest rain forest; when he is forced out of this home and into "civilization," apocalyptic violence results. He virtually destroys an entire town. In subsequent films, Rambo remains a wild man but is sent abroad to wage war against Communists in Vietnam and Afghanistan.

If the character Rambo is tied to the kernel word *Sylvester,* the character Rocky relates primarily to the word *Stallone. Stallone* calls to mind stallion, and, indeed, Rocky is nicknamed "the Italian stallion." This name evokes a rich range of associations. As a stallion, Rocky is full of animal power. As a stallion in the city, however, his animal powers are terribly frustrated. Much of the action of the film, as I discuss later, involves the release of these and other natural energies. Indeed, a definite high point of the film is the scene in which Rocky runs free and fast along the Delaware River waterfront. Much like the wild horses of the West, Rocky comes to serve as a symbol for a revitalized America, particularly for the immigrant working class. Thus, *Stallion* is not only a nickname, it also calls to mind potent animal metaphors and implies a heroic story. When linked to the word *Italian,* it evokes the immigrant experience and the dynamic story of the American Dream.

Whereas the characters Rambo and Rocky are distinct, they share a common conservative goal: defending the nation's dominant ideology against recent history. In confronting the ideological "crisis" caused by the 1960s, each hero concentrates primarily on one front of ideological combat, either foreign or domestic.[5] In the Rambo films made after *First Blood,* Rambo becomes a millennialist warrior in the American frontier tradition of Davy Crockett.[6] He directs violence against non-Western peoples. He reverses the history of decolonization and exorcises the "Vietnam syndrome," making a return to foreign intervention possible for the United States.[7]

Meanwhile, back home in the United States, Rocky fights the social movements that arose in the 1960s and that empowered traditionally segregated or subjugated Americans: non-European Americans and nonmales. The first three films of the Rocky cycle concern themselves with issues of race, class, and gender in the United States. After the upsetting chaos of the 1960s, Rocky has the urgent and unenviable task of getting everybody back in their place. His is the work of a European American male revitalization prophet. In contrast to Rambo, Rocky works within the system, fighting within the boxing ring—a space in which combat, although brutal, is regulated by rules. Despite this and other differences, Rocky and Rambo share a common ideological goal. Together, they help resacralize traditional power relationships abroad and at home. They participate in and encourage the conservative cultural and political backlash against the 1960s.

Although conservatives of the period wanted to turn back the clock, they had to acknowledge that struggles during the 1960s had irrevocably changed the terms of the debate concerning the proper shape of the social order. Among other things, the New Right realized it could no longer afford to endorse overt racism. This fact is well illustrated in the first and quintessential Stallone film. *Rocky* prominently features an articulate, confident, and financially successful African American man, Apollo Creed (Carl Weathers). By almost any measure, Creed is a respectable role model, and it would be a waste of energy to argue otherwise. Despite this positive image, the film expresses and directs European American working-class anger toward African Americans. It is important to see what the film makes of Creed's success. The film's narrative structure exploits Creed's success as one of a series of signs that the United States is racially out of order. With utter disregard for true socioeconomic facts about life in the United States (one-third of African Americans live in poverty), the film consistently portrays African Americans enjoying the good life while European Americans suffer. Rocky loses his locker to an

African American boxer. Unemployed European American youth mill about the streets. Working-class European Americans perform dirty jobs in degrading conditions (Rocky works for a loan shark and lives in an apartment that "stinks"; his brother-in-law tends cattle carcasses in a meat freezer). Meanwhile, African Americans work as newscasters, making common folks like Rocky look "stupid." In the conservative vision represented in *Rocky,* the boxing world champion, Apollo Creed, signifies scandal, pollution, a world turned upside down.

All of this is to say that *Rocky* aggressively and ideologically reinterprets recent history. As economists demonstrate, 1973 was the year in which post–World War II prosperity finally stopped. After this date, any increase in real income was offset by inflation. The American Dream was put on hold; expectations of greater wealth went unfulfilled; working-class and middle-class Americans grew frustrated. This frustration became the occasion for a new politics, but it was not clear what form this new politics would take. One could imagine, as did Martin Luther King Jr. in the last years of his life, the emergence of a new kind of working-class solidarity, solidarity that overcame racial divisions to empower a genuinely democratic recasting of U.S. society. Alternatively, drawing upon the tradition of Richard Nixon, one could posit a resentful middle-class "silent majority" and ground one's politics upon this reification. In any case, the promulgation and installation of a dominant wage-stagnation politics necessarily had to proceed through cultural production: the tapping of dreams, channeling of desire, and yoking of real frustrations to ideological explanations. It was here that film, particularly the films of Sylvester Stallone, proved indispensable and powerful.

Rocky symbolically resolved the crisis of wage stagnation by blaming the genuine woes of working class European Americans on the civil rights movement. In the post-1960s United States, the film argues, African Americans exercise improper power and enjoy too much visibility. In effect, they have stolen the American Dream from its rightful, European American heirs and have created a horrible American dystopia. Global economic shifts aside, African Americans and European American liberals have turned everything upside down; they have soiled the American flag and polluted its creed.

Rocky provides a program by which to overcome the 1960s, to escape dystopia. As Ryan and Kellner recognize, it is an ideologically conservative film. It provides a plausible interpretation of reality that simultaneously deflects attention away from the social order. Like other conservative films of the period, it represented the true suffering of Americans while at the same time pointing to spurious causes. Significantly, in *Rocky* this ideological labor relied upon the symbols and signs of religion. To understand the film, we need to do more than focus on ideology alone. We must go well beyond the kind of analysis offered by Ryan and Kellner, for *Rocky,* at its deepest level, offers a profound religious reconstruction of U.S. history. To appreciate this fully, we must draw upon the insights of scholars of religion, myth, and ritual.

The very first sounds and images of the film are unmistakably religious. The sound track features a flourish of trumpets as the screen provides a closeup of the countenance of a Byzantine Christ, represented in a mosaic on the wall of the gymnasium in which we first encounter Rocky. The gymnasium used to be a church, or, more accurately, the former has been installed within the latter. The startling and explicit use of Byzantine imagery testifies to the depth of the economic crisis wracking the West in the early 1970s. It is as if the West felt itself teetering upon such a dangerous precipice that it needed to go back to the very foundations of Western civilization, to Constantine and the sign of the cross. The camera tracks down from Christ to Rocky, the boxer in the ring. Thus, *Rocky's* opening scene links Christ to Rocky. As Rocky embarks on his road to the championship, we realize that it is actually Christ hiding in boxing shorts. He has temporarily descended to save the United States.

The Byzantine imagery and trumpet flourish suggest that this saviour is neither kind nor meek but is full of power and violence. To be precise, the opening shot suggests that the film's Christology may be docetic: The Son is only pretending to be weak—that is, in history.[8] This first impression is confirmed throughout the film with images of power that are momentarily bound and then triumphantly released. These images consistently concern vital animal powers, as exemplified in the dog Butkus, caged at the beginning of the film, later seen running. Likewise, Adrian (Talia Shire), a repressed and silent woman, suddenly becomes sexually active, liberating herself from her battering brother. Finally, the film's true star, Stallone's body, increasingly reveals its awesome muscular power.

These images of animal power give the film's docetic Christology a significantly original twist. Classical Docetism put down the flesh, equating it with finitude, weakness, the profane. Christ only pretended to be human, but his spirit never really entered matter. *Rocky's* Christology, in contrast, finds power in the flesh, which is secularized Docetism. It is still docetic, because we are given to understand that a fullness of sacred power is always already there, lurking beneath the surface. It is secular, however, because sacred power is no longer tied to a spiritual realm but is incarnated in the body. The body of the working-class hero merely feigns weakness; it restrains itself, waiting for the proper moment to reveal its awesome strength.

This docetic structure of restrained power that seeks violent release replicates itself in the movie's score, especially in the film's popular, chart-topping theme song (music by Bill Conti, words by Carol Connors and Ayn Robbins). The song evokes feelings of power, physical power, and it appropriately became the unofficial anthem of runners throughout the United States. In the film's deployment of this song, the melody sounds quietly at various brief moments in the first half of the film. As Rocky grows stronger, however, it waxes in volume and lengthens in duration. In the film's most memorable and inspiring moment, as Rocky races along the waterfront and heads toward the art museum, the music becomes overwhelming as the chorus exults "Gettin' strong now! Gonna fly now!"

Rocky is a film about the triumphant return of European Americans' power. Rocky's body stands for the body politic of European America. At the beginning of the film, when we see a tired, beaten Rocky, the film is suggesting that U.S. democracy has fallen into decay. As Rocky trains, he gains the support of working-class European Americans who provide him with food, money, moral support, and a place to work out. At an ideological level, this represents a renewal of democracy and, more generally, of European culture, an idea symbolized explicitly by having Rocky run to the art museum. In his dance on the museum's steps, Rocky revitalizes a stale Western culture and reclaims the decaying city for the people.[9]

This call for democratic cultural renewal perhaps explains the enormous popularity of *Rocky:* The film inspired its working-class and middle-class audiences to imagine a genuinely democratic movement, a movement of people power in the United States not unlike the one imagined by Martin Luther King Jr. However, if the film taps our utopian imagination,[10] it unfortunately contains these progressive energies within traditional repressive politics: the politics of racial oppression. Rocky cannot simply become strong and "fly," he must fight Apollo Creed— to the death, if necessary.

Thus, the film climaxes with one of the most painful and grotesque fight scenes ever filmed. It begins, oddly, with a sort of minstrel show. Apollo Creed, dressed as George Washington, is paraded around the gym on a float. This seems harmless enough, but I propose that this joviality and foolishness are intimately connected to the violence that follows. More precisely, the minstrel show and ensuing bloodbath constitute one unified ritual process. It is the ancient ritual process by which a community expels its demons through the means of a scapegoat. As in ancient Greek ceremonies, Creed is the *pharmakos,* the reviled individual the community uses as a sacrificial victim in a rite of purgation. True to form, before he is beaten, the community enthrones him as its mock king. As in the classic renewal ceremonies, there is a moment of chaos, an inversion of order, a time of foolishness; this is immediately followed by violence, a brutal violence that inverts the inversion to revivify an order grown stale and sterile.[11]

This interpretation is strongly and, indeed, directly authorized by the film, for during the fight scene a group of fans holds up a placard that declares "Creed is King." The placard's slogan not only confirms our identification of Creed as the mock king of the classical renewal ceremony, but it also urges us to equate Creed with yet another "king": Martin Luther King Jr. Thus, Creed may symbolically stand for the civil rights movement, a movement that serves in this film as a synecdoche of the 1960s; by beating him, the European American community can ritually exorcise cultural anomie and displace economic anxieties.

As the blows are exchanged by Creed and Rocky, the hoopla dies down and the real work begins. And it is work, a degraded and exhausting nose-to-the-grindstone task, performed under close supervision and carefully clocked. Rocky is compelled to put in a full day's "work." But it is also more than work. We sense something like hatred or rage flare in the ring. The boxers begin to fight as if some ancient score were being settled. The level of violence becomes unreal, physically unendurable. As we watch this onerous and painful passage, the film unavoidably registers the fact that the European American working class has nothing to gain by pursuing the politics of racism. The film, in spite of itself, gives representation to an antiracist or a utopian energy.

As the mutual beating produces bruises and cuts, this antiracist, anti-ideological message grows stronger and almost subverts the overarching racist message. When Rocky asks that his trainer cut his swollen eyelids and we learn that Creed is "bleeding inside," the film arrives at the fullness of its own contradictions and comes close to hemorrhaging. Torn between a utopian, genuinely democratic impulse—which would have Creed and Rocky simply stop the fight—and reactionary racism—which requires Rocky to fight to the death—the film resists the utopian impulse and opts for an ideological ending. The ritual requires blood sacrifice from the hero and the scapegoat.

Even so, the film can achieve its ideological resolution only with extraordinary effort. Because the utopian impulse is a real, historical possibility, the film must expend tremendous energy to suppress it. Because the visual imagery of the fight increasingly argues in favor of the utopian, antiracist option, the film must locate and unleash its repressive ideological energy in the only other place available: the sound track. In *Rocky*'s climax, the sound track actually opposes the visual. Such a conflict is unusual in film: "The general historical function of sound has been to confirm and support the image."[12] In *Rocky* sound contests image; ideology drowns out counterhegemonic, nonhierarchical possibilities. As Rocky and Creed destroy one another, the "Rocky Theme" waxes stronger, ensuring that the theme of white nationalism overcomes the potential of working-class solidarity. Rocky keeps on fighting, driven by the hymn. In the United States regeneration comes through violence against other races.[13]

Rocky does not win, and he walks away with eyes swollen, temporarily blinded. Thus, on an abstract, structural level, the film has moved from an initial situation in which European Americans saw too much of African Americans to a situation in which the European American hero who fought an African American cannot see at all. In this way, the first *Rocky* film at least registers the cost working-class African Americans and European Americans pay for racism. This subversive message did not survive, and was positively denied in subsequent films in the cycle. If Rocky did not win in the first film, he would in the second. His power, the power of European America, would rise again, not just in the cinema but also in politics and religion.

10

From Revelation to Dream:
Allegory in David Lynch's *Blue Velvet*

ELIZABETH MCLEMORE

IN THE INTRODUCTION to their book on Hollywood cinema, Michael Ryan and Douglas Kellner (1988) focus on the relationship between film and social history. Stressing the discourses that structure both cinema and society, they emphasize the connections between the systems of filmic and social representation. Their approach concentrates on the cultural representations common to a postmodern consumer society. According to Ryan and Kellner, these postmodern representations refuse any transparent or direct relationship to a (pre)signifying reality. Instead, postmodern representations problematize the very activity of reference. They blur or transgress such categories as "art" and "life" even as they refract other linguistic, artistic, and social codes. As a result, postmodern art—particularly film—bears the traces of its history in a complex process Ryan and Kellner term a "discursive transcoding" of various social discourses into structural narratives: "Rather than reflect a reality external to the film medium, films execute a transfer from one discursive field to another. As a result, films themselves become part of that broader cultural system of representations that construct social reality" (1988, 12–13).

Postmodern film borrows its material from other discursive registers, reworking, recontextualizing, and transcoding its material into new configurations. The result is a complex fabric that bears the imprint of cultural memory and loss—that is, the construction of histories—with regard to both the artistic work and the society within which it is produced, received, and consumed. As a postmodern film that explicitly maps filmic transcoding and social transgression onto the film itself, *Blue Velvet* foregrounds the crisis in representation that has become a topos in contemporary critical theory. As I hope to illustrate, *Blue Velvet* calls special attention to our understanding of the unconscious and of experience, of memory and of history.

As one of the most popular and controversial films of 1986, *Blue Velvet* has variously been described as a "cop flick, a teen-love paean, a horror movie and an American masterpiece" (Loder 1986, 44) and a "wondrously American combination of morbid obsession and true-blue sincerity" (Ansen 1986, 69). This peculiarly "American" combination, as many reviewers note, is not everyone's cup of tea. "In Chicago," Cathleen McGuigan reports, "two men fainted during the film. One of them, his pacemaker adjusted, rushed back into the theater to see how it ended" (1986, 100). At the same time many people were lined up outside ticket windows demanding their money back, managers at theaters across the country were adding matinee screenings to meet the demand for showings. Director and screenwriter David Lynch received an Oscar nomination for best director for the film, and the year-end issue of *Billboard* listed it as the twentieth most rented movie of 1987.

Viewer Reaction

Although box-office receipts were moderate, reactions to *Blue Velvet* were anything but lukewarm—as might be expected for a film whose unraveling of the "mysteries of life" takes us from the discovery of a severed ear in a vacant lot to sadomasochism and violence in a small town. Reviews, which compare the film to everything from the "evil twin of *It's a Wonderful Life*" to an updated version of "*Taxi Driver* with crabgrass" (Corliss 1986b, 12–13), are often hyperbolic and extreme: They are usually hostile or admiring but occasionally are downright confused.[1] Although the range among them is indeed wide, reviews of the film tend to fall into two general groups: those that describe the film as innovative and transgressive (often without any judgments regarding its social impact), and those that focus on the film as a parable or allegory of politics, religion, or history.

The first group, composed primarily of reviewers from the *New Yorker, Rolling Stone,* the *Nation,* the *Village Voice,* and *Newsweek,*[2] often describe the film as shocking in its unique and disturbing combination of "naïveté and kinkiness" (Ansen 1986, 69). For these reviewers, the film represents a clear break from Hollywood cinematic codes. From the oversaturated color in the opening shots of red roses and the white picket fence to the uncomfortable implication of the viewer in voyeuristic activities, the film is "nightmarish and therefore inescapable" (Rafferty 1986, 383). Not coincidentally, these reviewers often connect such nightmarishness to the psychological qualities of the film itself, calling it David Lynch's "unconscious" and praising Lynch as the "Frank Capra of dream logic" (Kael 1986, 99). Whereas each reviewer comments on the "kinky abusive Freudian psychodrama" (Ansen 1986, 69) played out among young Jeffrey, nightclub singer Dorothy, and the psychopathic Frank, the film's combination/violation of pornographic and psychological conventions is rarely addressed.

In contrast to these viewers, the allegorists point beyond the film text to some-thing else.[3] For these viewers, *Blue Velvet* is really about the "seamy underbelly of [1980s] Reaganite nostalgia" (Powers 1987, 47–48); the cosmic battle between good and evil for the soul of Jeffrey; or the failure of the struggle to view the past as a lived totality, thereby suggesting an inability to focus our own present.[4] Generally described as the unfolding of a metaphor in a narrative progression, allegory most often involves a figural representation or visual function.[5] As with metaphor, too, allegorical tropes are traditionally perceived as being supplanted by another meaning: Once the allegorical significance has been grasped, the figure recedes into the background, replaced by its anagogical, or "higher," meaning, be it in the realm of politics, religion, or history.

For many of these allegorical viewers, this higher meaning points to traditional bourgeois morality. Simultaneously, they claim the film's allegorical structure dis-tances the narrative from any immediate, referential reality. Richard Corliss's re-view in *Time* is the most representative of this group: "Blue Velvet is in no sense a realistic film. It is not modernist camp, either. Lynch believes every bit as much in the redemptive power of teen love—with families miraculously restored and two kids kissing to the crooning of a wedding-chapel organ—as he does in the force of evil" (1986a, 86). For some of these allegorical viewers, *Blue Velvet* presents a su-perb example of Christian typology, replete with Jeffrey as the "angelic choirboy," Adam in the garden, and Sandy as his Eve (Wall 1987, 8).[6] Lynch, according to this view, returns to the timeless "battle for purity over evil," indicting everyone in the struggle as sinners (Wall 1987, 7–8). Accordingly, as an allegory of the functioning of evil in the modern world, the film is ultimately didactic. In its graphically horri-fying portrait of sin, *Blue Velvet* is compared to Hieronymous Bosch's depiction of the Seven Deadly Sins (Wall 1987, 9)—a "must see" for Christian viewers.[7]

This allegorical view, although not completely incompatible with the psycho-logical struggle indicated in the first set of reviews,[8] differs in the function it at-tributes to the narrative—or, as Craig Owens would have it, the "counter-narra-tive" (1983, note 30, p. 80). In its view of history as an "irreversible process of dissolution and decay," allegory has been "condemned by modern aesthetics be-cause it speaks of the inevitable reclamation of the works of man by nature" (note 30, p. 80). Allegorical interpretation is precisely the revelation of a text's second (often "hidden") structure. As such, it is the "epitome of the anti-modern," al-though, as Owens reminds us, its "contemplative gaze ... need not ... be a sign of defeat; it may represent the superior wisdom of one who has relinquished all claims to mastery" (note 30, p. 80).

This reading of *Blue Velvet* as an allegory is particularly interesting in light of Jochen Schulte-Sasse's (1986–1987) definition of postmodern art as no longer overcoming the separateness of art and life. The attempt to locate an extra-narra-tive typological framework recuperates the functional significance of this film for this particular set of (re)viewers. This recuperative gesture is important here, sig-naling some crucial differences in reading strategies among viewers. Whereas the first set of reviewers indicated its discomfort with the ambiguous positioning of the film but made no attempt to assuage its anxiety, the traditional allegorists appear more eager to plug or close any gaps opened up by the narrative.

Allegorical Structure

In *Blue Velvet*, the dual narrative structure at times seems distinct: On the one hand, we have the surreal suburban banality of white, middle-class Lumberton, complete with apple pie and with Hope Lange as mom; on the other we have Frank Booth's violent, infantile rage, the joyride that turns into a nightmare.[9] However, the oscillation between these extremes—the line between good and evil is often blurred, and evil is particularly humorous at points in the film[10]—may generate anxiety, causing viewers to draw the anxiety-producing elements back neatly into an allegorical system, effectively neutralizing their threat. As Lynda K. Bundtzen puts it, "The campy veneer of *Blue Velvet*, coupled with dialogue that oscillates wildly between Frank's aggressive obscenity (almost every other word is 'fuck' or a variant thereof) and syrupy sentimentality (e.g., Sandy's dream about the robins), provokes nervous laughter, because we do not know whether the terrors of the film are to be viewed as real or pleasurable, even farcical, artifice, the characters as serious representations or cartoons from small-town American life" (1988, 188–189).

The differences in these approaches to the film are perhaps indicative of the differences between traditional allegory and postmodern allegory. Rather than the arbitrary representation of an idea, the "material" of allegory is the "concrete manifestation of that idea's material foundation" (Ulmer 1983, 97). According to Walter Benjamin, this "unity between the material and the transcendental object, which constitutes the paradox of the theological symbol, is distorted into a relationship between appearance and essence" (1977, 160). The result is, for Benjamin, a dialectic—not so much a synthesis between the two as "a *treuga dei* between the conflicting opinions" (Benjamin 1977, 177). Allegories do not erase the trope once the meaning has been perceived; as a result, postmodern allegorists do not cast off the allegory like "dross" but instead absorb it along with what is read. This difference between postmodern and traditional allegorists is further illustrated by Gregory Ulmer's distinction between "allegoresis" and "narrative allegory": "'Allegoresis,' the mode of commentary long practiced by traditional critics, 'suspends' the surface of the text, applying a terminology of 'verticalness, levels, hidden meaning, the hieratic difficulty of interpretation,' whereas 'narrative allegory' (practiced by post-critics) explores the literal—letteral—level of the language itself, in a horizontal investigation of the polysemous meanings simultaneously available in the words [or images] themselves ... narrative allegory favors the material of the signifier over the meanings of the signifieds" (1983, 95).

Ultimately, then, postmodern allegories call attention to the gap between sign and meaning, pointing not to interpretation (hermeneutics) but to the *failure* to read. If allegories exist in this gap between sign and meaning, they also function "in the gap between a present and a past" (Owens 1980, 68). Allegories are, almost by definition, fragmentary and melancholic. Vestiges of the past regularly appear in allegorical narratives, severed from their original context and resonating within a different discursive structure.[11] In *Blue Velvet,* this resonance takes the form of a pastiche of objects, images, and feelings from the American 1950s, 1960s, and 1980s.

From Allegory to Parody

Like parody, pastiche imitates or satirizes another work; however, according to Fredric Jameson, pastiche is "blank parody," "a neutral practice of such mimicry, without parody's ulterior motive ... without laughter, without that still latent feeling that there exists something *normal* compared to which what is being imitated is rather comic" (1983, 114). Pastiche is an imitation that calls attention to the original yet makes no explicit critique of it: Blank parody conspicuously draws attention to textual codes *as* codes. In *Blue Velvet* the effect is, at least for the viewer, a sense of being unmoored. Viewers of *Blue Velvet* are left simply with the parody of Hollywood codes and genres such as the pornographic film, the film noir detective serial, and the melodramatic romance.

The result—at least in *Blue Velvet*—is a perpetual deferral of meaning and a nostalgia for mythical origins: "Every metaphor is a metonymy of its own origin, its structure thrust into time by its very structurality" (Fineman 1980, 59). Craig Owens concurs: For him, twentieth-century allegory is anything but hermeneutics. Instead, allegorical art enacts the desire for history even as it points to a gap between the present and an irretrievable past. History in any conventional sense is no longer possible but, rather, is recognized as the unbridgeable gap between the sign and its referent. Accordingly, then, for these critics the "postmodern shift" in allegory is a "shift in elocutionary mode, from history to discourse" (Owens 1980, Part 2, p. 67)—or, perhaps, from (medieval) revelation to (postmodern) dream.

Not quite a nostalgia film, *Blue Velvet* still retains vestiges of our cultural past, although, as with dreams, in a form reworked and transformed in the process of remembering them. The film has been described by reviewer Pauline Kael (1986) as "David Lynch's unconscious," and, indeed, it seems quite consciously to foreground issues of memory and forgetfulness (both individual and collective), origin and loss. In fact, as many reviewers have noted, the film seems made-to-order as both an example and a subversion of the gaze depicted in Laura Mulvey's influential article, "Visual Pleasure and Narrative Cinema" (1975). Relying on concepts drawn from Freudian and Lacanian psychoanalysis, Mulvey explains that the desiring (male) subject is constructed through an awareness of his possession of the penis—a possession verified through the look. With the gaze as the structuring, organizing principle in the construction of the subject's symbolic, woman becomes the symbol of a biological lack that symbolically poses the threat of castration for the male. Faced with this threat, the male unconscious, Mulvey says, has only two alternatives: voyeurism/sadism (a preoccupation with "demystifying" the hidden mystery of woman), and fetishistic scopophilia ("the substitution of a fetish object or turning the represented figure itself into a fetish so that it becomes reassuring rather than dangerous)" (1975, 13–14).

Blue Velvet repeats and calls attention to both these avenues, foregrounding issues of representation and the construction of the subject. In his quest to "see things that have always remained hidden," Jeffrey attempts to unravel the mystery of Dorothy by turning her into an object for his gaze (he watches her from the closet). This look, however, is both inscribed and parodied as Dorothy reverses the positions of spectator and object, grabbing a butcher knife from the kitchen and ordering Jeffrey to disrobe as she holds the knife threateningly close to his exposed genitals.[12] Each inscription of male violence and scopophilia is undercut by its obviousness: As Lynda Bundtzen suggests, "Lynch is so bold in his exposure of [these] contradiction[s] that the 'neurotic needs of the male ego' are revealed as such" (1988, 202–203).

In addition to exposing the fetishization of woman in cinema, *Blue Velvet* is itself a filmic fetish that (un)consciously inscribes and parodies psychological/cinematic fetishism throughout the film.[13] In its unfolding of the mysteries of life (in this case infancy, sex, and death), *Blue Velvet* depicts the original trauma in the Oedipal mommy/daddy/baby psychodrama of violence in Dorothy and Frank/Jeffrey's relationship(s) (and, of course, in the homoerotic scenes between Frank and Jeffrey, all of which occur in the absence of Jeffrey's "real" father). On the other hand, the visual beauty of the film encourages its fetishization by the viewer. As the film moves from the neatly manicured lawns of Lumberton into the psychological underworld of Lumberton's citizens (the camera's zooming in and out of an ear frame the beginning and end of the narrative), the viewer is seduced into voyeurism of the sadomasochistic encounters between the characters. Moreover, the preoccupation with seeing (and the power it accords) is itself inscribed within the narrative: Frank's drug-induced, sadistic eroticism is signaled to the other characters and to the audience by his injunction "don't you fuckin' look at me!"

At the same time the film appears to be commenting on the contrived nature of scopophilia in its relentless exploration of Dorothy, we are forced to join in: The camera angles implicate us in the action. Although the spectacular color encourages us to watch, however, the noir scenes prevent us from seeing much. The desire to see and understand more, then, indicts us in Jeffrey's quest to unravel the mystery, to "gain knowledge and experience."[14] Once we have gained it, however, it is quickly snatched from our consuming jaws. The robin that signals the redemptive power of love and eternal happiness is, in fact, revealed to be a mechanical bird with a wriggling beetle in its beak, and the happy reunion of Dorothy and little Donny at the film's conclusion shows Dorothy gazing almost wistfully off the screen to the refrain, "I still can see blue velvet through my tears."

The film's refusal of an unalloyed happy ending is consistent with its parodic form. Rather than proffering any definitive commentary, *Blue Velvet* simply trails off into its musical score and its cycle of repetition and blank parody. Constantly pointing to other textual artifacts, *Blue Velvet's* aura and its "register of time" dissolve (Terdiman 1985, 25). Although the film's historical time is never stated, it conflates cultural vestiges of the past with those of the present.[15] The images of pastel dresses and 1950s suburban quiescence are shattered by the violent, Van Gogh–like[16] colors juxtaposed against 1980s images such as Jeffrey's earring. Similarly, Lynch's use of Roy Orbison's "In Dreams," Ketty Lester's "Love Letters," and Bobby Vinton's "Blue Velvet"—all sentimental love songs released around 1963[17]—reworks and decontextualizes the romanticized world the songs evoke. Whereas the songs still resonate with traces of their original context, the pastiche allows Lynch to imply that the world evoked by the songs was *always* tainted, *always* had an ugly underworld seething beneath its surface, thereby lending a nightmarish quality to the "dreamy" love songs. Our cultural memories of the past in *Blue Velvet* are charged with the metonymic residues of the present, reworking our sense of history (Jameson 1983, 116). Staircases remind us of Hitchcock thrillers; the face of Isabella Rossellini carries us back to the images of her mother, Ingrid Bergman, in addition to Rossellini's own Lancôme ads; Dennis Hopper reminds us of *Easy Rider, Giant,* and several American "B" movies. As Cathleen McGuigan wryly comments, "The sappy old Bobby Vinton song that echoes through the sound track will never again remind you of your senior prom" (1986, 102).

The decontextualization that is the result of these resonances serves to illustrate the process of memory and forgetfulness. "Cognition," Richard Terdiman reminds us, "cannot be divorced from the re/cognition of memory" (1985, 13), investing the present with haunting yet indelible traces of its past. *Blue Velvet* never completely reinvents that past for us: Instead, like dreams, it reinvents the feel and shape of what we remember from it (Jameson 1983, 116). Reverberating between the memory of our past and a present that is then set adrift, the film becomes a kind of "nightmare dreaming of the present by the past" (Terdiman 1985, 24) because of the "paradoxical inaccessibility" of that past (Terdiman 1985, 15). The manifestation of the past in *Blue Velvet* takes two forms: that of the histories of the characters as traced through their psychological struggles (and, as Freud would remind us, their—and our—subjectivities) and as traced through the references to our collective representational past. As Terdiman explains, "The structures which organize us are held in a memory which is virtually locked up. [Pierre] Bourdieu puts it this way: 'The "unconscious" is never anything other than the forgetting of history which history itself produces by incorporating the objective structures in the second nature of habitus'"(1985, 20).

This process of memory and forgetfulness repeats a history, a diachronicity, a narrative unfolding through time and space. As a form that by definition is intertextual, parody itself produces "a gap between sign and meaning" (Griggers

1990, vii), reproducing the process of memory by "simultaneously distancing its referent and calling back to mind that which is not present ... enact[ing] a displacement that brings the entire problem of representation into focus" (Terdiman 1985, 35). As such, parody becomes a dialogic form.[18] The result is the implosion of codes, a "turning in on itself, on its own history, its own past" (Griggers 1990, 140) in a way that allows the film to exceed its own representation (Griggers 1990, 142). If, as Terdiman suggests, the "fantasy of representation has important roots in th[e] technical development" of photography (1985, 22), then parody also calls attention to the fantasies of representation at the root of the filmic apparatus itself.

This pastiche, or "memory process," results in a change, a discursive transcoding that alters or blurs genres and practices. In transgressing these codes, *Blue Velvet* in part identifies itself as postmodern even as it marks its own history as a site of discursive transition. For Jameson, postmodernism is a "periodizing concept, a mark of the struggle for artistic form in the era of multinational consumer capitalism" (1983, 113). This struggle transforms and reinvents the history of mass culture through its own metonymic representation of our past—a re-creation Jameson bemoans as an inability to come to grips with history itself, revealing the "pathological symptom" of a collective unconscious through its effort and failure to identify its present. However, it is precisely through its artistic forms—allegory and blank parody[19]—that *Blue Velvet* rescues something of that past, although it illuminates the failure of any totalizing narrative and problematizes our notions of history. *Blue Velvet* exposes the fantasies at work in the desire for a stable past, a unifying and unmediated history.

11

Women Spoken For:
Images of Displaced Desire

IRENA MAKARUSHKA

IN A 1989 *New York Times* article on opera, Donal Henahan confesses to having had a conversion experience that he likens to that of Paul on the road to Damascus.[1] He describes how he "sat transfixed by Teresa Stratas' hair-raising performance ... in *Suor Angelica*." Suddenly, he came to the astonishing realization that in opera "women are perpetual, archetypal, dramatically necessary victims." Henahan expresses bewilderment that no one has ever mentioned this fact to him. With a tinge of regret, he remarks that opera will never again be the same for him. Henahan's somewhat belated revelation that in opera women are represented as "oppressed, manipulated and otherwise pitiable" is hardly news to feminists who for several decades have been concerned with the representation of women in the arts.

The fate of women that is common in opera is also present in film.[2] In her assessment of the 1940s genre frequently described as "woman's" film, Mary Ann Doane expands Foucault's analysis of the relationship between knowledge and pain. She argues that "disease and the woman have something in common—they are both socially devalued or undesirable, marginalized elements which constantly threaten to infiltrate and contaminate that which is more central, health and masculinity."[3] In the films Doane analyzes, women are regularly portrayed as marginal personality types, such as hysterics, who suffer from a wide variety of "women's troubles." Excessive sensuality, unbridled passion, or bad luck in relationships with men are common causes of suicidal tendencies or other psychological disorders in women. Represented as depressed, unstable, incompetent, and weak, women become objects of male scrutiny and power. Perceived as lacking the ability to control their emotions and, consequently, as unreliable narrators, these women fall under the care of men. In this genre, these men typically have the role of doctor or analyst. Exemplifying the voice of reason and scientific objectivity in the effort to save women from themselves, these men define women's identity and desires. In the process, they deny women their own language and voice. Doane points out that the "phenomenon of the mute woman is ... an extreme instance of a strategy whereby ... films manage simultaneously to grant the woman access to narration and withhold it from her."[4] In films such as these, women are invited to confide in men, men who distrust any woman's capacity for self-knowledge.

The offending representations of women, found in opera as well as in films made in the 1940s, reflect a perception of gender that does not acknowledge a possible difference between woman's experience and the representation of that experience as determined by a male symbolic order. Film scholar Constance Penley suggests that whereas classical films refused to raise the question of the construction of sexual difference, "the challenge for contemporary films is to address ... sexual difference as both a psychical and a social phenomenon."[5] Are there contemporary films that respond to this challenge? Are there films that are different from classical films, which Raymond Bellour describes as a "system of representation in which the woman occupies a central place only to the extent that it's a place assigned to her by the logic of masculine desire"?[6] Are women still spoken for? Is women's desire still displaced by the grammar of the male symbolic order?

In this chapter, I examine the construction of identity and selfhood in a contemporary film that both reflects and overcomes the reductive, belittling representation of women circumscribed by and confined to a male discourse. Adrian Lyne's *Nine and a Half Weeks* is a provocative film about a woman's journey from being "spoken for" to reclaiming her own voice. It describes the process and the price of coming to greater self-awareness and of attaining a greater degree of self-determination. When it was released in 1986, the film was criticized as abusive, manipulative, and sexist. I argue that *Nine and a Half Weeks* is as much about manipulation and loss of autonomy as it is about reclaiming autonomy. Lyne's representation of "woman" is more complex than that of earlier films feminists have criticized. His nuanced characterization of Elizabeth discloses an ambiguity of experience that resists the reductive dichotomies of either/or: either victim or victimizer, either good or evil, either oppressor or liberator, either fall or redemption.

Lyne's film portrays a woman on a journey to reclaim her own voice, to re-create her own identity within the psychic and cultural landscape she inhabits. Questions about freedom, virtue, and the creation of meaning raised in this film are part of the discourse of Western religious thought. Informed by a feminist critique of the normative values that anchor Western tradition, my analysis explores how these values are embedded in archetypal images of women and how they are reinterpreted within the contemporary urban culture Lyne re-creates.[7]

In *The Creation of Partriarchy*, feminist scholar Gerda Lerner argues that the history of patriarchy, and, therefore, the history of women as invisible and mute, begins as early as the second millennium B.C.E. in the cultures of the ancient Near East, where there is a distinct pattern of the commodification of women.[8] The power of patriarchy is located in the male hegemony or dominance over symbols system, which takes two forms: "educational deprivation of women and male monopoly on definition."[9] Male control and manipulation of the symbolic order places men at the center of the moral, political, and scientific discourse. The idea that male experience is normative determines the perception that women are deficient models of men. In the fifth century B.C.E., the predominant attitude of Athenian society assumed that "real people" were men. Women were not perceived as having an individual or a public identity.[10] Even Olympian goddesses were admired for qualities associated with men. Athena, for instance, exhibited military prowess, Artemis displayed skills as a hunter, and Aphrodite expressed an erotic and sensual nature rather than a maternal, reproductive one.[11]

The dominant archetypes that define the experience of women within Western traditions are the symbols of Eve, the temptress, and Mary, the unsexual handmaiden.[12] If the mythic Eve is perceived as the embodiment of human frailty and the loss of paradise, Mary is the promise of holiness and paradise regained. The Eve symbol is associated with disobedience of male authority, risk taking, sensuality, and moral ambiguity. These attitudes and behaviors (which women are warned to avoid) are constructed as evil. The Mary symbol is associated with subservience, compliance with male authority, virginity, and moral certitude. These characteristics constitute the core Western cultural categories of the good with regard to women. However, the Eve/Mary archetypes represent a curious cultural schizophrenia. Eve is described as a temptress, responsible for the fall from grace of humankind. Perceived as weak-natured and flawed, she is blamed for destroying the bond between God and man. At the same time, Eve is the originary, nurturing mother of us all, the creatrix of the human race. Similarly, the symbol of Mary, the Virgin Mother, is inherently conflicted. How are women to aspire to being virgin mothers? How can they avoid being punished for failing to live up to impossible and unhuman expectations?

Henahan's comment that women are archetypal victims raises some interesting questions with regard to the Eve/Mary symbols and suggests that these archetypes can be interpreted as representations of the victimization of women. Traditionally, Eve has been seen as a victim of her own weak nature. However, the feminist analyses of the patriarchal order proposed by Mary Daly, Elaine Pagels, and others have questioned the myth of Eve's "weak" nature.[13] If Eve is not a victim of her own weak nature, is she a victim of an effort to deflect attention from Adam's role in the drama of the fall? If so, who is the victimizer? God? The Serpent? Patriarchal assumptions? Similar questions arise with regard to the symbol of Mary, the immaculate mediatrix. By Mary being made an alternative to Eve, has she been burdened with the task of representing victory over the "weak," carnal nature of Eve? Has the Mary symbol been deprived of the possibility of representing the fullness of human experience?[14] Or, to raise these questions in a different way, is women's experience adequately represented by archetypal images, or is women's experience distorted? Are women the victims of archetypes created by the male desire to define the symbolic order to which women are meant to conform? Are women punished for failing to live up to either the norm located in male experience or the norm as male-defined women's experience? Can women's experience be reclaimed and named by women?

With regard to the representation of women in film, feminist critics have challenged culturally inscribed assumptions that anchor the archetypal images and define attitudes and experiences that are "natural" or "normal" for women. For instance, in their analysis of the place of woman in the films of director Raoul Walsh, Pam Cook and Claire Johnston argue that the identity of women is circumscribed within male discourse and that women do not determine what is natural for themselves. Women are spoken for rather than speaking for themselves.[15] The question of how identity becomes gendered is also raised by film scholar Laura Mulvey in her theory of the gaze. Using Freud and Lacan, Mulvey argues that the relationship between the spectator and the film's text is that of an active masculine gaze and a passive female object.[16] "The determining male gaze," she writes, "projects its phantasy on to the female figure which is styled accordingly. ... Women are simultaneously looked at and displayed ... so that they can be said to connote 'to-be-looked-at-ness'."[17] The gender of the spectator is not the issue for Mulvey; rather, she argues that the concept of visual pleasure is itself gendered.[18] Women spectators, as with women characters within the film's text, are placed in the position of being determined by what is normal by male standards. Women characters reinforce the sense of otherness that women experience as they become aware of the differences between their experiences and the way cultural images define their experiences.

The "otherness" women experience, therefore, is the otherness they see within themselves, their own sense of not fitting the external images that are purported to define all women. The archetypes of women defined by patriarchy, whether as Eve or Mary, become the "other women" women need to confront in order to begin to develop their own voices and their own sense of identity out of their own freedom. Confronting the other woman in oneself and taking responsibility for one's "self" are among the stories told in *Nine and a Half Weeks.*

Nine and a Half Weeks begins and ends with Elizabeth negotiating the streets of New York. The ambiguity of New York, with its sophistication and urban violence, is the context of Lyne's representation of a woman in crisis and for his critical overview of the values of contemporary culture. The encounter between Elizabeth and John, which lasts all of nine and a half weeks, is played out in a world controlled by power, money, and sex. Emblematic of the consumerism of contemporary culture, John works at buying and selling money; Elizabeth buys and sells artworks. Each spins fantasy worlds for the wealthy; for each, the risks are high. Explicitly and implicitly, sex is a factor both as power and as a commodity of exchange. This point is illustrated when the gallery owner where Elizabeth works suggests that if Molly, a less attractive coworker, were in the back room, they would sell more paintings. Similarly, the gifts John gives Elizabeth can be seen either as tokens of his affections or the price for her sexual favors.

In a consumer culture, relationships, after all, are treated like just one more commodity. Artworks and sex are commodities exchanged for money in pursuit of pleasure. Lyne extends the metaphor of consumerism as related to sex and power by juxtaposing the world of art with the world of pornography. Toward the end of their relationship, John hires a prostitute to join them, and Elizabeth is overcome with a feeling of self-loathing. Running away from John, she stumbles into a sex show on 42nd Street, where her sense of horror intensifies. From there, she goes to an opening at her gallery, only to discover that the behavior of the opening-night crowd is little different from that of the spectators on 42nd Street. For both art and pornography, the marketable product is a voiceless object.

Lyne charts the apparent distinction between pleasure and pain, love and obsession, sex and pornography through Elizabeth's relationship with John. Voice, object, and story play a significant role in the process of constituting an autonomous self. The narrative strategies suggest that the person who has a voice has power: to name is to constitute reality. How, then, does Lyne represent Elizabeth's recovery of her own voice? How is Elizabeth represented as more than an object of John's gaze?[19] How is her self-understanding constituted? Is she more than "the place where [John] ... deposits his words in a desire to 'know' himself through her?"[20]

The relationship between John and Elizabeth recalls the adage that children should be seen and not heard. John wants Elizabeth to be a "good little girl" who, created in the image of the father, is seen but not heard. At one point Elizabeth asks John how he knew she would respond to him the way she did. He tells her that he saw himself in her. To see the other as self is to deprive the other of an identity. To define another within the logic of one's own discourse is to deny the other her or his own story.

John defines Elizabeth as a projection of his fantasy. He sees her at the Chinese grocery and is attracted to her. He picks her out in the crowd at the flea market and decides, in effect, to acquire her. During the ensuing nine and a half weeks, he watches her as she is transmuted by his desire. The degree to which John offers to take care of her, to dress and undress her, brush her hair, feed and clothe her, nurse her in illness, and cater to her needs is the degree to which he controls her. John focuses her attention on his desire. He asks that she think of him at a specified time of day when she looks at the watch he gave her and that she relinquish her nights to him. Elizabeth becomes an extension of John to the exclusion of everything that constitutes her world beyond her relationship with him. She is distracted at work, her friendship with Molly suffers, she does not answer her telephone messages or keep dental appointments, and her plants die for lack of watering. The ordinariness of life comes to a standstill. John's acquisition of Elizabeth is complete when he buys her a dress. She asks whether he wants to know if she likes it. He says no. Elizabeth is spoken for.

Although women are culturally conditioned to submit to being an object of male desire and to remain silent, in Lyne's representation women are strong enough to recover their own voice and to constitute their own identity. What accounts for this possibility? What are the necessary conditions for such a possibility to come to fruition? How does Elizabeth transcend the "good little girl" image? Lyne represents the process as an arduous one, which, as with all pilgrimages, goes through several stages. Elizabeth experiences both exhilaration and love, as well as horror and despair. The descent and the dark night anticipate the dawn.

John comes into her life at a point of transition Molly describes as a readiness to return to the world after her divorce. Elizabeth is fascinated by his attention and frightened by his demands and violent reactions, yet she agrees to do as he asks. The underlying question is, How far is she willing to go before she knows it is time to stop? How far is too far? For Elizabeth, John evokes a world of risk, experimentation, sensuality, and transgression. She experiences herself as touched by a degree of danger and loss of control that is not a part of her ordinary experience. The line between playfulness and manipulation is often indiscernible. At times Elizabeth willingly submits to John's desire and even initiates some of their games. The scene in which Elizabeth, with eyes closed, indulges John's food fetishism, her desire to dress like a man, the striptease, and their visit to Bloomingdale's all constitute highly ambiguous experiences. Many scenes, however, are less ambiguous; these include John's punishment of Elizabeth for being a "nosy parker," her humiliation when he wants her to crawl to pick up the money he throws at her, and the incident with the prostitute, which clarifies for Elizabeth the difference between far enough and too far.

It is instructive to consider the degree to which Elizabeth is merely an object of John's desire and the degree to which she has a voice in defining the erotic games. Is her voice her own, or is it constituted as an object of John's voyeuristic gaze? John's gaze, his attempt to confine Elizabeth within the world of his desire, creates the condition for Elizabeth to glimpse a side of herself she had not previously allowed herself to see. With John she discovers that she is capable of sensuality and other hitherto forbidden behaviors such as theft (she steals a locket) and violence (she stabs one of their attackers). Breaking the rules, trespassing against the law or merely against social proprieties excites Elizabeth. What terrifies her is not John but, rather, the idea that her desire as spoken for and defined by John may actually be hers. Has she arrived at the point of seeing herself in John? Is it possible that she desires to be spoken for? She is horrified at the recognition of an otherness within herself, an otherness she cannot name.

The growing sense of terror Elizabeth experiences reaches its climax during the encounter John orchestrates with a prostitute. Elizabeth's experience of terror is not unlike Julia Kristeva's description of abjection in *Powers of Horror*.

> When I am beset by abjection, the twisted braid of affects and thoughts I call by such a name does not have, properly speaking, a definable *object*. The abject is not an ob-ject facing me, which I name or imagine. Nor is it an ob-jest, an otherness ceaselessly fleeing in a systematic quest of desire. What is abject is not my correlative, which, providing me with some one or something else for support, would allow me to be more or

less detached or autonomous. The abject has only one quality of the object—that of being opposed to the *I*. If the object, however, through its opposition, settles me within the fragile texture of a desire for meaning, which, as a matter of fact, makes me ceaselessly and infinitely homologous to it, what is *abject*, on the contrary, the jettisoned object, is radically excluded and draws me toward the place where meaning collapses.[21]

Seeing herself as she is reflected in John's games, Elizabeth sees her relationship with him rendered meaningless. Terrified, she experiences abjection and is over-whelmed with the desire to rid herself of its power over her and of her revulsion toward it.

Having experienced the 42nd Street sex show, Elizabeth next finds herself horri-fied and alone standing in the midst of a crowd at her art gallery. The familiar sur-roundings have become menacing. She notices that the painter, Farnsworth, is looking at her. Farnsworth, however, is not like John. His gaze is not self-referen-tial. He does not see himself in Elizabeth but sees Elizabeth's terror. Seeing herself beyond John's controlling gaze, she is empowered. Overcome with revulsion, she vomits, and her self-loathing is transformed into resolution. Having allowed John to speak for her, having descended into depths of abjection, she recovers her desire to live beyond John's gaze. Discovering that her relationship with John was devoid of virtue, she is free. Walking out of his apartment for the last time, Elizabeth ends the relationship in his space but in her own voice. John's eleventh-hour effort to redeem himself by beginning to disclose his own history comes too late to save him or to save their relationship.

Cultural and psychic displacement is encoded in the visual language that sus-tains the narrative. Displacement, rupture, and alienation become the visual met-aphors for a culture whose moral and social order is changing. From the opening shots to the closing credits, Lyne places elegantly framed images alongside one an-other as though he were showing slides. These discrete, marginally connected, self-enclosed images forefront the ruptures and discontinuities within the narra-tive.

The experience of Elizabeth's relationship with John is constituted as a series of ruptures or tears in the fabric of her existence and in her self-understanding. John's claim on her, his desire to control and possess her, is enacted through breaking the bonds that connect Elizabeth to the people and situations that center her life. The visual discontinuity Lyne creates by presenting images as though they were part of a slide show sustains the alienation disclosed in the narrative itself. John's control and manipulation of Elizabeth are facilitated, in part, through his refusal to take an interest in her past and her willingness to distance herself from her own history. Their relationship exists in a vacuum: disconnected from a wider sphere of influence. The commonplace, the familiar, the ordinary are excluded. When the past is recalled, it relates to experiences of violence and death. Early in their relationship, for instance, as he is feeding her linguini, John tells Elizabeth about the history of this "family" restaurant, a history that includes murder. Similarly, Elizabeth tells John about her uncle who died watching football on one of his twenty-seven television sets.

The ruptures that are a constitutive part of the fabric of the narrative are sustained visually by Lyne's use of abrupt scene changes. He denies the spectator the comfort that results from anticipating the next logical step in the unfolding of the narrative. The spectator sees the world as unstable and undependable. Wondering what will happen next, the spectator becomes more and more aware that continuity is an illusion. Anything can happen. Expect the unexpected. Elizabeth's relationship with John unfolds in a series of unanticipated and unexpected events that change the way she sees herself and her world. Having discovered through their relationship a level of sensuality she had not previously experienced, Elizabeth engages in autoeroticism while watching slides of artworks that flash before her eyes in ever more rapid succession. The spectator watches Elizabeth watching disconnected images of artworks projecting a multiplicity of sensual images. This scene gives the appearance of being a soft-porn peep show for the sophisticated voyeur. Lyne creates the condition wherein Elizabeth and the spectator are complicitous participants.

The sense of displacement and isolation is also sustained through Lyne's use of black and white, particularly in relation to John's world. Everything that pertains to John and to his attempts to re-create Elizabeth in his image is black and white. Snooping through closets and drawers in his apartment, Elizabeth discovers that everything about him—from his clothing, furnishings, and aesthetic sensibility to a picture of a former lover—is black and white. This positive/negative polarity is self-negating, since white is the presence of color and black is the absence of all color. Lyne's visual language is a commentary on seeing the world in monochrome. If the world is perceived in black and white, it becomes null and void. The emptiness of this world is represented by the many scenes between John and Elizabeth that are either backlit or take place at night. Their shadowy figures appear as insubstantial silhouettes against the horizon, rehearsing the tenuousness of their relationship.

Lyne's control over color is as striking as the significance of color in his visual vocabulary. The predominantly black-and-white images, with their muted shades of gray, are occasionally invaded by red. Elizabeth wears a red sweater at the art gallery during the early stages of her relationship with John. John sends Elizabeth red roses, feeds her red tomatoes and strawberries. Red appears on some of the canvases hung at the gallery. Lyne's use of red heightens the contrast between passion and self-referential eroticism. Lyne appears to ask whether there is a difference between love and obsession.

Through color, Lyne recalls the past that is part of either an individual or a collective historical memory. Elizabeth admires an exquisitely colored, old French shawl at a Soho flea market. Colorful balloons, reminiscent of the innocence of childhood, accompany Elizabeth when John suggests she take a ride on the ferris wheel. Perhaps the most dramatic immersion in color comes when Lyne shifts the visual space from the abstract geometry of a postmodern, monochromatic art world to the chromatic density of impressionism. The scene takes place when Elizabeth visits the painter, Farnsworth, at his home in the country. The richness of the painterly impressionistic palette recollects the historical roots of contemporary art. In this sequence, Elizabeth experiences doubts about her relationship with John. She looks to Farnsworth as she tries to find her footing on more solid, if somewhat nostalgic, ground.

Lyne does not offer solace in a nostalgia for the past. The chromatic world, he reminds the spectator, is no more substantial than the world in black and white. The world of childhood innocence imaged in colorful balloons is also the world of childish pranks and schemes. The ride Elizabeth takes on the ferris wheel holding on to the balloons turns into a terrifying experience, because John pays the attendant to leave her perched at the top. John buys her the antique French shawl she admires. Affirming the ambiguity implicit in their relationship, he says "don't say I didn't warn you!" as he wraps the shawl around her shoulders. Similarly, the impressionistic images of Farnsworth's idyllic painterly world include dead fish as well as luxuriant gardens. Not even Farnsworth's attempt to keep the world at bay by taking the phone off the hook fails to protect him from change and the inevitability of death.

The visual games of sensory deprivation Lyne plays with the spectator are consistent with the narrative's concern with power and control. The moral implications of Lyne's visual language, whether in color or black and white, are brought out in the narrative strategies that unfold the relationship between Elizabeth and John. *Nine and a Half Weeks* is about deprivation in its multiple manifestations, not least of which is John's attempt to deprive Elizabeth of her own voice. It is significant that John blindfolds Elizabeth during two of their erotic encounters and asks her to keep her eyes closed during the third. However, it is not as simple as black and white; it is not enough to say that John is evil and Elizabeth is good. Lyne tries to avoid a reductive binary representation of complex issues. Moral judgments may be unavoidable, but they are more instructive when they are based on a view of reality that credits its multifarious and complex nature.

Lyne's attentiveness to the ambiguity of experience and to the cultural construction of sexual difference helps explain his complex representation of women. He recognizes that women are culturally predisposed to be compliant, submissive, and sexually repressed. However, he also recognizes that women retain the will to recover their autonomous voice. He represents Elizabeth as more than a victim of a cultural construction of the idea of woman or the vicissitudes of contemporary culture or of John's manipulations. Elizabeth is presented as a divorced woman who in the past has taken responsibility for her life and has made choices. She may be predisposed toward being compliant, but she is not defeated. Her relationship with John is complex. She is as attracted to John as she is frightened of him. Although she says he has hypnotized her, she agrees to be the willing subject of his hypnotic power. In choosing to say yes, she becomes complicitous in John's manipulative behavior. She is both active and reactive, rebellious and compliant. Her attraction to John brings her pleasure, although she recognizes its potentially destructive nature. Lyne does not represent Elizabeth as merely spoken for; rather, she is seen as both spoken for and speaking.

The issue Lyne tackles in his portrayal of Elizabeth is the representation of woman as victim who, nevertheless, is in the process of reclaiming an autonomous voice. By rejecting the woman as victim–man as victimizer dichotomy, Lyne can be seen as supportive of the view of a number of feminists who emphasize the dangers of polarization. In her assessment of Woolf and Kristeva, feminist theorist Toril Moi argues that for each of them, "the goal of the feminist struggle must precisely be to deconstruct the death-dealing binary oppositions of masculinity and femininity."[22] It is useful to recall Kristeva's analysis of the stages of the feminist movement, which she describes in "Women's Time."[23] She notes that the feminist movement went from being a demand for equal access to the symbolic order to a rejection of the male symbolic order to its present rejection of the dichotomy of masculine/feminine as residual metaphysics. It is this present tendency to reject the binary opposition of masculine/feminine that is reflected in more complex characterizations of women in films such as *Nine and a Half Weeks*.

12

Conclusion:
Religion, Film, and Cultural Analysis

CONRAD E. OSTWALT JR.

Believing, with Max Weber, that man is an animal suspended in webs of significance he himself has spun, I take culture to be those webs, and the analysis of it to be therefore not an experimental science in search of law but an interpretive one in search of meaning.

— Clifford Geertz[1]

[The origins of culture are contained in] the moment when language, music, painting, dance, story-telling, ritual, moral regulation, religion, and social organization were undifferentiated and indissoluble. The compact of culture was society, the fusion of all practices into an unself-conscious whole. Society existed not only by art, religion, ritual, language; society existed in these forms of life.

— James W. Carey[2]

The introduction to this volume addresses questions of *why*—Why is a book on religion and film needed? Why is the material in this book organized in a certain way? Why is this investigation limited to certain films and methodologies? Throughout the heart of the book, the various authors deal with "what" questions—What is the cultural context of this investigation? What is it about any particular film that makes it a likely candidate for scrutiny in a book about religion and motion pictures? Now, at the end of this investigation, we must ask questions involving *how*—How does one carry forth a study of religion and film? How does one relate the two in scholarly inquiry and in cultural studies? How do religion and film interact in the broader context of culture? It may seem that the *how* questions should have come earlier. After all, we generally want to know how to do something before embarking on a job or how to get where we are going before leaving on a journey. Nevertheless, in our experience, the *how* questions can be dealt with only after considerable investigation of the more substantive issues. In this spirit, we conclude this study by placing it within the general context of cultural studies. Thus, this book attempts to influence *how* readers view films, *how* they understand the relation of religion and culture, and *how* they perceive the power of religion in society.

How do we justify combining religion and film as components of this study? This work takes the two quotations that opened this chapter seriously: Religion and film constitute two, but certainly not all, of those forms of life that define society and thereby constitute valid sources of investigation for the search for meaning in culture. Religion is "a descriptive category that names the process of creating meaning" and discovering value systems.[3] Religion describes the process of human beings "living and responding to the world."[4] This study demonstrates that films also participate in the process of creating and searching for order. Thus, these two cultural forms, religion and film, at times participate in the same activity and aid in discovering human understanding. How can religious studies students become involved in this interpretive analysis? They can couch the investigation in cultural forms that are engaging and relevant to them. This book attempts to do this by investigating popular films—the films college students are likely to view and know.

This study also takes popular films as its subject matter for a reason beyond the obvious appeal to students. Based on a belief that Americans encounter religion constantly through popular culture that confronts them daily, this study assumes a shift in the types of cultural forms that significantly impact society. Whereas in the nineteenth century popular novels and presses held the imagination of the American public, it seems that for contemporary Americans images are replacing texts in the ability to capture the imagination and to shape worldviews. Video images, movies, MTV-like programming, television in general, video games, interactive computer technology, virtual reality, and other visually stimulating technologies have captured the popular, intellectual, and religious imagination of Americans as books no longer do. Perhaps this is a comment on the postmodern context of our age: Visual images are replacing written texts as the conveyors of information and meaning.

In addition to offering a theory of culture that locates crucial existential meaning in popular modes of cultural expression, specifically in particular visual modes of cultural expression, this study does not isolate these modes of popular expression. Rather, it bases them in a theory of culture that is holistic and interrelated. Clifford Geertz described culture as "webs of significance ... spun" by human beings.[5] The webs are an intricate maze of interrelated cultural structures that work together to provide coherence and strength to the overall cultural framework. Each individual strand is somehow related to every other strand. The task of those who study human cultures—the ethnographers, literary critics, philosophers, theologians, and film analysts—is to unravel these webs so meaning can be gleaned from them. But the interpretive task is not one that can take place in isolation. The cultural critic must be sensitive to as many areas of cultural significance as possible, since religion, literature, film, art, media, and other areas are interdependent and partial expressions of a larger-order reality. To understand this reality critically requires an interdisciplinary effort that crosses the artificial lines of distinction that disciplines have drawn around themselves.

The paradigms and typologies employed throughout this study derive from critical methods appropriate to the academic study of religion, but the use of these methodologies is based upon a larger, broader concept of culture that views film itself as part of a cultural matrix, similarly inhabited by religion and other cultural forms. Yet this work is not primarily concerned with method and critical approaches to the study of film but, rather, with the way religion and film as cultural forms both shape and are shaped by society—with *how* cultural forms interact. Thus, when this work refers to theological criticism, it does not posit a critical methodology as such but, rather, a working, interpretive standard that focuses on *how* a dialogue among traditional, historical, and culture-bound religious themes and the secular medium of film takes place. When the topic is mythological criticism, the goal is to describe *how* universal myths are reappropriated for modern, secular audiences rather than to promote a methodological standard based upon myth criticism. Finally, when authors employ ideological criticism, they are looking at *how* films interact with societal and political issues rather than suggesting a methodological procedure that begins with and asserts a particular ideological framework or agenda. So our tripartite division into theological, mythological, and ideological criticism is not normative but, rather, is functional and descriptive. And when this study hints at a new criticism, it does not suggest methodological procedures that rely upon a narrow or constrained agenda but suggests one broad enough to deal with the interconnectedness of a complex cultural matrix—one that draws on strengths from film criticism, religious studies, and cultural studies in general.

This approach describes a phenomenological method for the study of religion and culture—an approach that invites participation by the cultural investigator and that seeks understanding through entering an "other" world empathetically.[6] The phenomenological approach assumes that "religion is a profoundly human activity" and that through "our shared humanity" we can begin to see and understand reality through the eyes and experiences of others "by lively use of the imagination."[7] The present work extends this approach and assumption beyond religion to other cultural forms in the attempt to understand human cultures through shared humanity. Film is particularly well suited for this religious function in that it invites the viewer to experience reality from an "other" perspective through an imaginative leap.

And why not? After all, the film industry is only one of many secular institutions that in contemporary U.S. life have challenged or begun to replace religious institutions in the scramble for societal attention and participation. In fact, it might even be argued that the movie theater has acted like some secular religion, complete with its sacred space and rituals that mediate an experience of otherness.

Consider the following Saturday evening ritual. People file into a movie theater at a specified time, choose a seat, and, with others gathered with them, prepare for the experience of cinema. There are rituals to be observed, behaviors that are deemed appropriate and expected, rules that govern the auditorium and the activities that occur there. Soon the moviegoers' attention is transfixed to the giant screen as the senses are filled by sights, sounds, and sensations, which are shared in part by the community of moviegoers in the auditorium. For an appointed time the crowd remains rooted and participates in the event of cinema, sometimes passively and sometimes with physical and emotional response. What happens when I am part of this community? We watch a movie, but we do more than that—we participate in a cultural and social phenomenon. To the extent that this event allows us to transcend mundane life for a prescribed period of time, we are part of a sacred space, a sacred time, and, transfixed by the experience, we are confronted by an alternative reality, a "not me," an otherness.

Film represents a particularly effective medium for providing this experience of otherness. For example, a close examination of the films included in this volume demonstrates that for all the differences in film types and methodological approaches, all of the films are characterized by excess. Indeed, a good portion of all popular U.S. films deal with situations of excess—murder, violence, comedy, perversity, apocalypse, encounter with the alien, war, cosmic battles, gender difference, sexuality, and similar issues. Perhaps this is crucial to establishing cultural myths and cultural connection with otherness. By focusing on the alien, the extraordinary, the extreme, these films articulate images of otherness, and thus of sacrality, by pushing experience beyond the known, familiar, and acceptable.

Film also provides a sense of otherness, as Janice Rushing argues, because the movie experience resembles the dream state and mythmaking: "We experience [films] in darkened conditions that are a respite from the everyday world; they have the plasticity and visual form of the dream; they are 'larger than life' myths. ... Films are to the cultural unconscious what dreams are to the personal unconscious. That is, films tell us truths about culture that we would often rather not see; they are compensatory to what we hide from view. ... Films are a blend of the archetypal and the ideological."[8] If this is true, films are one of the most effective cultural vehicles for expressing beliefs and values, for they operate at once on the mythic and the ideological levels, both affecting consumers unconsciously and consciously promoting or reflecting a particular value system. Matthew Fox argues that "culture needs myth to sustain itself" even in a secular age and that this myth harbors power over behavior and belief.[9]

The fundamental contention of our theory of religion and culture is that such experiences in popular culture that experiment with, reinforce, or alter reality perceptions can perform religious functions in U.S. society and that film, as a cultural standard-bearer, can communicate a society's major myths, rituals, and symbols. Of course, this quality of film is not limited to movies but can be extended to any secular institution. For example, when Michael Novak suggests that "sports is, somehow, a religion" in the United States[10] he receives no shortage of criticism from those who interpret cultural forms apart from their relations to other aspects of culture. Yet Novak's analysis strikes a chord with anyone trying to understand religiosity in a secular society. Some cultural elements, such as sports or movies, carry on some of the same functions as religion. That is, they participate in activities that provide "being, beauty, truth, excellence, transcendence ... a ritual elaborating some music of the human spirit."[11]

So all of this suggests that in this study we are not so much concerned with the critical viewpoint and how it is applied by individual scholars as we are with what happens or might happen when one watches a film and what consequences these happenings might hold for society. The movie industry constitutes a popular medium and an important one to modern life; film, therefore, has the ability and potential to do more than simply entertain. Film and other cultural forms have the potential to mirror, reinforce, challenge, create, overturn, or crystallize beliefs and fears. The bottom line is that a film can become, and sometimes does become, an important vehicle or critic of society's values and accepted truths, and popular films most assuredly reflect or otherwise interact with the "social and moral values" of the predominant culture.[12] In addition, popular films not only express values and identities but can also create them. As Catherine Albanese has stated, films and other popular media express or reinforce "powerful beliefs about life [and] provide a web of fundamental beliefs for Americans."[13] In fact, Albanese goes on to say that films might act like sacred religious stories because they establish "a world that makes sense and give people a feeling for their place in the scheme of things," and they introduce "what the world means and how it means."[14]

Thus, through the process of reflecting and creating values, films are meaning-laden, and when we look at films such as *JFK,* it is easy to see how. Not only does *JFK* tap into deep-seated fears and suspicions of the American public, it tends to undercut certain perceptions of reality and to posit a competing mythology about a historical event that has helped to define U.S. consciousness during the past several decades. By questioning the Warren Commission's version of events surrounding the assassination of President John F. Kennedy, *JFK* bolsters the legitimacy of conspiracy theories and questions the validity of the official explanation. In this way, *JFK* and other films accomplish the task of deconstructing and constructing American mythologies. For other examples, Peter Williams points out that motion pictures have been important in giving minority communities "respectability and acceptability in the minds of the general public."[15] Following Williams's suggestion, one could view a film such as *Dances with Wolves* in terms of its ambiguous presentation of Native Americans. The film might critique Western materialism through its presentation of Native American spirituality and nobility.[16] Conversely, others have chastised the film for racist stereotyping through "the celluloid residuals of Manifest Destiny."[17] Does *Dances with Wolves* reflect racist views, or does it create a new way of looking at Native Americans, or does it do both? In part, the response to this question depends upon the one who provides the answer.

Since this study assumes a theory of culture that is dynamic, interactive, and interdependent, it is obviously concerned with the impact of dialogue between cultural forms. This impact not only applies to society on a large scale, however, but also affects individual beliefs and attitudes. Therefore, a dominant concern is to begin to glimpse the potential film carries for communicating, reflecting, or changing individual, as well as collective, beliefs and values. In other words, the concern lies with what happens to the moviegoer, or, more appropriately, with what might happen. Let us return for a moment to Jack, the college classmate introduced at the beginning of this book. When Jack watched the movie *Rocky*, he was not merely entertained for a couple of hours. The event changed his life for a significant period of time—he participated in no less than a conversion experience. And without suggesting that every movie could have this effect on every moviegoer, we can assume that a good portion of the millions of people who watch movies are affected or changed in some way and that films can exert influence on attitudes, beliefs, and behaviors.

This is the reason this book is necessary and these chapters are important—this study initiates the exploration of the richness of the interrelationships between popular films and our beliefs and values. The authors assume that religion is an important part of our world and that films are powerful vehicles for communicating religious meanings, stories, and values to millions of people. In doing so, they teach us to recognize the presence of religion in our contemporary culture and demonstrate that the investment of religious longings, values, and engagement in the public sphere is alive and well. This knowledge should change the way we think about religion as well as about film—movies can no longer be viewed as simply secular entertainment, and religion can no longer be viewed as an antiquated or a peripheral institution in a dominantly secular society.

This view of the relationship among religion, film, and other cultural forms leads to a few observations about theories of secularization and religion. Twentieth-century Americans live in an awkward age. Secularists would have us believe that the enlightenment freed Western society from the shackles of religion, yet the centuries since the enlightenment have not destroyed the vigor and importance of religious traditions. In fact, many commentators on U.S. religion point to the vitality and variety of religion in a secular U.S. society.[18] Our society is defined by paradox. We are uncomfortable with religion, yet we are faced with it at every turn. It is not the case that religion is fading with the secularization of society; rather, religion is being popularized, scattered, and secularized through extra-ecclesiastical institutions. We find ourselves in a contradictory age in which secularity and religious images coexist.

As used here, the term *secularization* does not imply that the world is being rationalized so that religion must disappear and capitulate to science and empiricism. Rather, although some traditional religious institutions are losing power, religion is finding new life embedded more discreetly in cultural forms. Secularization, then, actually encourages a return of religion to ordinary life, leaving religion more powerful, diffused, and omnipresent. We might even view the age of secularization as the age of religious saturation. This paradox leads to interaction and dialogue between cultural forms and investigations such as this one that cross disciplinary and formalistic lines.

The present work does not try to suggest that the cinema has replaced the sanctuary nor that the screen has superseded the pulpit. Neither does it posit a reductionist theory of religion in which every element of society suddenly takes on a religious aura—where anything and everything can be religious. Nevertheless, these chapters do suggest that the power of film can allow movie theaters to become sanctuaries and the screen a pulpit, complete with their own rituals, sacred spaces, and heroes that influence a secular society. As the secularization process continues, many "secular" institutions and activities are taking on the functions formerly reserved for institutionalized religious ritual—namely, self-transcendence and self-actualization.

This theory of religious secularity holds that secular institutions can allow a fully authentic ontological and religious stance toward the world because they can provide an avenue for human development and wholeness. The secular worldview allows us to locate ultimate worth within the world and within human beings rather than in an otherworldly promise or deity. This worldview allows us to gain a greater appreciation for the natural environment and to place greater emphasis on human worth and interpersonal relationships.[19] Without placing a value judgment on this secular religiosity, we would like to assume that it exists and that secular cultural institutions, such as the film industry, participate in its operation.[20]

Many of the self-authenticating experiences secular institutions encourage are rooted in a society's popular culture. Why do people go to movies, watch sporting events, read novels, or turn to "extra-ecclesiastical (or, loosely, 'popular') religion?"[21] They participate in such activities because these and other forms of popular culture function in the same way traditional religion has always functioned: to provide ways for one to make sense of one's world and life.[22] And it is these types of popular activities that allow individuals to participate in that which provides meaning. In other words, popular religion and cultural events allow individuals to participate in their own reality construction.[23] This view of culture is a functional one, is becoming increasingly accepted in the academic world, and provides a valid basis for a serious study of popular cultural forms in general.

Popular culture provides the context for understanding the values, belief systems, religious imaginations, and myths of a particular people at a particular time. Popular culture is not only existentially crucial because, as Ralph Waldo Emerson suggested, "the popular mind supplies" the material for writers and artists but also because there is value in popular art itself.[24] Here we reject the elitism and egoism that view only classic writings and works of art as exhibiting intellectual value. Rather, in addition to the value a study of the classics offers (be it a film, literary, religious, or other study), an investigation of popular expressions of art and religion is integral to understanding the culture that produced them. As a result, if we are to attempt to understand the contemporary United States, we must study the books Americans are reading, the films they are paying to see, and the religious expressions that have found their ways into twentieth-century pews.

The task here, then, is to reflect upon the relatedness of popular film and religious expression in contemporary U.S. society. The question is not so much how are films religious, or what religious themes crop up in popular films, or how do films inform or support religious beliefs and vice-versa. Rather, the more appropriate question is, how are films and religious imagination related, and how does this relationship help us to understand contemporary society, cultural values, and individual beliefs. With this in mind, and through these reflections on theology, mythology, and ideology in popular U.S. film, this study challenges readers to seek responses to that spiritually, existentially, ideologically crucial question in the films they watch.

*   *   *

Screening the Sacred presents three different approaches to viewing the relationship among films, the religious imagination, and contemporary society. These three approaches, in turn, give rise to three methodologies for studying the relationship between religion and film: theological criticism, mythological criticism, and ideological criticism. The goal is to demonstrate that there are different ways of defining religion, different ways of viewing the relationship between religion and film, and, thus, different ways of approaching the study of religion and culture. These three methods are not definitive categories but are challenges to dialogue that will lead to more inclusive understandings of cultural forms within societal systems. From this point, the student of religion and film is limited only by the constraints of imagination. And when students allow their imaginations to navigate these cultural forms, they will learn that the age of secularization is also the era that witnesses the broad proliferation of religious attitudes throughout the cultural spectrum. It is through popular culture that we learn the values, symbols, and beliefs that inform both religion and society. And it is through immersion in those forms that we incorporate or redefine those values, symbols, and beliefs that define society.

Notes and References

NOTES FOR PREFACE

1. Peter W. Williams, *Popular Religion in America: Symbolic Change and the Moderniza-tion Process in Historical Perspective* (Englewood Cliffs, N.J.: Prentice-Hall, 1980), p. 12, "the idea of sacred time," p. 202.

NOTES FOR CHAPTER 1

1. Of the few books that notice religion, several are focused less on religion itself than on issues tied to ethnicity and cultural stereotypes. See Patricia Erens, *The Jew in American Cinema* (Bloomington: Indiana University Press, 1984); Lester Friedman, *The Jewish Image in American Film* (Secaucus, N.J.: Citadel Press, 1987); Lester J. Keyser and Barbara Keyser, *Hollywood and the Catholic Church: The Image of Roman Catholicism in American Movies* (Chicago: Loyola University Press, 1984). Theologically oriented studies include John C. Cooper and Carl Skrade, eds., *Celluloid and Symbols* (Philadelphia: Fortress Press, 1970); James M. Wall, *Church and Cinema: A Way of Viewing Film* (Grand Rapids: William B. Eerdman's Publishing Company, 1971); Neil P. Hurley, *Theology Through Film* (New York: Harper and Row, 1970); Ernest Ferlita and John May, *Film Odyssey: The Art of Film as Search for Meaning* (New York: Paulist Press, 1976); Thomas M. Martin, *Images and Imageless: A Study in Religious Consciousness and Film* (Lewisburg, Pa.: Bucknell University Press, 1981); John R. May and Michael Bird, eds., *Religion in Film* (Knoxville: University of Tennessee, 1982). Most of these works focus on European films. An exception is John R. May, ed., *Images and Likeness: Religious Visions in American Film Classics* (Mahwah, N.J.: Paulist Press, 1991).

2. Bryan Wilson, "Reflections on a Many Sided Cotroversy," in *Religion and Moderniza-tion: Sociologists and Historians Debate the Secularization Thesis*, ed. Steve Bruce (Oxford: Oxford University Press, 1993), p. 210.

3. Robert Stam, Robert Burgoyne, and Sandy Flitterman-Lewis, *New Vocabularies in Film Semiotics: Structuralism, Post-structuralism and Beyond* (New York: Routledge, 1992).

4. Ibid., p. ii.

5. Bruce B. Lawrence, *Defenders of God: The Fundamentalist Revolt Against the Modern Age* (New York: Harper and Row, 1989).

6. Karl Marx and Friedrich Engels, *On Religion* (New York: Schocken Books, 1964); Sigmund Freud, *The Future of an Illusion* (New York: Norton, 1961); Julia Kristeva, *Powers of Horror: An Essay* (New York: Columbia University Press, 1982); Harold Coward and Toby Foshay, eds., *Derrida and Negative Theology* (Albany: State University of New York Press, 1992).

7. Louis Althusser, *For Marx* (New York: Vintage Books, 1970), p. 231.

8. Stam, Burgoyne, and Flitterman-Lewis, *New Vocabularies in Film Semiotics*, pp. 21–22.

9. Deborah Knight, "Reconsidering Film Theory and Method," *New Literary History* 24 (1993): 326–327.

10. Joseph Cunneen, "Film and the Sacred," *Cross Currents* (Spring 1993): 93.

11. Gregory Evans Dowd, *A Spirited Resistance: The North American Struggle for Unity, 1745–1815* (Baltimore: Johns Hopkins University Press, 1992), p. 14.

12. Daniel L. Pals, "Is Religion a Sui Generis Phenomenon?" *Journal of the American Academy of Religion* 2 (1987): 278.

13. The discussion of the basic forms of religion is drawn from William E. Paden, *Religious Worlds: The Comparative Study of Religion* (Boston: Beacon Press, 1988).

14. Eric Sharpe, *Comparative Religion: A History* (LaSalle, Ill.: Open Court, 1986); Jacque Waardenburg, *Classical Approaches to the Study of Religion*, vol. 1 (The Hague: Mouton, 1973); Frank Whaling, ed., *Contemporary Approaches to the Study of Religion*, 2 vols. (Berlin: Mouton, 1984, 1985); Jan de Vries, *Perspectives in the History of Religions*, trans. Kees W. Bolle (Berkeley: University of California Press, 1967).

15. Paden, *Religious Worlds*, pp. 15–33.

16. Catherine Albanese, *America: Religions and Religion* (Belmont, Calif.: Wadsworth, 1992), p. xxii.

17. Cunneen, "Film and the Sacred," p. 95.

18. Mircea Eliade, *The Sacred and the Profane: The Nature of Religion*, trans. William R. Trask (New York: Harcourt Brace Jovanovich, 1959), p. 205.

19. Quoted in Robert A. Segal, *Joseph Campbell: An Introduction* (New York: Penguin, 1990), p. 32; see also pp. 22, 269.

20. Campbell has been charged with anti-Semitism (ibid., p. 24); Eliade has been accused of being complicit with fascism. For criticisms of Jung and a defense of his theory, see Janice Hocker Rushing and Thomas S. Frentz, "Integrating Ideology and Archetype in Rhetorical Criticism," *Quarterly Journal of Speech* 77 (1991): 389.

21. Michael Ryan and Douglas Kellner, *Camera Politica: The Politics and Ideology of Contemporary Hollywood Film* (Bloomington: Indiana University Press, 1988), pp. 54, 55, 59, 65, 134.

22. Ibid., pp. 112–119.

23. C. G. Jung and Carl Kerenyi, *Essays on a Science of Mythology*, trans. R.F.C. Hull (New York: Pantheon/Bollingen Series 22, 1949), p. 146.

NOTES FOR PART 1

1. Melvyn Bragg, *The Seventh Seal* (London: British Film Institute, 1993), pp. 10–11.

2. Quoted in ibid., p. 10.

3. Fredric Jameson, *The Political Unconscious: Narrative as a Socially Symbolic Act* (Ithaca, N.Y.: Cornell University Press, 1981), pp. 29–30.

4. See Frank Kermode, *The Sense of an Ending: Studies in the Theory of Fiction* (London: Oxford University Press, 1967); Robert Scholes and Robert Kellogg, *The Nature of Narrative* (New York: Oxford University Press, 1966); and Wesley Kort, *Narrative Elements and Religious Meaning* (Philadelphia: Fortress Press, 1975).

5. Kort, *Narrative Elements and Religious Meaning*, pp. 20–21.

6. Ibid., p. 40.

7. Ibid., p. 59.

8. Ibid., pp. 86–87.

9. Mary Pat Kelly, *Martin Scorsese: A Journey* (New York: Thunder's Mouth Press, 1991), p. 71.

NOTES FOR CHAPTER 2

1. François Truffaut, *Hitchcock/Truffaut* (New York: Simon and Schuster, 1983), p. 269. All future references to the Truffaut interview are to this, the revised edition.

2. Ibid., p. 32.

3. See especially chapters on *Psycho* reprinted in Marshall Deutelbaum and Leland Poague, eds., *A Hitchcock Reader* (Ames: Iowa State University Press, 1986). It should also be noted that in Robin Wood's *Hitchcock's Films Revisited* (New York: Columbia University Press, 1989), he says "*Psycho* is much nearer being a masterpiece (the first half, up to the point where Marion's car sinks into the swamp, is certainly among the most extraordinary achievements in American cinema)," p. 219. Thomas M. Leitch, in *Find the Director and Other Hitchcock Games* (Athens: University of Georgia Press, 1991), treats *Psycho* as if the Marion/Norman part were the entire film, pp. 215–221.

4. J. Hillis Miller, *Fiction and Repetition* (Cambridge: Harvard University Press, 1982), p. 155.

5. Donald Spoto, *The Dark Side of Genius: The Life of Alfred Hitchcock* (Boston: Little, Brown, 1983), pp. 426–427.

6. Deutelbaum and Poague, *A Hitchcock Reader*, pp. 343–344.

7. Athanasius, "On the Incarnation," in *Christology of the Later Fathers*, ed. Edward R. Hardy, Library of Christian Classics, Vol. 3 (Philadelphia: Westminster Press, 1954), p. 60.

8. Anselm of Canterbury, "Why God Became Man," in *A Scholastic Miscellany*, ed. Eugene R. Fairweather, Library of Christian Classics, Vol. 10 (Philadelphia: Westminster Press, 1956), pp. 136–137.

9. Ibid., p. 176.

10. Truffaut, *Hitchcock/Truffaut*, pp. 43–44.

11. William Rothman, *Hitchcock: The Murderous Gaze* (Cambridge: Harvard University Press, 1982), p. 341.

REFERENCES FOR CHAPTER 3

Calvino, Italo. 1986. *The Uses of Literature*. Trans. Patrick Creagh. New York: Harcourt Brace Jovanovich.

Dante, Alighieri. 1983. *Purgatorio*. Trans. Allen Mandelbaum. New York: Bantam Books.

"Dialogue on Film." 1986. *American Film* 2 (April): 13–15.

Dimmock, G. E., Jr. 1956. "The Name of Odysseus." *Hudson Review* 9 (Spring): 52–70.

Edinger, Claudio. 1988. *The Making of Ironweed*. New York: Penguin Books.

Gibbs, Robert. 1986. "The Life of the Soul: William Kennedy, Magical Realist." Dissertation, Lehigh University.

Ironweed. 1987. Dir. Hector Babenco. Taft Entertainment.

Kennedy, William. 1984. *Ironweed*. New York: Penguin Books.

———. 1987. "Be Reasonable—Unless You're a Writer." *New York Times Book Review*, January 25, pp. 3–4.

———. 1988. "Ironweed." *American Film* 4 (January–February): 19–25.

REFERENCES FOR CHAPTER 4

Auster, Albert, and Leonard Quart. 1988. *How the War Was Remembered: Hollywood and Vietnam*. New York: Praeger.

Cimino, Michael. 1977. *The Deer Hunter* [screenplay] (5th and final draft). Los Angeles: [property of] EMI Films, Inc., June 7.

Combs, Richard. 1987. "Beating God to the Draw: Salvador and *Platoon*." *Sight & Sound* 56, 2: 136–138.

Hellman, John. 1986. *American Myth and the Legacy of Vietnam*. New York: Columbia University Press.

Herr, Michael, Stanley Kubrick, and Gustav Hasford. 1987. *Full Metal Jacket* [screenplay]. New York: Knopf.

The Holy Bible. n.d. Authorized, or King James, Version. Philadelphia: John C. Winston.

Kael, Pauline. 1987. "The Current Cinema." *New Yorker* 62 (January 12): 94–96.

McGilligan, Pat. 1987. "Point Man: Oliver Stone Interviewed." *Film Comment* 23 (February): 11.

O'Brien, Tom. 1987. "Reel Politics: Miss Mary, Weeping, and *Platoon*." *Commonweal* (January): 17.

Pfeiffer, Chuck. 1987. "Interview with Oliver Stone." *Interview* 17, 2 (February 7): 73.

Rosenstone, Robert A. 1988. "History in Images/History in Words: Reflections on the Possibility of Really Putting History onto Film." *American Historical Review* 93 (December): 1173–1185.

Stone, Oliver. 1986. *Platoon* [screenplay]. Platoon and Salvador. New York: Vintage, 1987.

White, Hayden. 1988. "Historiography and Historiophoty." *American Historical Review* 93 (December): 1193–1199.

NOTES FOR CHAPTER 5

1. For a good treatment of the characteristics of the Judeo-Christian apocalyptic imagination (upon which modern film bases its own apocalyptic themes), see John J. Collins, *The Apocalyptic Imagination: An Introduction to the Jewish Matrix of Christianity* (New York: Crossroad, 1987), pp. 7–31. See also Norman Cohn, *The Pursuit of the Millennium* (Oxford: Oxford University Press, 1980 [1957]).

2. Joel 2:29–31. This and other scriptural references are taken from the Revised Standard Version of the *Bible*.

3. See Louis Ginzberg, *The Legends of the Jews*, 6 vols. (Philadelphia: Jewish Publication Society of America, 1925, 1953), 5: p. 75; Rappoport, (1966), p. 20; Ephraim E. Urbach, *The Sages: The World and Wisdom of the Rabbis of the Talmud* (Cambridge: Harvard University Press, 1987), p. 237. See Yebamot 62a, 2 Enoch 58:5, Apocalypse of Baruch 23:5, 4 Ezra 4:35.

4. For this version of the Legend of the Wandering Jew, see Frederick William Hackwood, *Christ Lore: Being the Legends, Traditions, Myths, Symbols, Customs, and Superstitions of the Christian Church* (Milwaukee: Young Churchman Co., 1902), pp. 111–113.

5. See Kermode, (1967), p. 17; and Wesley A. Kort, *Modern Fiction and Human Time: A Study in Narrative and Belief* (Tampa: University of South Florida Press, 1985), pp. 3–4, 169.

6. See Robert Scholes and Robert Kellogg, *The Nature of Narrative* (New York: Oxford University Press, 1966), pp. 207–208.

7. See George Foot Moore, *Judaism in the First Centuries of the Christian Era: The Age of the Tannaim*, 3 vols. (Cambridge: Harvard University Press, 1958), 2: p. 338; H. L. Strack and P. Billerbeck, *Kommetar zum Neuen Testament aus Talmud und Midrasch*, 6 vols. (Munich: C. H. Beck, 1965), 3: pp. 842–847.

REFERENCES FOR CHAPTER 5

Cohn, Norman. 1980. *The Pursuit of the Millennium.* Oxford: Oxford University Press, reprint ed.

Collins, John J. 1987. *The Apocalyptic Imagination: An Introduction to the Jewish Matrix of Christianity.* New York: Crossroad.

Ginzberg, Louis. 1925, 1953. *The Legends of the Jews.* Philadelphia: Jewish Publication Society of America.

Greeley, Andrew. 1988. *God in Popular Culture.* Chicago: The Thomas More Press.

Hackwood, Frederick William. 1902. *Christ Lore: Being the Legends, Traditions, Myths, Symbols, Customs, and Superstitions of the Christian Church.* Milwaukee: Young Churchman Co.

Kermode, Frank. 1985. *The Sense of an Ending: Studies in the Theory of Fiction.* London: Oxford University Press, 1967.

Kort, Wesley A. 1985. *Modern Fiction and Human Time: A Study in Narrative and Belief.* Tampa: University of South Florida Press.

Moore, George Foot. 1958. *Judaism in the First Centuries of the Christian Era: The Age of the Tannaim.* 3 vols. Cambridge: Harvard University Press.

Rappoport, Angelo S. 1966. *Myth and Legend of Ancient Israel.* 3 vols. New York: Ktav Publishing House.

Scholes, Robert, and Robert Kellogg. 1966. *The Nature of Narrative.* New York: Oxford University Press.

Strack, H. L., and P. Billerbeck. 1965. *Kommetar zum Neuen Testament aus Talmud und Midrasch.* Munich: C. H. Beck.

Urbach, Ephraim E. 1987. *The Sages: The World and Wisdom of the Rabbis of the Talmud.* Cambridge: Harvard University Press.

Yeats, William Butler. 1957. "The Second Coming." In *The Variorum Edition of the Poems of W. B. Yeats.* Edited by Peter Allt and Russell K. Alspach. New York: Macmillan.

NOTES FOR PART 2

1. Geoffrey O'Brien, *The Phantom Empire* (New York: W. W. Norton 1993), p. 101.

2. Ibid., p. 109.

3. On the relationship of myth and religion, see William Paden, *Religious Worlds: The Comparative Study of Religion* (Boston: Beacon Press, 1988), pp. 69–92.

4. Bryan R. Wilson, "Reflections on a Many Sided Controversy," in *Religion and Modernization: Sociologists and Historians Debate the Secularization Thesis,* ed. Steve Bruce (Oxford: Clarendon Press, 1992), pp. 208–210.

5. Sallie McFague, *Theology for an Ecological, Nuclear Age* (Philadelphia: Fortress Press, 1987); Gordon D. Kaufman, *In the Face of Mystery: A Constructive Theology* (Cambridge: Harvard University Press, 1993). See also Marsha Witten, *All Is Forgiven: The Secular Message in American Protestantism* (Princeton: Princeton University Press, 1993).

6. Joseph Campbell, with Bill Moyers, *The Power of Myth* (New York: Doubleday, 1988), pp. 18, 129, 144–147.

7. See Richard Poirier, *A World Elsewhere: The Place of Style in American Literature* (London: Oxford University Press, 1966). See also Giles Gunn, *The Interpretation of Otherness: Literature, Religion, and the American Imagination* (New York: Oxford University Press, 1979).

8. Mircea Eliade, *The Sacred and the Profane: The Nature of Religion,* trans. Willard R. Trask (New York: Harcourt Brace and World, 1959), pp. 9–10, Chapter 1.

9. Mark Rose, *Alien Encounters: Anatomy of Science Fiction* (Cambridge: Harvard University Press, 1981), p. 45. Andrew Gordon called attention to this source and has influenced our thinking about science fiction.

10. Martin M. Winkler, "Classical Mythology and the Western Film," *Comparative Literature Studies* 22 (1985): 516–540; Leonard Engel, "Space and Enclosure in Cooper and Peckinpah: Regeneration in the Open Spaces," *Journal of American Culture* 14 (1991): 86–93; Jane Tompkins, "West of Everything," *South Atlantic Quarterly* 86 (1987): 357–377.

11. Linda Dittman and Gene Michaud, *From Hanoi to Hollywood: The Vietnam War in American Film* (Rutgers, N.J.: Rutgers University Press, 1990); John Hellman, *American Myth and the Legacy of Vietnam* (New York: Columbia University Press, 1986).

12. Ken Cartwright and Mary McElroy, "Malamud's 'The Natural' and the Appeal of Baseball in American Culture," *Journal of American Culture* 8 (Summer 1985): 47–55; Kevin Thomas Curtin, "*The Natural:* Our *Iliad* and *Odyssey,*" *Antioch Review* 43 (Spring 1985): 225–241.

13. Campbell, with Moyers, *The Power of Myth,* p. 3.

NOTES FOR CHAPTER 6

1. Richard Corliss, "A Cool Look at a Hot 'Star,'" *New Times,* June 24, 1977, p. 65.

2. Stanley Kauffmann, "Innocences," *New Republic,* June 18, 1977, p. 22.

3. Molly Haskell, *Village Voice,* June 13, 1977, p. 40.

4. See Robert M. Adams, "The Hobbit Habit," *New York Review of Books,* November 24, 1977, p. 24. Adams compares the appeal of *Star Wars* to that of Tolkien.

5. Interview with George Lucas printed in the *Star Wars* souvenir program (New York: S. W. Ventures, 1977).

6. Paul Scanlon, "The Force Behind George Lucas," interview with George Lucas, *Rolling Stone,* August 25, 1977, p. 43.

7. Ibid.

8. Stephen Zito, "George Lucas Goes Far Out," *American Film,* April 1977, p. 13.

9. *Star Wars* souvenir program.

10. Brian Aldiss, *Space Opera* (London: Futura, 1974), pp. 9, 15.

11. Ibid., p. 10.

12. Sam J. Lundwall, *Science Fiction: What It's All About* (New York: Ace, 1971), p. 102.

13. Ibid.

14. Ibid., p. 103.

15. Corliss, "A Cool Look," p. 65. We might also note that heroic epics traditionally begin in medias res.

16. "*Star Wars:* The Year's Best Movie," *Time,* May 30, 1977, p. 56.

17. Roger Copeland, "When Films 'Quote' Films, They Create a New Mythology," *New York Times,* Sunday, December 25, 1977, Section D, p. 1.

18. Scanlon, "The Force Behind George Lucas," p. 45.

19. Ibid., p. 43.

20. According to *Newsweek,* May 30, 1977, p. 61.

21. "*Star Wars:* The Year's Best Movie," p. 62.

22. Jack Kroll, "Fun in Space," *Newsweek,* May 30, 1977, p. 60.

23. Scanlon, "The Force Behind George Lucas," p. 47.

24. Copeland, "When Films 'Quote' Films," p. 1.

25. Zito, "George Lucas Goes Far Out," p. 12.

26. Ibid., p. 10.

27. Aldiss, *Space Opera*, p. 10.

28. Joseph Campbell, *Hero with a Thousand Faces* (New York: World, 1956), p. 17.

29. Ibid., pp. 17, 38.

30. Ibid., p. 51.

31. Ibid., pp. 72–73.

32. Otto Rank, *The Myth of the Birth of the Hero and Other Writings,* ed. Philip Freund (New York: Vintage, 1959), pp. 71, 79.

33. Campbell, *The Hero with a Thousand Faces,* p. 77.

34. Ibid., p. 90.

35. Ibid., p. 97.

36. Ibid., p. 101.

37. Ibid., pp. 102, 103.

38. Ibid., pp. 257–258.

39. Ibid., p. 182.

40. Ibid., p. 193.

41. Ibid., p. 196.

42. Ibid., p. 229.

43. Ibid., p. 352.

44. See also Copeland,"When Films 'Quote' Films," p. 24: "Modern artist, in a world which has largely repudiated mythology, found himself with no shared public foundation on which to build. The artists I'm discussing [Lucas is one] have begun to build on older works of art. Having lost a mythological tradition, they have created their own tradition."

45. See also Jesse Kornbluth, "The Gleaming of America," *New Times,* June 24, 1977, pp. 24–29. Kornbluth says that "thanks to *Star Wars,* I'm temporarily inclined to believe that technology isn't soulless."

46. Kroll, "Fun in Space," p. 60.

NOTES FOR CHAPTER 7

1. Science-fiction films did not suddenly appear in 1950. Some of the earliest moviemakers experimented with notions of space travel, as seen in *A Trip to the Moon* (Georges Melies 1902). Nor have the past forty years neglected space exploration and exploitation on the part of earthlings, beginning with what is widely considered the progenitor of modern, "sophisticated" space-travel movies, *Destination Moon* (Irving Pichel 1950). *Forbidden Planet* (Fred McLeod Wilcox 1956), *2001: A Space Odyssey* (Stanley Kubrick 1968), and the *Star Trek* epics of the 1970s (Robert Wise) and 1980s (Nicholas Meyer, Leonard Nimoy) are some other notables.

2. For an interesting, book-length analysis of this trend, see Nora Sayre, *Running Time: Films of the Cold War* (New York: Dial Press, 1982).

3. Vivan Sobchack, "Science Fiction," in *Handbook of American Film Genres,* ed. Wes D. Gehring (New York: Greenwood Press, 1988), p. 232.

4. Ibid., p. 235. Sobchack's *Screening Space: The American Science Fiction Film*, 2d enl. ed. (New York: Ungar, 1987) is an excellent introduction to and overview of the science-fiction film genre.

5. It can be argued that Klaatu, the "gnostic messenger" of *The Day the Earth Stood Still* (Robert Wise 1951), who bears a grave warning for earthlings, also looks human. His "normal" physical appearance and "beneficent" role are very unusual for a space alien of the early 1950s, going against the expectations of an evil, ugly invader. I will not include Klaatu in this analysis, because I do not consider him part of the recent trend discussed here.

6. As Mircea Eliade refers to manifestations of the holy. See especially *Patterns in Comparative Religion*, trans. Rosemary Sheed (New York: New American Library, 1958), pp. 1–4.

7. As described by Rudolf Otto. See *The Idea of the Holy* (London: Oxford University Press, 1950), especially Chapters 2–6, pp. 5–40.

8. Stuart M. Kaminsky, *American Film Genres*, 2d ed. (Chicago: Nelson-Hall, 1985), p. 3.

9. Ibid.

10. Here I am relying on Eliade's definition of myth as "'true story' and, beyond that, a story that is a most precious possession because it is sacred, exemplary, significant." *Myth and Reality*, trans. Willard R. Trask (New York: Harper Torchbooks, Harper and Row, 1963), p. 1. Myth, as interpreted this way, is truth, reality, the way things are.

11. Paul G. Hewitt, *Conceptual Physics*, 5th ed. (Boston: Little, Brown, 1985), p. 591.

12. Ibid., p. 151.

13. Vivian Sobchack, "Genre Film: Myth Ritual, and Sociodrama," in *Film/Culture: Explorations of Cinema in Its Social Context*, ed. Sari Thomas (Metuchen, N.J.: Scarecrow Press, 1982), p. 151.

14. See Otto, *Idea of the Holy*, pp. 5–40.

15. Mircea Eliade, *The Two and the One*, trans. J. M. Cohen (Chicago: University of Chicago Press, 1962), pp. 101–111.

16. Ibid., p. 114.

17. Otto, *Idea of the Holy*, p. 26.

18. It seems likely that he really bought the telescope out of sadness and homesickness, to search the skies for his own planet. However, it also serves as a symbol, perhaps, of the human need to look beyond the limited horizons of humanness and to find Otherness, as is reflected in the character of Newton.

19. A noteworthy visual pun on Bergman's character of Death in *The Seventh Seal* (1957).

20. He also presents one to Jenny for their son because "the baby will know" what to do with it.

21. As Gerardus van der Leeuw puts it, "*Tabu* is thus a sort of warning: 'Danger! High voltage!'" in *Religion in Essence and Manifestation*, trans. J. E. Turner (Princeton: Princeton University Press, 1986), p. 44.

22. This appears to be a manifestation of the famous Mozhukhin Experiment. In the early 1920s Russian filmmaker Lev Kuleshov put together a short film by splicing together alternating shots of actor Ivan Mozhukhin with a neutral facial expression and clips of a child playing with a toy, a bowl of soup, and an old woman in a coffin. Audiences felt he was a terrific actor, expressing affection, hunger, and grief in a very subtle manner. Screen performance ever since has emphasized underacting. See Bruce F. Kawin, *How Movies Work* (New York: Macmillan, 1987), pp. 227–228.

23. That no one, including the film audience, witnesses his arrival leads to a greater ambiguity of Rantes's character. Indeed, some people in the film are never convinced of his extraterrestriality.

24. Mircea Eliade, *The Sacred and the Profane,* trans. Willard R. Trask (New York: Harcourt Brace Jovanovich, 1959), pp. 118–119.

25. Ibid., pp. 121–122. For more detail on "absent gods," see Eliade, *Patterns,* pp. 46–50.

26. Because of his muteness he appears to embody the often-expressed feeling that the gods no longer speak to humankind, particularly the familiar Western biblical God, who some contend ceased communicating with humankind after the time of the prophets.

27. This time frame of three days will be familiar to Westerners used to Christian mythology: Jesus's trial with death lasts three days, after which he, like the Starman, returns to the heavens.

28. Here the smiling, joyful Rantes's claim to have no feelings does not really work. But it is a delightful scene nonetheless.

29. Eliade, *The Sacred and the Profane,* p. 122. In the West, the Word meant to explain creation, in the form of sacred scriptures, descends from the heavens and is revealed in high places: the Torah on Mt. Sinai and the Qu'ran on Mt. Hira. Yet the most obvious Western manifestation of the completer of creation can be found in the myth of Jesus. I do not mean to imply that every Westerner is Jewish, Christian, or Muslim but merely to indicate how religious mythology suffuses culture.

30. Yet another allusion to Jesus in terms of his Parousia, his Second Coming.

31. Again, I recognize that not every Westerner has read the *Bible.* This notion of appearance is simply a part of the undeniable and inescapable undercurrent of our culture.

32. Eliade, *Myth and Reality,* p. 32.

33. G. Simon Harak, "One Nation, Under God: The Soteriology of SDI," *Journal of the American Academy of Religion,* 56 (Fall 1988): 504.

34. Ibid.

35. See Ira Chernus, *Dr. Strangegod: On the Symbolic Meaning of Nuclear Weapons* (Columbia: University of South Carolina Press, 1986).

36. Darrol M. Bryant, "Cinema, Religion, and Popular Culture," in *Religion in Film,* ed. John R. May and Michael Bird (Knoxville: University of Tennessee Press, 1982), p. 102.

REFERENCES FOR CHAPTER 7

Giannetti, Louis. 1987. *Understanding Movies,* 4th ed. Englewood Cliffs, N.J.: Prentice-Hall.
Hillman, James. 1975. *Re-Visioning Psychology.* New York: Perennial Library, Harper and Row.
Jarvie, I. C. 1970. *Movies and Society.* New York: Basic Books.

FILMOGRAPHY

The Man Who Fell to Earth. Screenplay by Paul Meyersberg from the novel by Walter Tevis. Directed by Nicholas Roeg. Released by British Lion Films, 1976.
The Brother from Another Planet. Written, directed, and edited by John Sayles. Released by A-Train Films, 1984.
Starman. Written by Bruce A. Evans and Raynold Gideon. Directed by John Carpenter. Released by Columbia Pictures, 1984.
Man Facing Southeast. Written and directed by Eliseo Subiela. Released by FilmDallas, 1986.

NOTES FOR CHAPTER 8

1. Ronald H. Carpenter, "Frederick Jackson Turner and the Rhetorical Impact of the Frontier Thesis," *Quarterly Journal of Speech* 63 (1977): 117–129; "America's Opinion Leader Historians on Behalf of Success," *Quarterly Journal of Speech* 69 (1983): 111–126; Walter R. Fisher, "Romantic Democracy, Ronald Reagan, and Presidential Heroes," *Western Journal of Speech Communication* 46 (1982): 297–310; Janice Hocker Rushing, "The Rhetoric of the American Western Myth," *Communication Monographs* 50 (1983): 14–32; Richard Slotkin, *Regeneration Through Violence: The Mythology of the American Frontier, 1600–1860* (Middletown, Conn.: Wesleyan University Press, 1975); Richard Slotkin, *The Fatal Environment: The Myth of the Frontier in the Age of Industrialization* (New York: Atheneum, 1985); Henry Nash Smith, *Virgin Land: The American West as Symbol and Myth* (Cambridge: Harvard University Press, 1950); Frederick Jackson Turner, "The Significance of the Frontier in American History," in *The Turner Thesis*, ed. George Rogers Taylor (Boston: D. C. Heath, 1956).

2. Joanna L. Stratton, *Pioneer Women: Voices from the Kansas Frontier* (New York: Simon and Schuster, 1981); Jenni Calder, *There Must Be a Lone Ranger* (London: Hamish Hamilton, 1974), pp. 165–166; Peter Homans, "Puritanism Revisited: An Analysis of the Contemporary Screen-Image Western," in *The Popular Arts in America: A Reader*, 2d ed., ed. William Hammel (Dubuque, Iowa: William C. Brown, 1961), p. 102.

3. Annette Kolodny, *The Lay of the Land: Metaphor as Experience and History in American Life and Letters* (Chapel Hill: University of North Carolina Press, 1975), p. 150; for an account of women's symbolic experience of the land, see Annette Kolodny, *The Land Before Her: Fantasy and Experience of the American Frontiers, 1630–1860* (Chapel Hill: University of North Carolina Press, 1984).

4. Kolodny, *The Lay of the Land*, pp. 4, 7.

5. Michael Osborn, "The Evolution of the Archetypal Sea in Rhetoric and Poetic," *Quarterly Journal of Speech* 63 (1977): 347–363; Rushing, "American Western Myth."

6. Janice Hocker Rushing, "Mythic Evolution of 'The New Frontier' in Mass Mediated Rhetoric," *Critical Studies in Mass Communication* 3 (1986): 265–296; see also Janice Hocker Rushing, "E.T. as Rhetorical Transcendence," *Quarterly Journal of Speech* 71 (1985): 188–203.

7. Alasdair MacIntyre, *After Virtue: A Study in Moral Theory* (Notre Dame, Ind.: University of Notre Dame Press, 1981), p. 203.

8. C. G. Jung, *Four Archetypes* (Princeton, N.J.: Princeton University Press/Bollingen Series, 1970), pp. 3–14; see also Edward C. Whitmont, *The Symbolic Quest: Basic Concepts of Analytical Psychology* (Princeton, N.J.: Princeton University Press, 1978), pp. 73–83; Campbell is cited in Slotkin, *Regeneration Through Violence*, p. 14.

9. Erich Neumann, *The Origins and History of Consciousness*, trans. R.F.C. Hull (Princeton, N.J.: Princeton University Press/Bollingen Series, 1954); Ken Wilber, *Up from Eden* (Boulder: Shambhala Press, 1983).

10. Whitmont, *The Symbolic Quest*, p. 77.

11. Slotkin, *Regeneration Through Violence*, p. 14.

12. J. D. Bass and Richard Cherwitz, "Imperial Mission and Manifest Destiny: A Case Study of Political Myth in Rhetorical Discourse," *Southern Speech Communication Journal* 43 (1978): 213–232; Martha Solomon, "The Positive Woman's Journey: A Mythic Analysis of the Rhetoric of STOP ERA," *Quarterly Journal of Speech* 65 (1979): 262–274.

13. Whitmont, *The Symbolic Quest*, p. 80.

14. M. Esther Harding, *Woman's Mysteries: Ancient and Modern* (New York: Harper Colophon, 1976), pp. 124–125.

15. Sylvia Brinton Perera, *Descent to the Goddess: A Way of Initiation for Women* (Toronto: Inner City Books, 1981), p. 16.

16. Ibid., p. 18.

17. Edward C. Whitmont, *The Return of the Goddess* (New York: Crossroad, 1986), p. viii.

18. Perera, *Descent to the Goddess*, p. 16.

19. Ibid., pp. 89, 99.

20. Whitmont, *The Return of the Goddess*, p. 7.

21. Ibid., pp. 49–68.

22. Wilber, *Up from Eden*, p. 123.

23. Barbara G. Walker, *The Woman's Encyclopedia of Myths and Secrets* (San Francisco: Harper and Row, 1983), p. 1066; Harding, *Woman's Mysteries*, p. 128.

24. In *The Land Before Her*, Kolodny notes that women did not begin to relate to their husbands' paradisal myth until they moved out of the woods and onto the prairies. They then revised the myth and "proclaimed a paradise in which the garden and the home were one" (p. 6). It is intriguing to speculate whether a reason for their new interest in the land as paradise might have been their intuitive awareness that the plains were more amenable to being collectively imagined as the Great Goddess than were the dark, enclosing forests.

25. See Osborn, "Evolution of the Archetypal Sea," pp. 352–353, for examples of how the sea was fused with the land in frontier metaphors.

26. Whitmont, *The Return of the Goddess*, p. 50. See also Gerda Lerner, *The Creation of Patriarchy* (New York: Oxford University Press, 1986).

27. Whitmont, *The Return of the Goddess*, p. 71.

28. Ibid.

29. Neumann, *Origins*, p. 95. This does not mean the entire unconscious is feminine in character or that women are unconscious and men are conscious. In depth psychology, the feminine and masculine principles are archetypal a priori polarities akin to the Oriental Yin and Yang; they express existential value systems and modes of perception that are present in both sexes. The repression of the feminine by the patriarchy thus occurs in men as well as women and affects the relationship between humanity and the cosmos, as well as that between men and women. Furthermore, certain aspects of the masculine exist as unconscious potentialities within men and women. But most historians of myth agree that the aspects of humanity associated with the feminine are more repressed (forgotten) and oppressed (dominated) than those associated with the masculine. For clarification, including a revision of the patriarchal bias in C. G. Jung's discussion of the masculine and feminine archetypes, see Whitmont, *The Return of the Goddess*, pp. 121–144; Demaris Wehr, *Jung and Feminism: Liberating Archetypes* (Boston: Beacon Press, 1987), especially pp. 116–117.

30. Pamela Berger, *The Goddess Obscured: Transformation of the Grain Protectress from Goddess to Saint* (Boston: Beacon Press, 1985); Wilber, *Up from Eden*, pp. 133–150, 189–190.

31. Perera, *Descent to the Goddess*, pp. 12–13.

32. Whitmont, *The Return of the Goddess*, p. 136.

33. Ibid., p. 66.

34. Ibid., pp. 105–120.

35. Kolodny, *The Lay of the Land*, p. 7.

36. Ibid., pp. 66–67.

37. Ibid., p. 133.

38. Ibid., p. 137.

39. See Rushing, "Mythic Evolution," p. 270.

40. Kolodny, *The Lay of the Land*, p. xv.

41. Slotkin, *Regeneration Through Violence*, p. 12; see also pp. 57–58, 552–553.

42. Paul Zweig, *The Adventurer* (Princeton, N.J.: Princeton University Press, 1981), p. 68.

43. Whitmont, *The Return of the Goddess*, pp. 149–178.

44. See Helen M. Luke, *Woman Earth and Spirit: The Feminine in Symbol and Myth* (New York: Crossroad, 1986), pp. 51–71; C. G. Jung and C. Kerenyi, *Essays on a Science of Mythology: The Myth of the Divine Child and the Mysteries of Eleusis*, trans. R.F.C. Hull (Princeton: Princeton University Press/Bollingen Series, 1969), pp. 113–183.

45. Perera, *Descent to the Goddess*, pp. 9, 13.

46. Ibid., pp. 20–62.

47. Ibid., p. 30.

48. Ibid., p. 20. I would like to thank Professor G. Thomas Goodnight for suggesting to me the relationship between the Furies and the mother monster in *Aliens*.

49. Luke, *Woman Earth and Spirit*, pp. 96–97.

50. Wilber, *Up from Eden*, p. 231.

51. Whitmont, *The Return of the Goddess*, p. 102.

52. These characteristics of space, without the feminine connotations, are outlined in Rushing, "Mythic Evolution," p. 283.

53. Whitmont, *The Symbolic Quest*, p. 222.

54. Fritjof Capra, *The Turning Point: Science, Society, and the Rising Culture* (Toronto: Bantam Books, 1983), pp. 284–285; Walker, *The Woman's Encyclopedia*, p. 332.

55. Rebecca Bell-Metereau, *Hollywood Androgyny* (New York: Columbia University Press, 1985), p. 222.

56. Quoted in Ruth Prigozy, "*Aliens* Alienates ... Disaster for Women," *New Directions for Women*, (November–December 1986): 6.

57. Ari Korpivaara, "To See, Or Not to See: Roll Over, Rambo," *Ms.*, September 8, 1986, p. 14.

58. David Edelstein, "Mother of the Year," *Rolling Stone* 481, August 28, 1986, pp. 41–42.

59. Prigozy, "*Aliens* Alienates," p. 6.

60. Edelstein, "Mother of the Year," p. 42.

61. Barbara Creed, "Horrors and the Monstrous-Feminine: An Imaginary Abjection," *Screen* 27 (1986): 44–70.

62. Rushing, "Mythic Evolution," pp. 271–281.

63. Edelstein, "Mother of the Year," p. 41.

64. Joseph Campbell, *The Inner Reaches of Outer Space: Metaphor as Myth and Religion* (New York: Alfred van der Marck Editions, 1986).

65. Creed, "Horrors," p. 56.

66. Ibid., p. 58.

67. Ibid., p. 63.

68. Ibid., p. 60.

69. Ibid., p. 63.

70. Bell-Metereau, *Hollywood Androgyny*, pp. 213, 219.

71. Creed, "Horrors," pp. 65–68.

72. Neumann, *Origins*, p. 83.

73. Ibid., pp. 61, 87.

74. Wilber, *Up from Eden,* p. 210.

75. Neumann, *Origins,* p. 388.

76. Perera, *Descent to the Goddess,* p. 63.

77. Carol P. Christ, "Why Women Need the Goddess: Phenomenological, Psychological, and Political Reflections," in *Womanspirit Rising: A Feminist Reader in Religion,* eds. Carol P. Christ and Judith Plaskow (New York: Harper and Row, 1979), pp. 273–287.

78. Bell-Metereau exhaustively analyzes the critical responses to *Alien* (*Hollywood Androgyny,* pp. 209–224) and finds not only that most of the reviews were negative but that none responded to the movie as one of the first science-fiction films to present a strong heroine survivor. Only one critic, in fact, mentioned heroic rather than anatomical virtues in Ripley.

79. Carol Pearson, *The Hero Within: Six Archetypes We Live By* (San Francisco: Harper and Row, 1986).

80. Homans, "Puritanism Revisited," p. 104.

81. Tom Wolfe, *The Right Stuff* (Toronto: Bantam Books, 1980), pp. 101–105.

82. Christ, "Why Women Need the Goddess," p. 284.

83. Solomon, "The Positive Woman's Journey."

84. Eric Berne, *Games People Play* (New York: Grove Press, 1964), pp. 123–124.

85. Thomas B. Farrell, "The Tradition of Rhetoric and the Philosophy of Communication," *Communication* 7 (1983): 170.

86. William Barrett, *Irrational Man: A Study in Existential Philosophy* (Garden City, N.Y.: Doubleday Anchor Books, 1962), p. 279.

87. Irene Claremont de Castillejo, *Knowing Woman: A Feminine Psychology* (New York: Harper and Row, 1973), p. 86.

88. Aeschylus, *The Orestes Plays of Aeschylus,* trans. P. Roche (New York: New American Library, 1962), p. 167.

89. Luke, *Woman Earth and Spirit,* p. 98.

90. Aeschylus, *The Orestes Plays,* p. 179.

91. Barrett, *Irrational Man,* p. 280.

NOTES FOR PART 3

1. James H. Kavanagh, "Ideology," in *Critical Terms for Literary Study,* eds. Frank Lentricchia and Thomas McLaughlin (Chicago: University of Chicago Press, 1990), pp. 309–310.

2. Ibid., p. 306.

3. Ibid.

4. Louis Althusser, *For Marx* (New York: Vintage Books, 1970), p. 232.

5. Mike Cormack, *Ideology* (Ann Arbor: University of Michigan Press, 1992), p. 12.

6. Althusser, *For Marx,* p. 231.

7. Kavanagh, "Ideology," p. 310.

8. Ibid., p. 311. It must be stressed that there are many varieties of criticism examining gender, race, and class, and not all are influenced by Althusser. For an overview of gender analysis in film criticism, see "The Spectatrix," eds. Janet Bergstrom and Mary Ann Doane (Baltimore: Johns Hopkins University Press, 1990) [Special Issue of *Camera Obscura,* nos. 20–21 (1989)]. See also Teresa de Lauretis, *Alice Doesn't: Feminism, Semiotics, Cinema* (Bloomington: Indiana University Press, 1984); Mary Ann Doane, *The Desire to Desire: The*

Woman's Film of the 1940s (Bloomington: Indiana University Press, 1987); Patricia Erens, ed., *Issues in Feminist Film Criticism* (Bloomington: Indiana University Press, 1990); Molly Haskell, *From Reverence to Rape: The Treatment of Women in the Movies,* 2d ed. (Chicago: University of Chicago Press, 1987); Constance Penley, ed., *Feminism and Film Theory* (New York: Routledge, 1988). For the study of class representations in film, see Michael Ryan and Douglas Kellner, *Camera Politica: The Politics and Ideology of Contemporary Hollywood Film* (Bloomington: Indiana University Press, 1988); Tom O'Brien, *The Screening of America: Movies and Values from Rocky to Rain Man* (New York: Continuum, 1990); Stephen Prince, *Visions of Empire: Political Imagery in Contemporary American Film* (Westport, Conn.: Praeger, 1992). For analyses of race in film, see Donald Bogle, *Toms, Coons, Mulattoes, Mammies, and Bucks: An Interpretive History of Blacks in American Films* (New York: Viking, 1973); Thomas R. Cripps, *Making Movies Black: The Hollywood Message Movies from World War II to the Civil Rights Era* (New York: Oxford University Press, 1992).

9. Fredric Jameson, "Reification and Utopia in Mass Culture," *Social Text* 1 (Winter 1979): 130–148.

10. Ryan and Kellner, *Camera Politica,* p. 14.

11. Ibid., pp. 111–112.

12. In recent critical debates, the category *postmodern* has been used in many different ways, including some imprecise ones. In his book-length study of the category, Thomas Docherty notes that "for some, postmodern equates with 'nihilistic' or 'anarchic'; for others, it refers to a culture dominated by the banality of televisual representations and Las Vegas–style neon-signs whose presence everywhere reminds us of the McDonaldsization of an otherwise vegetarian world; yet others think of that explosion of poststructuralist theory which arose in the 1960s and 1970s as a postmodern manner of thinking. The prevalence of such populist, rather superficial and essentially misleading characterizations of 'the postmodern' is troubling for anyone who would take the issues of contemporary culture seriously." Thomas Docherty, ed., *Postmodernism: A Reader* (New York: Columbia University Press, 1993), p. xiii. Used in so many sloppy ways, the category of *the postmodern* can confuse more than it clarifies.

McLemore's use of the category, however, is carefully considered and altogether appropriate. Her understanding of the category comes very close to that described by one of its leading theorists. "Postmodernism," according to Peter Brooker, "splices high with low culture, it raids and parodies past art, it questions all absolutes, it swamps reality in a culture of recycled images, it has to do with deconstruction, with consumerism, with television and the information society, with the end of communism." Peter Brooker, ed., *Modernism/Postmodernism* (New York: Longman, 1992), p. 3. Most, if not all, of these tendencies are prominent in *Blue Velvet.* In the film, they have the effect of undermining meaning and questioning the ways male subjectivity is formed. The film suggests that male subjectivity is artificial, a historical construct, unanchorable in reality. Perhaps this is why the film generated anxiety in so many viewers: It called into question our established order of gender identities.

13. See Irena Makarushka, "Framing the Text: A Reflection on Meanings and Methods," unpublished paper, October 11, 1993.

NOTES FOR CHAPTER 9

1. Michael Ryan and Douglas Kellner, *Camera Politica: The Politics and Ideology of Contemporary Hollywood Film* (Bloomington: Indiana University Press, 1988), pp. 12–16.

2. See Harvey Greenberg, "Dangerous Recuperations: Red Dawn, Rambo, and the New Decaturism," *Journal of Popular Film and Television* 16 (1987): 60–70.

3. Michael Riffaterre, "On the Diegetic Functions of the Descriptive," *Style* 20 (1986): 282.

4. Ibid., "proffers a link" p. 286, "womb of narrative," p. 293.

5. The classic description of this kind of religious movement is provided in Anthony F.C. Wallace, "Revitalization Movements," *American Anthropologist* 57 (1956): 264–281.

6. Catherine L. Albanese, "Savage, Sinner, and Saved: Davy Crockett, Camp Meetings, and the Wild Frontier," *American Quarterly* 33 (1981): 482–501.

7. Of course this desire to reassert American chosenness is not limited to popular film but is also strongly evidenced in contemporary evangelical religion. As Stewart M. Hoover has demonstrated in *Mass Media Religion* (Newbury Park, Calif.: Sage, 1988), the rise of the religious right and the electronic church may be fruitfully interpreted as a "Protestant Revitalization Movement."

8. Also termed Illusionism, Docetism was a third-century teaching, considered heterodox by the church, that held that Christ only "appeared" or "seemed" to be a man, to have been born, to have lived and suffered. "Docetae," *The Catholic Encyclopedia* (New York: Encyclopedia Press, 1913), p. 70.

9. In U.S. culture, fitness has long been linked to nationalism. See Harvey Green, *Fit for America: Health, Fitness, Sport, and American Society* (New York: Pantheon Books, 1986). On a much more advanced theoretical level, Michel Foucault explores the relation of the body to modern systems of power in *Discipline and Punish: The Birth of the Prison,* trans. by Alan Sheridan (New York: Vintage Books, 1979); and *The History of Sexuality, Vol. 1: An Introduction,* trans. Robert Hurley (New York: Vintage Books, 1980).

10. Fredric Jameson, "Reification and Utopia in Mass Culture," *Social Text* 1 (Winter 1979): 130–148.

11. Mircea Eliade, *The Myth of the Eternal Return,* trans. Willard R. Trask (Princeton, N.J.: Princeton University Press, 1974), pp. 53–54, 61–62; Rene Girard, *Violence and the Sacred* (Baltimore: Johns Hopkins University Press, 1974), p. 95.

12. Dana B. Polan, "'Above All Else to Make You See': Cinema and the Ideology of Spectacle," in *Postmodernism and Politics,* ed. Jonathan Arac (Minneapolis: University of Minnesota Press, 1986), p. 69, n. 18. See also Mary Ann Doane, "The Voice in the Cinema: The Articulation of Body and Space," *Yale French Studies,* no. 60 (1980): 33–50.

13. This pattern is centuries old. See Richard Slotkin, *Regeneration Through Violence: The Mythology of the American Frontier, 1600–1860* (Middletown, Conn.: Wesleyan University Press, 1973).

NOTES FOR CHAPTER 10

1. David Chute's review illustrates some of these mixed reactions: In many cases they demonstrate a disparity between the opinions of the audience and those of the reviewer. Noting that whereas sneak previewers in the Valley claimed the film was "disgusting and sick," Chute says they missed the film's "other" side, its presentation of the power of good. Although Chute's later comment that the character Jeffrey is "so amorally awestruck by crime and horror that he could be accused of fraternizing with the forces of human soul-rot" (1986, 32) could be a concession to these viewers, elsewhere his tone is one of genuine admiration.

Blue Velvet reviews also illustrate how time and memory alter our images and opinions. For example, Janet Maslin's initial review in the *New York Times* (1986a) indicates traces of bewilderment, yet she covered the film twice more in other *Times* reviews. These later reviews (1986b, 1986c) are decidedly more positive in tone.

As perhaps a side note, it should also be mentioned that reviewers occasionally get details from the film completely wrong, thereby skewing their interpretations. (Jameson's references to the crawling beetles under the "bushes surrounding the house" and his mention of handcuffs in the film are two such examples.) Greil Marcus's comment on *Blue Velvet* film reviews—that they fetishize the film and make you "doubt the power of what you've just seen" (1986, 12)—should be kept in mind. He attributes this fetishization to the power of the film to evoke sensations rather than ideas, claiming that the film accordingly "dramatizes displacement" (1986, 12).

2. The editors of *Newsweek* felt compelled to print two reviews of the film, one in September and the other in October 1986, after the film had had a more general release across the country. Whereas both reviews comment on *Blue Velvet* as a morality tale, the first (by David Ansen) is the more negative, calling it a kind of Hardy Boys meet the Marquis de Sade and noting that the "film will surely be reviled" (although he adds that the film demands respect for its "dramatic and technical vocabulary" [1986, 86]). The second (by Cathleen McGuigan) summarizes viewer reactions to the film, praising it as a "cult hit."

3. The etymology of the term *allegory* is illuminating in this context: *allos* = other + *agoreuei* = to speak (Owens 1980, part 1, p. 69).

4. These allegories—of politics, religion, and history/nature—are discussed in articles by Powers (1987), Wall (1987), and Jameson (1983, 1989), respectively.

5. Although allegory often employs symbols, it lacks their "momentariness." Walter Benjamin describes allegory as a "progression in a series of moments," connecting—although not identifying—it with myth (1977, 165).

6. Interestingly, the figure of Dorothy eludes this neat schema: She is described by one review simply as "a slightly disturbed mother of a small child" (Wall 1987, 8).

7. This comparison is borrowed from Lynch himself, who reported that his favorite view of the film was that of one of the sound mixers from the set, who claimed *Blue Velvet* was "like Norman Rockwell meets Hieronymous Bosch" (Chute 1986, 32).

8. Often the same narrative conventions discussed by the first set of reviewers—the dream-like quality of the film, Jeffrey's quest to "gain knowledge and experience," the winding staircases, the psychomachia—are also targeted as identifiable features of allegory by the second set of reviewers.

9. *Blue Velvet* has often been described as incorporating elements of surrealism (the ants crawling on the severed ear illustrates this claim most graphically), and many reviewers compare Lynch to Dali or Bunuel because of his almost clinical attention to gory details.

10. The film is rife with puns and oddball images: Jeffrey's question, "So what do you know about the [severed] ear?" is answered by Sandy: "I don't know much but bits and pieces ... I hear things." Moreover, Jeffrey's chicken walk, as well as the woman dancing on the roof of the car to Roy Orbison's "In Dreams" during the joyride, is simultaneously humorous, disturbing, and disjunctive.

11. As an example, Benjamin notes that the use of Greek gods in Christian allegory is "not an epigonal victory monument; but rather the word which is intended to exorcise a surviving remnant of antique life" (1977, 233). "An appreciation of the transience of things, and the concern to rescue them for eternity," he claims, "is one of the strongest impulses in allegory" (1977, 223).

12. Greg Tate's comments in the *Village Voice* are worth repeating here. Although Tate claims the film does not "challenge the power invested in the male gaze ... [it] do[es] in fact

exploit female sexual aggression for purposes of subverting mainstream cinema" (1986, 78). He summarizes his own reaction to the scene of Dorothy with the knife as depicting "sexual terror, submission to the female versus female objectivity," reporting that as a male viewer he "went for [his] nuts watching those scenes"—"figuratively," of course (1986, 78). Steve Jenkins's reaction in the *Monthly Film Bulletin* is less visceral and more theoretical but nonetheless echoes Tate's: "The absolute, inextricable link between the film's moral concerns and its investment in the guilty pleasures of looking is crucial, and seems carefully calculated to force male spectators into moralising confusion" (1987, 100).

13. Blue velvet, Frank's fetish in the film, is also *our* fetish, "covering" the film like a curtain rising and falling before and after the performance.

14. Jeffrey is the "private eye" in the film—or, depending upon your gendered perspective, the "private dick." At one point Sandy tells Jeffrey that she is not sure whether he is a detective or a pervert, and Jeffrey retorts, "That's for me to know and you to find out." The point, of course, is that he—and we—are both.

15. Lynch's response to an interview question corroborates this: "Film to me is like feelings. So much of the innocence and the naive quality of Jeffrey and Sandy are from the '50s, so that's where some of it comes from. But when you go into a small town in America and you start looking closer, you don't see too much of today. You go into any house and it's like the '60s or '40s or '30s, depending on how old the people are or what they've collected, the mood of the place and the old neighborhoods. They just seem like they're in the past. So if you pick and choose, you know, based on feelings, pretty soon you say, my god, this is starting to feel like an older picture, but you don't worry if a modern car drives through. It frees you" (Borden 1986, 62, 66).

16. In particular, the lurid reds and yellows of the final sequence in Dorothy's living room (with the bodies of Gordon and Don) are eerily reminiscent of Van Gogh's work. Other parallels and references to Van Gogh are also present throughout the film. Lynch himself began as a painter; in addition, the older Donny is referred to by Frank as "Van Gogh" after Frank removes the man's ear with scissors.

17. Paul Monaco (n.d.) theorizes that 1963—the year of John F. Kennedy's assassination—was a turning point in U.S. consciousness. The throwback to 1963 in the film, then, serves nicely as a representation of rupture.

18. Dialogism is defined by Richard Terdiman as a "memory model" because it "seeks to recall the semantic and social history carried by a culture's language, but which tends to be forgotten, to be blanked, in the characteristic form of cultural mystification since the revolutions of the nineteenth century" (1985, 23). In addition, Catherine Griggers (1990) maps the links among dialogism, parody, and "the sign in struggle" in various mass-culture texts, among them *Blue Velvet*.

19. "What is most proper" to allegory, claims Owens, is "its capacity to rescue from historical oblivion that which threatens to disappear" (1980, part 1, p. 68). In addition, Linda Hutcheon celebrates parody for its ability to "both enshrine the past and to question it" (1988, 126).

REFERENCES FOR CHAPTER 10

Ansen, David. 1986. "Stranger Than Paradise: Lynch's Nightmare Tour of Homespun Americana." *Newsweek,* September 15, p. 69.

Aufderheide, Pat. 1987. "Down on Main Street." *The Progressive* 51: 36–37.

Benjamin, Walter. 1977. *The Origin of German Tragic Drama.* Trans. John Osborne. London: New Left Books.

Berry, Betsy. 1988. "Forever, in My Dreams: Generic Conventions and the Subversive Imagination in *Blue Velvet.*" *Film/Literature Quarterly* 16(2): 82–90.

Biga, Tracy. 1987. "*Blue Velvet.*" *Film Quarterly* 41(1): 44–49.

Borden, Lizzie. 1986. "The World According to Lynch." (Interview) *Village Voice,* September 23, 62.

Bundtzen, Lynda K. 1988. "'Don't Look at Me!' Woman's Body, Woman's Voice in *Blue Velvet.*" *Western Humanities Review* 42(3): 187–203.

Chute, David. 1986. "Out to Lynch." (Interview) *Film Comment* 22(5): 32–35.

Combs, Richard. 1987. "Crude Thoughts and Fierce Forces: On First Looking into the World of David Lynch, Kitty-Corner from the City Morgue." *Monthly Film Bulletin* 54 (April): 100–104.

Corliss, Richard. 1986a. "It's a Strange World, Isn't It." *Time,* September 22, p. 86.

——. 1986b. "Our Town: George Bailey Meets 'True,' 'Blue,' and 'Peggy Sue.'" *Film Comment* 22(6): 9–13.

Fineman, Joel. 1980. "The Structure of Allegorical Desire." *October* 12 (Spring): 46–66.

French, Sean. 1987. "The Heart of the Cavern." *Sight & Sound* 56(2): 101–104.

Gold, Richard. 1986. "Lynch Confident About Velvet; Plans 4-Hour Dune Videocassette." (Interview) *Variety,* September 24, p. 5.

Griggers, Catherine. 1990. "Reinventing the Popular: Inscriptions of the Feminine Subject in Postmodern Genres." Dissertation. University of Florida.

——. 1989. "Bearing the Sign in Struggle: Pornography, Parody, and Mainstream Cinema." *American Journal of Semiotics* 6(4): 95–107.

Hoberman, J. 1986. "Return to Normalcy." *Village Voice,* September 23, p. 58.

Hutcheon, Linda. 1988. *A Poetics of Postmodernism: History, Theory, Fiction.* New York: Routledge.

Jaehne, Karen. 1987. "*Blue Velvet.*" *Cineaste* 15(3): 38.

Jameson, Fredric. 1989. "Nostalgia for the Present." *South Atlantic Quarterly* 88(2): 517–537.

——. 1987. "Reification and Utopia in Mass Culture." *Social Text* 1 (Winter): 130–148.

——. 1983. "Postmodernism and Consumer Society." In *The Anti-Aesthetic: Essays on Postmodern Culture.* Ed. Hal Foster. Port Townsend, Wash.: Bay Press.

Jenkins, Steve. 1987. "*Blue Velvet.*" *Monthly Film Bulletin* 54 (April): 99–100.

Kael, Pauline. 1986. "The Current Cinema: Out There and In Here." *New Yorker* 62: 99–103.

Kuzniar, Alice. 1989. "'Ears Looking at You: E.T.A. Hoffman's *The Sandman* and David Lynch's *Blue Velvet.*" South Atlantic Review 54(2): 7–21.

Loder, Kurt. 1986. "David Lynch's *Blue Velvet.*" *Rolling Stone,* October 23, pp. 44–45.

Lynch, David, dir. 1986. *Blue Velvet.* De Laurentiis prod.

Marcus, Greil. 1986. "Speaker to Speaker." *Artforum* 25(1): 11–12.

Maslin, Janet. 1986a. "*Blue Velvet:* Comedy of the Eccentric." *New York Times,* September 19, sec. C, p. 12.

——. 1986b. "Individuality Rears Its Oh-So-Welcome Head." *New York Times,* October 12, sec. 2, p. 19.

——. 1986c. "New Films Rethink the Small Town." *New York Times,* sec. 2, p. 1.

McCarthy, T. 1986. "*Blue Velvet.*" *Variety,* September 3, p. 16.

McGuigan, Cathleen, with Janet Huck. 1986. "Black and Blue Is Beautiful? David Lynch's Strange Film Divides Moviegoers." *Newsweek,* October 27, pp. 104–105.

Monaco, Paul. n.d. *Ribbons in Time: Movies and Society Since 1945.* Bloomington: Indiana University Press.

Mulvey, Laura. 1975. "Visual Pleasure and Narrative Cinema." *Screen* 16(3): 6–18.

Owens, Craig. 1983. "The Discourse of Others: Feminists and Postmodernism." In *The Anti-Aesthetic: Essays on Postmodern Culture*. Ed. Hal Foster. Port Townsend, Wash.: Bay Press.

———. 1980. "The Allegorical Impulse: Toward a Theory of Postmodernism." Parts 1 and 2. October 12 and 13 (Spring and Summer): 67–86, 58–80.

Powers, John. 1987. "Bleak Chic." *American Film* 12(5): 47–51.

Rafferty, Terrence. 1986. "*Blue Velvet*." *The Nation*. October 18, pp. 383–385.

Robertson, Nan. 1986. "The All-American Guy Behind '*Blue Velvet*.'" (Interview) *New York Times*, October 11, p. 11.

Ryan, Michael, and Douglas Kellner. 1988. *Camera Politica: The Politics and Ideology of Contemporary Hollywood Film*. Bloomington: Indiana University Press.

Schulte-Sasse, Jochen. 1986–1987. "Modernity and Modernism, Postmodernity and Postmodernism: Framing the Issue." *Cultural Critique* 5 (Winter): 5–22.

Tate, Greg. 1986. "Revenge of the Nerds: Making Betty Blue." *Village Voice*, December 30, p. 78.

Terdiman, Richard. 1985. "Deconstructing Memory: On Representing the Past and Theorizing Culture in France Since the Revolution." *Diacritics* (Winter): 13–36.

Testa, Bart. 1987. "The Remaindered Surrealist." *The Idler* 14 (September–October): 28–33.

Ulmer, Gregory. 1983. "The Object of Post-Criticism." In *The Anti-Aesthetic: Essays on Postmodern Culture*. Ed. Hal Foster. Port Townsend, Wash.: Bay Press.

Wall, James M. 1987. "The Best Film of 1986: Probing the Depths of Evil." *Christian Century*, January 7–14, pp. 7–9.

Winer, Laurie. 1986. "Isabella Rossellini Assesses the Role That Haunted Her." (Interview) *New York Times*, November 23, sec. 2, p. 1.

NOTES FOR CHAPTER 11

1. Donal Henahan, "Oppressed Women, Your Name Is Opera," *New York Times*, October 8, 1989, sec. 2, p. 34.

2. For an overview of the representation of women in film from the early 1920s to the present, see Molly Haskell, *From Reverence to Rape: The Treatment of Women in the Movies*, rev. 2d ed. (Chicago: University of Chicago Press, 1987), and Mary Ann Doane, *The Desire to Desire: The Woman's Film of the 1940's* (Bloomington: Indiana University Press, 1987).

3. Doane, *The Desire to Desire*, p. 38.

4. Ibid., p. 56.

5. Constance Penley, "'A Certain Refusal of Difference': Feminism and Film Theory," in *The Future of an Illusion: Film, Feminism and Psychoanalysis* (Minneapolis: University of Minnesota Press, 1989), p. 53.

6. Quoted in ibid., p. 47.

7. My analysis is influenced by semiotician Julia Kristeva, who understands the subject as being in process "within plural and heterogeneous universes." See Julia Kristeva, *Revolution in Poetic Language*, trans. Margaret Waller (New York: Columbia University Press, 1984), p. 14.

8. Gerda Lerner, *The Creation of Patriarchy* (New York: Oxford University Press, 1986), pp. 213–216.

9. Ibid., p. 219.

10. Elizabeth Clark and Herbert Richardson, *Women and Religion: A Feminist Sourcebook of Christian Thought* (New York: Harper and Row, 1977), p. 3.

11. Ibid., p. 4.

12. Marilyn French, *Beyond Power: On Women, Men and Morals* (New York: Ballantine Books, 1985), p. 162. See also: Mary Daly, *Beyond God the Father: Toward a Philosophy of Women's Liberation,* 2d ed. (Boston: Beacon Press, 1985), pp. 44–68, 81–97; John Phillips, *Eve: The History of an Idea* (New York: Harper and Row, 1984); Marina Warner, *Alone of All Her Sex: The Myth and Cult of the Virgin Mary* (New York: Vintage Books, 1976); Elaine Pagels, *Adam, Eve and the Serpent* (New York: Random House, 1988); and Mieke Bal, *Lethal Love: Feminist Literary Readings of Biblical Love Stories* (Bloomington: Indiana University Press, 1987), Chapter 5.

13. French, *Beyond Power.*

14. Daly, *Beyond God the Father,* p. 81.

15. Pam Cook and Claire Johnston, "The Place of Woman in the Cinema of Raoul Walsh," in *Feminism and Film Theory,* ed. Constance Penley (New York: Routledge, 1988), p. 27.

16. Among postmodern feminists influenced by the works of Lacan I include Hélène Cixous, Luce Irigaray, and Julia Kristeva. See Toril Moi, *Sexual/Textual Politics: Feminist Literary Theory* (London: Methuen, 1985), pp. 89–167. Also Rosemarie Tong, *Feminist Thought: A Comprehensive Introduction* (Boulder: Westview Press, 1988), pp. 217–230. For feminist film critics who rely on Lacan, see, for example, Cook and Johnston, "The Place of Woman in the Cinema of Raoul Walsh," p. 25; and Laura Mulvey, "Visual Pleasure and Narrative Cinema," in *Feminism and Film Theory,* ed. Penley, p. 57.

17. Mulvey, "Visual Pleasure," p. 62.

18. See ibid., pp. 69–72.

19. This use of the concept of the gaze is indebted to Mulvey. However, in this instance it does not refer to the relationship between the spectator and the filmic text. Rather, it describes the construction of woman as object determined by the projections of a male fantasy.

20. Quoted in Cook and Johnston, "The Place of Woman in the Cinema of Raoul Walsh," p. 27.

21. Julia Kristeva, *Powers of Horror: An Essay on Abjection,* trans. Leon Roudiez (New York: Columbia University Press, 1982), p. 1.

22. Moi, *Sexual/Textual Politics,* p. 13.

23. Julia Kristeva, "Women's Time," in *The Kristeva Reader,* ed. Toril Moi (New York: Columbia University Press, 1986), pp. 187–213.

NOTES FOR CHAPTER 12

1. Clifford Geertz, "Thick Description: Toward an Interpretive Theory of Culture," in *The Interpretation of Cultures* (New York: Basic Books, 1973), p. 5.

2. James W. Carey, "Taking Culture Seriously," in *Media, Myths, and Narratives: Television and the Press,* ed. James W. Carey (London: Sage Publications, 1988), p. 11.

3. Irena Makarushka, "Framing the Text: A Reflection on Meanings and Methods," unpublished paper, Brunswick, Maine, October 11, 1993, p. 1.

4. Matthew Fox, *Religion U.S.A.: Religion and Culture by Way of TIME Magazine* (Dubuque, Iowa: Listening Press, 1971), p. 4.

5. Geertz, "Thick Description," p. 5.

6. Of course, phenomenological studies and methodologies in the study of religion abound, and we think this will offer a helpful perspective to the study of religion and film. It is also a helpful perspective for students encountering religious studies for the first time. For a description of a phenomenological approach that is accessible to undergraduate students, see Julia Mitchell Corbett, *Religion in America* (Englewood Cliffs, N.J.: Prentice-Hall, 1990), pp. 8–10. Corbett describes the phenomenological approach as descriptive, analytic, and empathetic. It is the empathetic goal of phenomenology of religion that particularly suits it as an approach to understanding human cultures.

7. Ibid., p. 8.

8. Janice Rushing, "Introduction to 'Evolution of the New Frontier' in Alien and Aliens: Patriarchal Cooptation of the Feminine Archetype," unpublished paper, Fayetteville, Ark., September 1, 1993, p. 2.

9. Fox, *Religion U.S.A.*, pp. 7–10.

10. Michael Novak, *The Joy of Sports: End Zones, Bases, Baskets, Balls, and the Consecration of the American Spirit* (New York: Basic Books, 1976), p. xi.

11. Ibid., pp. xii, xv.

12. This argument is common in studies dealing with popular literature. Kathryn Presley's work on popular literature in the Gilded Age draws upon a variety of works that establish a connection between popular literature and the social and moral values of an age. For further discussion see William Darby, *Necessary American Fiction: Popular Literature of the 1850s* (Bowling Green, Ohio: Bowling Green University Press, 1987), and Louis Schneider and Sanford M. Dornbush, *Popular Religion: Inspirational Books in America* (Chicago: University of Chicago Press, 1958).

13. Catherine Albanese, *America: Religions and Religion,* 2d ed. (Belmont, Calif.: Wadsworth Publishing Company, 1992), pp. 469, 471.

14. Ibid., p. 469.

15. Peter W. Williams, *Popular Religion in America: Symbolic Change and the Modernization Process in Historical Perspective* (Chicago: University of Illinois Press, 1989), p. 203.

16. Conrad Ostwalt, "Dances with Wolves: An American Heart of Darkness," paper presented at SECSOR, Atlanta, March 1992.

17. David Seals, "The New Custerism," *The Nation,* May 13, 1991, pp. 634–638.

18. See George M. Marsden, *Religion and American Culture* (San Diego: Harcourt Brace Jovanovich, 1990), pp. 1–6.

19. Conrad Ostwalt, *After Eden: The Secularization of American Space in the Fiction of Willa Cather and Theodore Dreiser* (Lewisburg, Pa.: Bucknell University Press, 1990).

20. See Albanese, *America: Religions and Religion,* and Williams, *Popular Religion in America.*

21. Williams, *Popular Religion in America,* p. 9.

22. See Peter Berger, *The Sacred Canopy: Elements of a Sociological Theory of Religion* (Garden City, N.Y.: Doubleday, 1967). In this very important study, Berger describes the way religion functions to render reality constructions meaningful. He also deals with the institutionalization of religion in the modern, secular world. Following Berger's theories, we might surmise that religion, if it is to remain a meaningful institution, must adapt to and participate in secular society.

23. See ibid. Berger describes a social process of reality construction and maintenance that preserves social and cultural meaning. Without constructive and maintenance tech-

niques, society would dissolve into anomy. Films and other cultural forms provide the opportunity for construction and maintenance of ideas and attitudes that give meaning to individual lives and society. Likewise, Elizabeth Traube describes a model of cultural processes based on Richard Johnson's "circuit of the production, circulation and consumption of cultural products." See Richard Johnson, "What Is Cultural Studies Anyway?" *Social Text* 16 (1986–1987): 38–80; quote on p. 46. When culture is viewed as a "circuit, neither its producers nor its receivers appear as its sole possessors." Elizabeth Traube, *Dreaming Identities: Class, Gender, and Generation in 1980s Hollywood Movies* (Boulder: Westview Press, 1992), p. 4. As a result, culture and meaning are the products of cultural amalgamation and dialogue as members of society actively participate in the creation and maintenance of culture.

24. Ralph Waldo Emerson, *Emerson in His Journals*, ed. Joel Porte (Cambridge: Harvard University Press, 1982), p. 344. See David S. Reynolds, *Beneath the American Renaissance: The Subversive Imagination in the Age of Emerson and Melville* (Cambridge: Harvard University Press, 1989), pp. 3–4, 6–7.

About the Book and Editors

What are the religious impulses in the 1976 film *Rocky,* and how can they work to shape one's social identity? Do the films *Alien* and *Aliens* signify the reemergence of the earth goddess as a vital cultural power? What female archetypes, borne out of male desire, inform the experience of women in *Nine and a Half Weeks?*

These are among the several compelling questions the authors of this volume consider as they explore the way popular American film relates to religion. Oddly, religion and film—two pervasive elements of American culture—have seldom been studied in connection with each other. In this first, systematic exploration, the authors look beyond surface religious themes and imagery in film, discovering a deeper, implicit presence of religion. They employ theological, mythological, and social and political criticism to analyze the influence of religion, in all its rich variety and diversity, on popular film. Perhaps more important, they consider how the medium of film has helped influence and shape American religious culture, secular or otherwise.

More than a random collection of essays, this volume brings to the study of religion and film a carefully constructed analytic framework that advances our understanding of both. *Screening the Sacred* provides fresh and welcome insight for film criticism; it also holds far-reaching relevance for the study of religion. Progressive in its approach, instructive in its analyses, this book is written for students, scholars, and other readers interested in religion, popular film, and the impact of each on American culture.

Joel W. Martin is associate professor of American studies and religious studies at Franklin and Marshall College. He is the author of *Sacred Revolt: The Muskogees' Struggle for a New World.* **Conrad E. Ostwalt Jr.** is associate professor of religious studies at Appalachian State University. He is the author of *After Eden: The Secularization of American Space in the Fiction of Willa Cather and Theodore Dreiser.*

Index